U.S. Africa Policy
beyond the Bush Years

Significant Issues Series
Timely books presenting current CSIS research and analysis of interest to the academic, business, government, and policy communities.
Managing Editor: Roberta Howard Fauriol

About CSIS
In an era of ever-changing global opportunities and challenges, the Center for Strategic and International Studies (CSIS) provides strategic insights and practical policy solutions to decisionmakers. CSIS conducts research and analysis and develops policy initiatives that look into the future and anticipate change.

Founded by David M. Abshire and Admiral Arleigh Burke at the height of the Cold War, CSIS was dedicated to the simple but urgent goal of finding ways for America to survive as a nation and prosper as a people. Since 1962, CSIS has grown to become one of the world's preeminent public policy institutions.

Today, CSIS is a bipartisan, nonprofit organization headquartered in Washington, D.C. More than 220 full-time staff and a large network of affiliated scholars focus their expertise on defense and security; on the world's regions and the unique challenges inherent to them; and on the issues that know no boundary in an increasingly connected world.

Former U.S. senator Sam Nunn became chairman of the CSIS Board of Trustees in 1999, and John J. Hamre has led CSIS as its president and chief executive officer since 2000.

CSIS does not take specific policy positions; accordingly, all views expressed herein should be understood to be solely those of the author(s).

The CSIS Press
Center for Strategic and International Studies
1800 K Street, N.W., Washington, D.C. 20006
Tel: (202) 775-3119   Fax: (202) 775-3199
E-mail: books@csis.org   Web: www.csis.org

U.S. Africa Policy beyond the Bush Years

Critical Challenges for the Obama Administration

Edited by Jennifer G. Cooke and J. Stephen Morrison

THE CSIS PRESS

**Center for Strategic
and International Studies**
Washington, D.C.

Significant Issues Series, Volume 31, Number 3
© 2009 by Center for Strategic and International Studies
Washington, D.C.
Printed on recycled paper in the United States of America
Cover design by Robert L. Wiser, Silver Spring, Md.
Cover photo: © istockphoto.com/Peeterv/Peeter Viisimaa

12 11 10 09 08   5 4 3 2 1

ISSN 0736-7136
ISBN 978-0-89206-564-6

Library of Congress Cataloging-in-publication Data
U.S. Africa policy beyond the Bush years : critical choices for the Obama
administration / edited by Jennifer G. Cooke and J. Stephen Morrison.
    p. cm. — (Significant issues series ; v. 31, no. 3)
  Includes bibliographical references and index.
  ISBN 978-0-89206-564-6 (pbk. : alk. paper) 1. Africa—Foreign relations—United
States. 2. United States—Foreign relations—Africa. 3. United States—Foreign
relations—2001–2009. 4. United States—Foreign relations—2009– 5. National
security—United States. 6. National security—Africa. I. Cooke, Jennifer G.
II. Morrison, J. Stephen. III. Title: United States Africa Policy beyond the Bush
Years. IV. Series.

  DT38.7.U16 2009
  327.7306—dc22   2009008000

CONTENTS

ACKNOWLEDGMENTS

"Beyond the Bush Administration's Africa Policy: Critical Choices for the Obama Administration," the CSIS project that produced this volume, was cochaired by Jennifer G. Cooke, CSIS Africa Program director, and J. Stephen Morrison, CSIS Global Health Program director and senior vice president, and was ably managed by David Henek, CSIS Africa Program coordinator. The project was divided into eight working groups, each chaired by a distinguished expert in a particular area of U.S. Africa policy: Joel D. Barkan, William Mark Bellamy, Timothy M. Carney, Michelle D. Gavin, David L. Goldwyn, Princeton N. Lyman, Phillip Nieburg, J. Stephen Morrison, and David H. Shinn.

Between May and December 2008, these experts convened up to six working groups on their respective topics, soliciting participation from a broad array of senior policymakers, congressional staff, and representatives from academia, nongovernmental organizations, and the private sector in order to produce the chapters written for this publication. In addition to these individual working group sessions, our authors directly engaged with senior Bush administration officials responsible for U.S. Africa policy to solicit their thoughts and reflections on the Bush administration's legacies and challenges for the Obama administration. There are thus many contributors to this book, and for their advice on shaping the overall project, the time they were willing to commit, and their thoughtful participation in working group discussions, we are deeply grateful.

CSIS is indebted to several individuals who helped provide critical advice and analysis throughout the project's duration, all of whom are close friends of the CSIS Africa Program. A special thanks is owed to Akwe Amosu, senior policy analyst for Africa at the Open Society Policy Center; Dorina Bekoe, senior research associate of the Center for Conflict Analysis and Prevention at the U.S. Institute of Peace; Chester A. Crocker, the James R. Schlesinger professor of strategic studies at Georgetown University's Walsh School of Foreign Service; Paul Hare, executive director of the U.S.-Angola Chamber of Commerce; Robert Houdek, former national intelligence officer for Africa; Walter Kansteiner, founding principal of the Scowcroft Group and former assistant secretary of state for African affairs; Stephen Lande and Tony Carroll, president and vice president of Manchester Trade Ltd.; Peter Lewis, director of the Africa Studies Program at the Johns Hopkins University School of Advanced International Studies; Mauro de Lorenzo, resident fellow at the American Enterprise Institute; Simeon Moats, international government relations manager at Exxon Mobil; Sola Omole, international government affairs manager at Chevron Corporation; Lange Schermerhorn, retired U.S. ambassador to Djibouti; and Witney Schneidman, former assistant secretary of state for African affairs and adviser to the Obama Transition Team.

Several individuals should also be singled out for exceptional commitment and outstanding contributions to our individual working group sessions, including Wendy Baldwin, program manager for poverty, gender, and youth at the Population Council; Mark Billera, regional coordinator for Africa at the U.S. Agency for International Development (USAID); Maria Blair, associate vice president and managing director of the Rockefeller Foundation; Joanne Carter, legislative director of Results; Peter Chaveas, former director of the Africa Center for Strategic Studies at the National Defense University (NDU); Richard Cincotta, consulting demographer for the Long-Range Analysis Unit of the National Intelligence Council; Daryl Edwards, policy director at the Coalition for Neglected Tropical Diseases at the Sabin Institute; Monica Enfield, PFC Energy; Janet Fleischman, chair of the CSIS HIV/AIDS Gender Committee Task Force; Chris Fomunyoh, senior associate and regional director for Central and West Africa at the National Democratic Institute; John Furlow, climate change specialist at USAID; Tony Gambino, former USAID mission director for the Democratic Republic of the Congo and independent consultant; Arvind Ganesan, director of Human Rights Watch's business and human rights program; Ian Gary, policy adviser for extractive industries for Oxfam; Patrick Gonzalez, climate change scientist for the Nature Conservancy; Doug Hengel, deputy assistant secretary of state for energy, sanctions, and commodities; Jim Herrington, director of international relations at the Fogarty International Center; Gerald Hyman, president of the CSIS Hills Program on Governance; Cate Johnson, deputy director of the Office of Democracy and Governance at USAID; Richard Joseph, John Evans Professor of International History and Politics at Northwestern University; Jennifer Kates, director of the HIV Policy Program at the Kaiser Family Foundation; Judith Kauffman, independent consultant; Kyle Kinner, senior policy adviser at CARE; Jeffrey Krilla, deputy assistant secretary for democracy, human rights, and labor; Elizabeth Leahy, research associate at Population Action International; Andre Le Sage, researcher at the Africa Center for Strategic Studies at NDU; Sasha Lezhnev, policy adviser at Global Witness; Terry Lyons, professor at George Mason University; Mark Malan, researcher at the Strategic Studies Institute of the U.S. Army War College; Sean McFate, consultant; Tom Melia, deputy executive director of Freedom House; Allen Moore, distinguished fellow at the Stimson Center and senior associate at CSIS; Todd Moss, former deputy assistant secretary of state for African affairs; Monde Muyangwa, academic dean of the Africa Center for Strategic Studies at NDU; Rachel Nugent, deputy director for global health at the Center for Global Development; Willy Olsen, member of the Revenue Watch Institute Governing Board; Dan Pike, director for African affairs at the Department of Defense; Lauren Ploch, Africa policy analyst at the Congressional Research Service; David Pumphrey, deputy director of the CSIS Energy Program; Richard Roth, senior vice president of NDU; Andy Sisson, NDU; Mike Smith, program director for the Global Peace Operations Initiative at the U.S. Department of State; Charlie Snyder, deputy assistant secretary of state for international narcotics and law enforcement; Marc Sommers, associate research professor of the Humanitarian Studies Institute of Human Security at the Fletcher School at Tufts University; Jim Swan, former deputy assistant secretary of state for African affairs; Ronald J. Waldman, professor of clinical population and family health at the Mailman School of Public Health at Columbia University; David Waskow, climate change program director at Oxfam; and Lauren Weeth, consultant at the Center for Global Development.

Support from a number of senior Bush administration officials involved with U.S. Africa policy was essential to the success of this project, and CSIS is deeply indebted to those who shared a willingness to talk honestly and constructively with our authors about the achievements and limitations of the Bush legacy in off-the-record sessions. CSIS would like particularly to thank the following Bush administration officials: Johnnie Carson, national intelligence officer for Africa; Phil Carter, principal deputy assistant secretary of state for African affairs; Malik Chaka, director of threshold countries at the Millennium Challenge Corporation; Senator John Danforth, former U.S. special envoy to Sudan; Mark Dybul, U.S. global AIDS coordinator; Jendayi Frazer, assistant secretary of state for African affairs; David Gordon, director of policy planning at the U.S. Department of State; Maureen Harrington, vice president for policy and international relations at the Millennium Challenge Corporation; Florizelle Liser, assistant U.S. trade representative for Africa; Tim Shortley, senior adviser for conflict resolution to the Africa Bureau at the U.S. Department of State; and Theresa Whelan, deputy assistant secretary of defense for African affairs.

CSIS is also grateful for U.S. congressional interest in our project and the opportunity to brief staffers interested in Africa on the early findings of our project. CSIS would like to thank the Office of Senator Russ Feingold, particularly Peter Quaranto, junior legislative assistant, and Sarah Margon, legislative assistant, for helping organize a briefing for interested House and Senate staff.

We are especially indebted to the working group chairs, who, when they first agreed to participate, perhaps did not anticipate just how much we would ask of them. Their sustained effort, intellectual focus, openness to differing viewpoints, and ability to distill group discussions into thoughtful written analysis helped ensure consistent and exceptional participation by working group contributors and are reflected in the quality and balance of the final volume. Our authors would like to acknowledge Sheila Moynihan, Goldwyn International Strategies, and Katy Robinette , research associate at the Council on Foreign Relations, for their research contributions to the chapters on energy security and on aid and trade and, respectively.

CSIS wishes to thank Exxon Mobil and Chevron, the donors whose generous financial support made the project possible. The contents of this volume are, of course, the responsibility of the CSIS Africa Program and do not reflect the views of donor organizations or CSIS as a whole.

Within CSIS, we are most grateful for the help and advice of the CSIS Press, including James Dunton, Donna Spitler, and Emma Davies, and the CSIS Africa Program interns, particularly Wilson Aiwuyor, Matt Borman, Max Bruner, Hailey Flynn, Decky Kipuka Kabongi, Canaan McCaslin, Robert Mylroie, Elisa Prosperetti, Nikki Sepesi, and Heather Texeira, whose help was critical to the success of the project. A special thanks is owed to Kate Hofler, former program manager, and Suzanne Brundage, research assistant, of the CSIS Global Health Policy Center for their contributions to the chapter on public health in Africa. Finally, this project would not have been brought to a successful conclusion were it not for the prodigious, sustained efforts and substantive input of David Henek, program coordinator of the CSIS Africa Program.

A SMARTER U.S. APPROACH TO AFRICA

JENNIFER G. COOKE AND J. STEPHEN MORRISON

THE POWERFUL LEGACY OF THE BUSH ERA

During President George W. Bush's eight-year tenure, U.S. policy toward Africa underwent a dramatic transformation characterized by an expansion of U.S. interests, a high-level diplomatic push on Sudan, unprecedented resource flows, and the establishment of several historic initiatives. These changes came about in an era in which security, energy, and health emerged as new, near-strategic U.S. interests in Africa and in which U.S. Africa policy ascended to a position far closer to mainstream foreign policy than ever before. The U.S. constituency for an activist Africa policy broadened considerably to include public health institutions, powerful new foundations, vocal religious groups, and a more active corporate sector. Although U.S. Africa policy attracted consistently strong bipartisan support, it was also criticized for imbalanced, unsustained, underpowered, and inconsistent approaches.

Expectations for the Bush administration vis-à-vis Africa were initially low. Yet almost immediately upon taking office, beginning first with a major diplomatic investment to end the north-south civil war in Sudan, President Bush lent his leadership and sustained commitment to high-profile signature initiatives that each had a heavy or predominant focus on Africa: the President's Emergency Plan for AIDS Relief (PEPFAR), the Millennium Challenge Corporation (MCC), and the U.S. Africa Command (AFRICOM). Assistance to Africa trebled, and favorable opinion toward the United States held, especially in those states where the administration made its greatest commitments. The

U.S. reputation in Africa remained better than in other regions of the world where U.S. policy approaches on counterterrorism, the wars in Afghanistan and Iraq, allegations of torture and prisoner abuse, and climate change, among other issues, undermined U.S. standing.

Over time, PEPFAR and MCC became symbols of the value of investing substantially in soft power in Africa and, in the case of PEPFAR, became commonly regarded as among the most positive of Bush-era legacies. These initiatives created new models for the delivery of U.S. foreign aid and established public health as a dominant new foreign assistance priority.

Despite these significant achievements, there were limitations in U.S. policy approaches to Africa. Competing demands of other U.S. foreign policy priorities impeded the sustained high-level attention essential to achieving results in Africa. Hesitation and innate skepticism persisted among senior policymakers, grounded in awareness of the tough, enduring obstacles to sustainable policy successes in Africa. The new administration will have to confront these fundamental realities.

Much work lies ahead, and many questions do not yet have answers. It is not clear how the important but unfinished Bush-era legacies are to be refined and sustained effectively into the future and how essential support from both U.S. governing institutions and African partners is to be ensured, especially in a time of worsening economic crisis at home and around the world. Nor is it evident how rising U.S. security engagement in Africa is to be reconciled with commitments to reducing poverty and promoting democracy, human rights, and good governance: no integrated U.S. policy strategy has yet to be set out. Institutionally, it is not certain how PEPFAR, MCC, and USAID are to better integrated, less encumbered by fragmentation, and buoyed by a renewed effort to place them within a single, overarching development frame.

PARADOX AND WEAKNESS

Paradoxically, the Bush era revealed that in a period of significantly enlarged U.S. engagement in Africa, U.S. influence actually declined. This situation came about because U.S. policy contains significant weaknesses, because Africa has become a far more intensely competitive political and economic marketplace, and because a number of African states have embraced a problematic and defiant mode of malgovernance and found other external partners to support them. U.S. sway on the continent has become objectively less than it was in the Cold War era.

Power and alliances in Africa have become more broadly distributed, driven by new trade and investment relationships, an area where U.S. attention has lagged. Western funding for humanitarian aid and public health is often taken as a given and seen as an obligation for wealthy, developed countries. African states have become more sensitive to U.S. unilateralism and any appearance of Western presumption. African energy and commodity producers have enjoyed heightened revenue flows, and African states are today actively courted by a range of new partners and suitors from Brazil, China, India, Malaysia, Russia, and others.

Africa has also seen a decline in strong democratic and human rights leadership, in South Africa and Nigeria especially; a willful disregard of democratic norms; and a deliberate turning back to harsh, authoritarian tactics: witness coups in Guinea and Mauritania and profoundly flawed elections in Ethiopia, Kenya, Nigeria, Uganda, and Zimbabwe, accompanied by violent repression.

In addition, the Bush era exposed serious limitations in U.S. approaches. A massive U.S. investment in HIV/AIDS—despite its immeasurable human impact—carries little U.S. leverage: a large-scale life-sustainment project cannot, for obvious ethical reasons, be easily suspended or reduced in retaliation for a recipient country's behavior on other sensitive governance issues. In the Bush years, U.S. diplomatic skill and leadership have often been weak, and bilateral relations with critically important African states—Angola, Nigeria, South Africa— have withered. Conspicuously insufficient U.S. diplomatic capacities vis-à-vis Africa made it difficult, if not impossible, for the State Department to provide effective policy oversight and to create coherence across institutionally fragmented initiatives.

Important gaps emerged, most notably in U.S. energy policy toward Africa and in U.S. engagement with China. Counterterrorism approaches were at critical moments narrowly defined, imbalanced, and costly to conflict-resolution efforts in Somalia and promotion of democratic governance in Kenya and Ethiopia. A vocal and well-organized U.S. domestic constituency on the Darfur crisis in Sudan maintained pressure for leadership on that conflict but at the same time gravely limited the leeway essential to U.S. diplomatic efforts and undermined the work of U.S. envoys. The absorption by the Bush administration in

Sudan also meant that chronic crises in Somalia and the Democratic Republic of Congo (DRC) did not receive the senior-level attention and sustained, robust engagement that they warranted, given their humanitarian import, the scale of atrocities and abuses, and the destabilizing threat they pose to their neighbors. Robert Mugabe's tyranny in Zimbabwe and protracted, enabling support from South Africa also never became a consistent policy priority.

President Bush's commitments on HIV/AIDS and malaria, on a massive scale and at massive cost, have had the appearance if not the reality of crowding out other important health priorities and straining health systems. These initiatives unfolded in a period when U.S. investments in basic development needs and democracy promotion in Africa were relatively static, provoking calls for renewed commitments in these areas and greater balance in foreign assistance approaches.

OPPORTUNITIES FOR THE OBAMA ADMINISTRATION

The new administration of President Barack Obama inherits from the Bush administration major institutional legacies that will require active efforts to sustain and refine. It faces expectations that the United States will carry forward a highly activist African agenda matched by adequate new resources. As it considers its own signature priorities, the newly formed Obama administration is under pressure to be careful in preserving major gains. Internal pressures have mounted for the introduction of a broad new development framework that would encompass PEPFAR, MCC, and basic needs and governance and that could elevate development as a top priority, give it greater institutional heft and independence, and grant it higher-level political leadership. How these ambitions play out, whether they enjoy adequate high-level backing and consensus, whether they can be instituted quickly and effectively, and how they ultimately shape U.S. approaches to Africa remain key questions that will require time to resolve. Hasty overcommitment to structural reform of U.S. foreign aid would be a costly mistake.

President Obama's arrival on the world stage stirs considerable enthusiasm, expectation, and goodwill from within Africa and may create an opening for an Obama administration to build systematically on the Bush administration's legacy, better bridge U.S. security concerns with long-term development and governance issues, and lay down significant achievements of its own.

At the same time, the incoming administration confronts a wall of new, high-order demands inside Africa: an arc of worsening instability and conflict including the DRC, Somalia, Sudan, and Zimbabwe, with grave uncertainty hanging over Ethiopia, Nigeria, and Uganda. It confronts domestic and global demands as well: an uncertain and dangerous global recession and severe economic downturn in the United States; active U.S.-led wars in Afghanistan and Iraq; and daunting security challenges in North Korea, Iran, and elsewhere in the Middle East. In this context, President Obama's entry may create outsized expectations that rapidly lead to disillusion. That disillusion could be acute if the global economic downturn results in worsening poverty, malnutrition, and instability among vulnerable African states and if the United States and other Western powers are perceived as indifferent.

The tough realities before the Obama administration may downgrade Africa as a foreign policy priority. These challenges may obscure what is at stake, how much progress has been achieved through higher U.S. engagement, and how much additional special effort may be needed to mitigate the impacts a global recession will have on the continent. At a minimum, the economic crisis at home in the United States, the price of a domestic stimulus and recovery package, and the broader global economic downturn argue for a sober realism. There can and should be a redoubling of effort in U.S. engagement with Africa, giving priority to preserving recent gains, gauging and documenting results from U.S. investments, working to achieve higher efficiencies in U.S. funding, adhering to long-term goals, and making smart, balanced, short-term adjustments. To be successful, the Obama administration will require a strategic approach and must give highest priority to selecting the very best, the most competent and respected policy leadership both in Washington and in U.S. missions in Africa.

THE ELEMENTS OF A SMART U.S. APPROACH TO AFRICA

The chapters in this volume cover in depth a range of key Africa policy areas: aid and trade; energy; crisis diplomacy; security engagement; public health; China in Africa; democratization and governance; and climate change, demographics, and food insecurity. In each, the author was asked to review the key developments in that sector since 2001, assess the major approaches and impacts of the Bush policy, and propose specific high-priority policy initiatives for the new administration.

Across these diverse chapters emerge five core elements that should underpin the new administration's approach to Africa:

- *Be strategic, openly acknowledge the gravity of the global economic crisis, and align rhetoric with reality.* High expectations and grave fiscal constraints may create a gap between rhetorical assurances and actual resources and attention. The new administration should guard against this tendency. Rather than a proliferation of new programs or commitment to structural reform of foreign aid, the new administration should outline early a limited set of strategic priorities. In our view, these should include fixing clarifying AFRICOM's rationale and placing it coherently within a balanced U.S. foreign policy strategy; sustaining critical health commitments, improving their efficiency, and linking them more firmly to long-term development; creating a new multilateral diplomacy that better addresses Africa's chronic violent crises; promoting a renewal of ethical governance in Africa; and establishing rural development as a priority. These priorities should be set within a reaffirmation of U.S. national interests in Africa: promotion of human dignity and democratic norms, economic growth and alleviation of poverty, and stability and security. These priorities should be cast as a continuation of success in pursuing "smart" power in Africa.

  The new administration should demonstrate its seriousness about investing in its core African interests while signaling that it is poised to reengage at a higher level on other important priorities when the economic crisis has subsided. Presidential leadership will be the *sine qua non* for driving forward an activist engagement in Africa, for winning continued support from the American people and Congress, for building on the successes and institutional legacies of the Bush administration, and for preserving bipartisan cooperation on Africa.

- *Create effective, robust U.S. diplomatic capacities.* Diplomacy should be the strongest leg of U.S. government engagement in Africa—but today it decidedly is not. At present, the Africa Bureau at the Department of State and its counterpart bureau in USAID are woefully deficient in financial, leadership, and human resources. Today the Africa Bureau cannot effectively manage the multiple challenges confronting U.S. policymakers and exert leadership over the fragmented "silos" of institutional power centers. The bureau is 30 percent under strength, underpowered and overstretched. Embassies are far too often fortresses separated for security reasons from the very societies they are charged with understanding. Targeted recruitment and retention programs are required if the hollowing out of capacity at the State Department and USAID is to be reversed and a cadre of seasoned Africanists is to be cultivated and empowered to lead.

- *Forge a new multilateral diplomacy.* As U.S. leverage on the continent diminishes, the new administration needs to engage creatively with other partner countries and with the African Union, the European Union, and the United Nations. Strengthening and coordinating better with UN institutions and the EU should be a priority. Forging common ground within the Security Council will be essential, particularly on new emerging threats such as narcotics and piracy; on long-standing common priorities like African peacekeeping; and on divisive and complex crises like the DRC, Somalia, Sudan, and Zimbabwe. To be successful, this effort will require sustained commitment, leadership, and restraint. The administration should place special emphasis on collaborating with China on security, development, and conflict resolution.

- *Reinvigorate governance and accountability.* Virtually every U.S. interest in Africa will best be served by partnerships with participatory, capable, and accountable African governments. Reprioritizing democracy will require a rebalancing of the U.S. approach, particularly with strategic partners or individual leaders who have enjoyed U.S. support. It will require a comprehensive approach toward energy security that shifts from an emphasis on oil to one that integrates governance, transparency, and anticorruption measures. It will require a counterterrorism and security approach that adequately acknowledges and supports the centrality of participatory government and human rights. It will require sustained investments in institutions of countervailing power: namely, parliaments, civil society, and media. And it will require a move away from the uncritical embrace of autocrats.

- *Push hard to strengthen African agriculture.* The 2008 food crisis carries forward into 2009 and underscores the need for a comprehensive strategy on African agricultural development. It has generated an opportunity to reengage Congress and powerful U.S. constituencies on how the United States delivers food aid, on trade and protection issues, and on longer-term investments to build viable, sustainable agricultural sectors in Africa. Building agricultural capacity can serve as a path to address employment for the continent's burgeoning youth populations and to mitigate chronic food insecurity and debilitating micronutrient deficiencies. A broad U.S. approach on agriculture and food security can begin to tackle land reform, climate change and environmental stewardship, trade capacity, urban-rural linkages, and critical inputs for raising productivity.

The United States retains considerable prestige and legitimacy in Africa and can point to major concrete gains in the Bush years. The new administration has an important opportunity to build on that legacy, to harness rising domestic interest in Africa, and to craft a balanced, "smart power" approach to Africa that gives primacy to diplomatic engagement. In that endeavor, it must draw on the capacities and experience of African and other international partners, both to address immediate crises and to address collectively longer-term challenges in which African, U.S., and global interests are at stake.

2

MAKING BETTER SENSE OF U.S. SECURITY ENGAGEMENT IN AFRICA

WILLIAM MARK BELLAMY

A significant development in Africa over the past decade has been the generalized lessening of violent conflict. Revitalized, expanded international peacekeeping, bolstered by the determination of a newly launched African Union (AU) to tackle security challenges, has reinforced this trend. U.S. diplomacy scored some successes as well, notably in driving the negotiations that ended the civil war in Sudan in 2005 and in removing Charles Taylor from power in Liberia in 2003. U.S. and international efforts to render security assistance more effective provided several African governments with increased peacekeeping capacity.

It is far from certain, however, that this positive security trend will continue or that U.S. security assistance programs will have the desired long-term impact. Parts of Africa remain as conflict ridden as before, and in others unresolved conflicts are resurfacing. The ongoing disintegration of Somalia now rates as the world's worst humanitarian crisis. Rebellion and repression in Darfur continue to generate international outrage. The prospect of a renewed civil war in Sudan, where a referendum on secession is scheduled for 2011, looms larger with each forfeited opportunity of reconciliation between Khartoum and south Sudan. And renewed fighting and mass displacements in the eastern Congo are a reminder of the difficulties facing the UN's largest peacekeeping operation globally.

The Obama administration will have little choice but to confront these ongoing crises early. Less spectacular but equally important will be a host of new and less conventional security challenges that have received scant policy attention. Piracy, for example, has increased dramatically in African waters, threatening commerce and disrupting humanitarian relief operations. Narco-trafficking and other criminal activities—including illegal fishing, human trafficking, and grand-scale theft of oil in the Niger Delta—have expanded markedly across West Africa, threatening to destabilize already fragile governments. An uncharted danger is the extent to which strong economic growth across Africa in recent years will be reversed as a result of a worsening global financial crisis. Shortages of affordable food and fuel, intensified competition for diminishing natural resources such as water, and dislocations caused by environmental stress and climate change seem certain to bring more pressure to bear on already overburdened African governments.

The new administration will inherit from its predecessor a significantly enlarged U.S. security engagement in Africa. This legacy includes a U.S. military base in Djibouti, active counterterror programs, a massive expansion of UN peace operations, and the launch of the U.S. Africa Command (AFRICOM). This inheritance is unfinished and subject to controversy. Security enlargement has not been effectively integrated with U.S. political and long-term developmental aims. Indeed, stark tensions persist across these three domains. The expanded security engagement has not been effectively managed on an interagency basis and fails to take account of new and unconventional threats that besiege parts of Africa. The legitimacy of U.S. security engagement in Africa is mixed, as are understanding and support among senior U.S. policymakers and key U.S. constituencies.

More vigorous, better-resourced diplomacy is essential to an effective U.S. response to Africa's security challenges, in addition to well-targeted and sustained assistance programs. The new administration, though, will be called upon to move beyond these traditional remedies. Too often, U.S. interventions have been reactive and compartmentalized, a weakness typified by post-9/11 counterterrorism programs in Africa and by almost all forms of nonmilitary security assistance. To address adequately the increasingly complex security challenges in Africa, the new administration will need to be more anticipatory in its actions and more coherent in bringing civilian and military resources to bear. Without improvement in interagency planning and execution, stronger State Department leadership, and more forceful and effective

White House oversight, the new administration is unlikely to improve on the record of its predecessors in Africa.

One ambition behind the creation of AFRICOM was better integration of U.S. civilian and military responses to security challenges in Africa, although critics quickly disputed the notion that AFRICOM or the Department of Defense (DOD) should lead this effort. Nonetheless, AFRICOM is a promising undertaking, which could bring additional resources and capabilities to overall U.S. efforts to address Africa's evolving security needs. It has a valuable contribution to make in building African peacekeeping capacities, advancing maritime security, assisting security sector reform, and supporting responses to humanitarian emergencies. It will no doubt also be called upon to respond in time of security crises that threaten U.S. interests. If successful, AFRICOM will bring greater coherence and efficiencies to U.S. security programs and help consolidate a U.S. constituency for sustained U.S. engagement in Africa. Marshaling AFRICOM's special assets and melding them with diplomatic and developmental interests should be an overarching priority of the new administration's Africa team.

THE CHANGING CONTEXT: VIOLENCE EBBS

As this volume's predecessor study noted, Africa was "riddled with wars" at the beginning of the first Bush administration.[1] Eight years later, the new U.S. administration inherits a situation that has changed dramatically for the better. Many conflicts raging at the outset of the Bush years have been contained, and casualty counts across Africa are well down compared to the late 1990s.

Whereas in 2000 many worried that a number of African states were on the verge of collapse, fears of state failure have receded today. External investment and economic growth rates have climbed in every region of Africa, changes due at least in part to an improved security climate. Few observers in 2000 would have dared predict such a remarkably hopeful turnaround in so short a period.

In most cases, however, progress made in peacemaking remains fragile and tentative. In very few instances have conflicts ended definitively. More often, rebellions and insurgencies have been contained by negotiated agreements that have not been followed by meaningful political accommodations and other forms of compliance. Thus peace in south Sudan, for example, remains acutely brittle because of the many unfulfilled reciprocal obligations of the comprehensive north-south peace accord. An armed insurgency persists in Burundi because Hutu rebels and the Burundi government, despite mutual observance of a ceasefire for more than three years, cannot agree on a way to end the war. In the Democratic Republic of Congo (DRC), most of the grievances and rivalries that fueled a chaotic regional war in the 1990s remain unaddressed. Fighting continues in Darfur, albeit at much lower levels than previously. In 2006, the Darfur conflict spilled over into neighboring Chad and the Central African Republic, destabilizing both nations. With Ethiopian occupying forces withdrawing from Somalia, heavily armed Islamist militias have gained the upper hand over a feckless and dysfunctional transitional government. An estimated 3 million Somalis have been displaced by the fighting.

It is thus far too soon to assume that African states have found permanent solutions to the political rivalries and governance problems that lie at the root of most recent conflicts. Indeed, the new administration enters office in a period in which armed conflicts are flaring anew.

THE UNITED NATIONS REBOUNDS AND THE AFRICAN UNION EMERGES

In contrast to the Clinton years, when public and congressional hostility to UN peacekeeping was prevalent, the Bush administration quietly supported a surge in UN peacekeeping in Africa.

The first turnaround was in Sierra Leone, where, despite initial humiliation at the hands of rag-tag militias of the Revolutionary United Front (RUF), a credible UN force was eventually deployed to contested areas of the country by mid-2001. Large UN peacekeeping operations followed in the DRC in 2001, in Liberia in 2003, and in Côte d'Ivoire in 2004. All were "Chapter 7" missions authorizing the use of force.[2] All were generally "successful" in that they either checked violence, helped establish conditions in which conflict could be contained, or contributed to postconflict stabilization.

UN operations were most successful where they were effectively "sponsored" by members of the Security Council willing to deploy resources unilaterally in support of them. Thus, the UK military presence in Sierra Leone, French military activities in Côte d'Ivoire, and strong U.S. backing for the UN operation in Liberia all appear to have worked to create a more permissive operating environment for international peacekeeping forces.

During this same period, the newly formed African Union legitimized for the first time the principle of collective armed intervention under AU auspices to restore peace or rectify egregious violations of human rights or humanitarian law. A new Peace and Security Council was established to oversee peace support operations, institute sanctions, and facilitate humanitarian action. Five standby brigades were also to provide capability for armed intervention, one in each African subregion, supplemented by a continent-wide reserve force of observers, police, and civilian personnel.

Consistent with this new regional thinking, the AU launched several peace support operations after 2000. A small, one-year deployment to Burundi provided some measure of security following a ceasefire in 2003, although it failed to achieve its main objective of disarming rebels and facilitating political dialogue. AU missions to embattled Darfur and Somalia were far more ambitious and less successful. Their shortcomings offer poignant lessons.

The AU's Darfur intervention (AMIS), which the U.S. among others strongly urged the AU to undertake, was dependent from the outset on funding, airlift, and ongoing logistical support from donor states. This meant that the AU force was subject to continuing uncertainty and held hostage to national political and budgetary decisions over which it had no influence. The mission was plagued by command and operational problems from the beginning, to the extent that communication within the force and cooperation among different national elements were judged dangerously deficient at times. Further compromising the mission was the AU's stubborn reluctance to cede responsibility or authority to UN peacekeepers even after it became apparent that there were urgent operational reasons for doing so.

The real problem facing AMIS, however, was the disinclination of the AU and of the UN Security Council to demand that the Sudanese government provide the minimum level of cooperation necessary for AU (and later UN) peacekeeping forces to carry out their mission. It was the placement of blue-helmeted forces in similar no-win situations in the 1990s that so discredited the entire concept of UN peacekeeping. Although AMIS may well be remembered as a praiseworthy attempt by the AU to respond forcefully to a genuine humanitarian emergency, it also stands as an example of how not to use an underresourced, ill-prepared, and poorly mandated military mission to compensate for a collective diplomatic failure to confront directly the offending state parties to a conflict.

Worse still in this regard is the AU mission to Somalia (AMISOM), launched in late 2006 with a handful of Ugandan troops, later reinforced by a small contingent of Burundians. This was another venture called for and funded by the United States and other donors in the absence of any peace agreement or realistic prospect of achieving one. Outgunned, surrounded by potentially hostile forces, and lacking any clear or achievable military mission, AMISOM has for the most part hunkered down and given top priority to keeping its forces out of harm's way.

As 2009 unfolds, where does this legacy leave the UN and African Union? UN peace operations appear to be at their upper limit in Africa and globally: close to 90,000 UN peacekeeping personnel are today committed to 16 UN operations worldwide; some 70 percent of those personnel are in Africa for seven operations. A growing gap between expectations and demands placed on peace operations argues strongly for a broad reassessment of UN peacekeeping in Africa and a new strategy for easing current excess commitments. It also argues for renewed multilateral thinking on how to assist the African Union in sustaining confidence and enthusiasm for playing an active operational role in ending conflicts on the continent.

THE POST-9/11 PARADIGM: TERRORISM IN AFRICA

Following the attacks of 9/11, concerns about terrorist threats taking root in or emanating from Africa came to dominate U.S. thinking about security challenges in Africa. An immediate post-9/11 concern was that Africa, in particular ungoverned Somalia, could become a refuge for al Qaeda fighters or their allies. Urgent steps were taken to reestablish intelligence and operational links in Somalia. The United States also moved rapidly to step up intelligence sharing and solicit cooperation from counterpart services in a number of African countries to identify and track potential threats. Despite the technical and operational limitations, the overall cooperation of these services with the United States was reportedly highly satisfactory.

The 9/11 attacks also awakened U.S. officials to Africa's broader vulnerabilities. With its porous borders, ungoverned spaces, social tensions, and law enforcement shortcomings, Africa appeared to offer ideal territory in which terrorist or criminal organizations could seek refuge, acquire and stockpile weapons, recruit members, conduct training, and plan operations without much fear of official interference. Besides these weaknesses, some African countries, like Kenya, the site of al Qaeda attacks in 1998 and 2002, offered good international transportation links, relatively sophisticated communications, financial and support networks, and a wealth of high-value targets as well.

Many observers considered Africa potentially vulnerable to Islamist extremism. More Muslims live in Africa than in the Middle East. Where they live in communities undermined by poverty, unemployment, and a sense of exclusion and official neglect (a situation that applies to many non-Muslim communities in Africa as well), it can be argued that they are prey to extremist messages and eventually to terrorist recruitment. A template drawn from European, North African, and Middle Eastern experiences was thus placed over sub-Saharan Africa. From this perspective, Somalia, much of the Horn of Africa, most of the Sahel, northern Nigeria, and parts of West Africa were considered potential breeding grounds for international terrorists.

Programs were implemented to address all these concerns: enhanced intelligence cooperation, generous new offers of bilateral antiterrorism assistance, more aggressive developmental and public diplomacy projects to target supposed "root causes" of radicalism and extremism, and the standing up of a combined joint task force in Djibouti that, for the first time since the early years of the Cold War, put U.S. forces on the ground in Africa in semipermanent fashion. Announcement of the creation of AFRICOM—the first U.S. combatant command dedicated solely to Africa—followed in 2007.

Many African governments welcomed the initial surge of U.S. interest in African security matters, even if the focus on terrorism did not correspond entirely to what most of them considered the continent's most pressing security problems. One feature of the shifting U.S. policy focus after 9/11 was a new rhetorical emphasis on the strategic importance of Africa and on U.S. strategic interests there, outlined in the Bush administration's 2002 National Security Strategy, which identified weak and failed states as the central threat to global security emanating from the developing world. Subsequent policy statements, including DOD directive 3000.05 (2005), which for the first time defined stability operations as a core DOD mission, further entrenched the idea that U.S. security depends as much on the success of preventive measures in weak states as on "kinetic" (i.e., combat) operations against clearly defined enemies.

Thus, chronic weaknesses that had previously attracted the attention mainly of humanitarians and development experts—poverty, joblessness, disease, illiteracy, corruption, weak governance—were discovered to have new strategic importance. This fed a tendency to conflate all forms of U.S. assistance to Africa—security, developmental, and humanitarian—with overriding counterterrorism objectives.

At the close of the Bush administration, the counterterrorism balance sheet is mostly a positive one in Africa, if only because so many of the worst-case assumptions made in 2001 proved unfounded. Osama Bin Laden and his associates did not seek refuge in Africa. No sub-Saharan nation has become a reliable safe haven for international terrorists. Nowhere in sub-Saharan Africa has there been any rallying, in Islamic communities or elsewhere, to calls for international jihad. Very few Africans have volunteered to fight against the United States in Iraq or elsewhere. The African experience strongly suggests that few links exist between poverty and underdevelopment on the one hand and political extremism and terrorism on the other.

As 2009 opens, reports proliferate that foreign fighters are again active in Somalia alongside Al-Shabab and Islamist militias. Eritreans, ethnic Somalis from Ethiopia, combatants from different Arab states, and Gulf State financiers have to some degree helped "internationalize" the internal power struggle within Somalia. Given irredentist claims against Ethiopia from within the militant Islamist movement in Somalia, and Somalia's history as a staging zone for al Qaeda attacks in Kenya and Tanzania, Somalia's potential as a terrorist safe haven remains real and will be an immediate challenge for the new administration, especially if Al-Shabab seizes Mogadishu and asserts control in central and southern Somalia. Less clear is whether Al-Shabab can consolidate its primacy, whether an alternative vision of moderate Islamists joined with remnants of the transitional government is at all viable, and whether Somalia proves to be a hospitable, long-term safe zone for international terrorists.

What might all this mean for the small al Qaeda cell in East Africa? It has been disrupted, some of its members have been apprehended, and its leaders have been kept on the run by a steady application of U.S. pressure, supported by African governments. Opportunistic air strikes in Somalia by U.S. forces in 2007 and 2008 were directed at high-value al Qaeda or affiliated targets. Weakened and harried, the cell nonetheless remains active and capable of regrouping and striking if pressure against it is relaxed. Three suicide car bomb attacks in Hargeisa, Somaliland, on October 29, 2008—the most serious terrorist attacks in sub-Saharan Africa in almost six years—are very likely a reminder that the al Qaeda–affiliated threat in the Horn of Africa is still present.

North Africa faces a different terrorist threat. Al Qaeda and al Qaeda–related terrorism in North Africa appear to spring from the same set of sociopolitical conditions present in much of the Middle East or in other areas where international Islamist terrorism has taken root. Driven by a sense of injustice and humiliation and by disgust with authoritarian regimes judged complicit in the penetration of traditional Muslim societies by Western cultural influence, North African extremists do not have many counterparts in sub-Saharan Africa, and their motivations do not resonate there.

Despite this cultural divide, al Qaeda elements have nonetheless attempted to extend their reach in the Sahel, to establish contacts in Nigeria, and to explore relationships with potential sympathizers in southern Africa.

THE NEW THREATS

Apart from armed conflicts and episodes of terrorism, new threats constitute a third area of legitimate and serious concern about Africa's security. Multiple loosely related threats have come to the fore in the past decade, some traditional and some relatively new. None has been a serious U.S. policy priority, nor have African countries, Western powers, or international organizations yet come up with feasible responses.

Transnational and domestic crime, ranging from drug trafficking to financial fraud to escalating violent urban street crime, is the most obvious of these new threats. Rising criminality is not unique to Africa, but few African states have the institutional infrastructure—the policing mechanisms, the judicial systems, the correctional services—required to confront this phenomenon.

Though Africans are not significant consumers of illegal drugs, a growing number of African states have in recent years become important transit points for narcotics moving from South Asia and South America to European markets. The problem appears to be especially acute in West Africa, where several nations have emerged as major transshipment centers for Europe-bound hard drugs. By some estimates Guinea-Bissau, and possibly neighboring Guinea as well, are today de facto "narco-states" captured by drug syndicates able to expand their operations with impunity under the protection of, and in partnership with, senior governmental figures.

According to the UN Office on Drugs and Crime (UNODC), evidence suggests that the drug bosses and networks controlling this trade are rarely African. However, transnational syndicates benefit from porous borders, lax law enforcement, and the vulnerability of poor African populations. According to the UN, not only are increasing quantities of heroin and cocaine reaching Europe from Africa, but also arrests of individual Africans carrying narcotics in Europe have increased steeply in recent years.

Money laundering, now estimated by the International Monetary Fund to equal a staggering 2.5 percent of global gross domestic product, is believed to be on the increase throughout Africa. Even those African states with relatively advanced financial sectors generally lack the surveillance and enforcement capabilities required to thwart money-laundering operations within their territory. Other forms of white-collar crime on the rise include financial fraud. UNODC estimates that 58 percent of fraudulent insurance claims in the United States are made by Nigerians.

Despite years of concerted international efforts, relatively little progress has been made in controlling the illegal flow of small arms into and through Africa. Omnipresent and cheap automatic weapons have fundamentally transformed the nature of violent conflict in Africa, making them deadlier, harder to contain, and more destabilizing for societies as a whole. Human trafficking in Africa has received greater attention, but prevention in this area has been episodic at best. Piracy is another criminal activity that has outpaced sporadic African efforts at containment, with dramatic increases in major incidents off the coast of Somalia and heightened media attention in 2008. UN Security Council measures have opened the way for more aggressive retaliatory action inside Somalia waters, and the multilateral naval escorts have been expanded, including for the first time a Chinese component. Piracy in the Gulf of Guinea is likewise on the rise, reflecting both increasing sophistication and brazenness on the part of the pirates and an almost complete lack of governmental capacity to respond.

Official corruption remains an important contributing factor to the spread of criminal activities in Africa. Yet, even when governments are determined to combat criminal influences, profound institutional deficiencies often prevent effective action. Africa has the lowest percentage of police officers (180 per 100,000 population) and judges per capita of any global region. This shortage is compounded by the generally poor pay and training provided African police forces, a well-documented tendency of police forces to prey upon civilian populations, and an understandable lack of public confidence in the police. Understaffed, underfunded, and politically pressed judiciaries in most African states are often unable to manage successful prosecutions in those instances where police bring cases to trial.

In coming years, as spelled out in chapter 9 of this volume, nothing is likely to expose these governance weaknesses more emphatically than the impact of environmental degradation on chronically vulnerable and still mostly rural African populations. Across Africa, coastal erosion, desertification, deforestation, and increasingly severe shortages of water, pasture, and arable land have already heightened local conflicts over resources and begun to trigger population displacements that are likely to prove permanent. When aggravated by the impact of accelerating climate change, social disturbances witnessed today could assume tectonic proportions. It is difficult to predict how corrosion of traditional livelihoods and cultures may affect stability. But almost certainly, the concept of "security" will change, as millions of ordinary Africans are forced to cope with major disruptions to their way of life with only limited governmental help to cushion the shocks.

SECURITY POLICY AND ASSISTANCE STRATEGIES IN THE BUSH YEARS: SUPPORTING AFRICAN FORCES

When the Bush administration came into office in 2001, it inherited an ongoing peacekeeping training program, the African Crisis Response Initiative (ACRI) and an ambitious peacekeeping project in embattled Sierra Leone known as Operation Focus Relief (OFR). Both were managed by the State Department's Bureau of African Affairs in close coordination with DOD. ACRI offered a curriculum of peacekeeping training and exercises to a handful of interested African countries, along with the provision of some personal military equipment. The idea was to create the nucleus of a pan-African response capability, whereby African military units, with logistical backing from the United States or other capable outsiders, could intervene to restore order, check the spread of violence, or stabilize endangered African states. OFR, however, was an unprecedented $86 million undertaking to train seven West African battalions for UN peacekeeping service in the hostile environment of Sierra Leone. Unlike ACRI, in which civilian contractors did most of the training of African forces, OFR's "train and equip" program was conducted by U.S. army special forces at bases in West Africa. ACRI was a generic program; OFR was tailored to a specific crisis. Both were adopted and sustained by the new Bush administration (OFR was completed in 2002).

As the flagship U.S. program for building African crisis response capabilities, ACRI underwent two evolutions during the Bush administration. In 2002, it was redesigned to become more flexible, more focused on "training the trainer" (hence ensuring sustainability), and sharper in terms of "peace enforcement" skills. Renamed ACOTA, the Africa Contingency Operations Training and Assistance Program, the program garnered congressional support, expanded to encompass 122 African states, and claimed, by 2008, to have trained over 58,000 African troops.

In 2004, at the G-8 Summit in Sea Isle, Georgia, President Bush announced the Global Peace Operations Initiative (GPOI), designed to boost yet again the available pool of international peacekeepers. ACOTA was subsumed by GPOI but retained its separate identity as the African component of the plan. GPOI proposed to train 75,000 international peacekeepers, two-thirds of them from Africa, over five years. The novelty of GPOI lay in its attempt to address long-standing issues of poor follow-up training for African forces and to provide new mechanisms for transporting and giving logistical support to deploying African forces. GPOI further proposed to spread the responsibilities and costs for this enhanced support more widely within the donor community.

To the credit of the Bush administration, support and funding for African security assistance programs, especially peacekeeping training, remained strong even after the post-9/11 shift of U.S. strategic priorities. By consistently meeting assessed obligations to UN peacekeeping, the administration further helped put African peacekeeping on a more solid footing than was the case in the 1990s.

Yet despite these efforts, questions persist about the overall effectiveness of U.S. assistance programs. Programs to train the trainer and build sustainable capabilities within African militaries have instead continued to churn out "just in time" trainees for rotation into current UN peacekeeping operations. This focus on current operations at the expense of long-term capacity building is a an understandable trade-off but also a well-recognized problem for U.S. and other donor programs. Maintaining the cohesion and effectiveness of U.S.-trained units—that is, preventing the dispersal and dissipation of skills once training is completed and beyond an initial deployment—is likewise a recurrent problem. Contractors rather than U.S. forces conduct most of the training, making it more difficult to gain objective assessments of the quality of the programs or to set their eventual endpoints.

GPOI was designed in part to address these ongoing weaknesses but does not appear to have achieved that result. Congressional studies have noted other problems with GPOI, including difficulties monitoring the actual readiness of African units trained under the program, continuing deficiencies in operational training for senior leaders, inadequate equipment and transportation support, and limited G-8 and international participation in the plan.

Given these shortcomings, the new administration should seek answers to multiple questions, among them how to measure actual improvements in African peace enforcement capabilities and how to judge whether African governments and militaries are demonstrably more capable today of responding to security crises in Africa than they were a decade ago. Better measures are needed of whether longstanding problems of command and control, interoperability of forces, and transportation and logistical requirements have been addressed. A better understanding is needed of what it will take for the AU to mount future peace enforcement operations on its own terms, without relying on funding, mobility, and sustainment of donor states. The slowness with which AU member states are assembling the African standby brigades is one indication that summoning political will and pairing it with enhanced capabilities is still very much a future aspiration.

COUNTERTERRORISM INITIATIVES

By 2002, the State Department's budget justifications had begun to highlight the war on terrorism as the nation's top global foreign policy priority. In line with this, new security assistance programs launched in Africa focused initially on a handful of designated "front line states" in the Horn of Africa. The East Africa Counter-Terrorism Initiative, unveiled on the eve of President Bush's first trip to Africa in June 2003, was a $100 million program, which, while impressive on paper, was in fact largely a repackaging of monies previously budgeted for a diverse mix of security, governance, and developmental projects across East Africa. The initiative was parceled out into 20 or 30 projects sprinkled across Djibouti, Ethiopia, Kenya, Tanzania, and Uganda. Projects ranged from improvements in airport security to helping pastoralists in remote rural areas bring their animals to market.

The Pan Sahel Initiative (PSI), undertaken in 2003, was a more modest initiative, limited to Chad, Mali, Mauritania, and Niger and focused closely on helping these nations' small militaries track and neutralize suspected terrorist targets in remote areas of the Sahel. In 2004 the PSI evolved into the Trans Saharan Counter Terrorism Partnership (TSCTP), a five-year, $500 million initiative, whose focus expanded from training host nation militaries to include a range of governance and public diplomacy programs. These were designed, among other things, to "deny terrorists safe havens, operational bases and recruitment opportunities, and to enable African governments to resist attempts by Al Qaida and others to impose their radical ideology on traditionally moderate and tolerant Muslim populations in the region."

A distinctive feature of post-9/11 security assistance programs in Africa was the Bush administration's transfer to DOD of authorities once vested exclusively in civilian agencies, namely State and USAID. So-called section "1206" and "1207" authorities (referring to the relevant sections of the Defense Authorization Act of 2006) permit DOD in certain limited circumstances to train and equip nonmilitary foreign counterparts (police forces, for example) and to transfer DOD funds to the State Department to meet a range of security and stabilization requirements. The perceived need for this flexibility derived from experiences in Iraq and Afghanistan. In 2006, $6.8 million in DOD funds was obligated for Nigeria and Sao Tomé and Principe for programs to "counter threats to U.S. energy security." Another $6.2 million was allocated for North Africa under the TSCTP program. In 2007, DOD transferred to State $25 million for "civilian police reform, security and justice infrastructure rehabilitation, youth unemployment, and income generation" projects in Somalia. An additional $15 million was transferred in the same fashion for TSCTP programs in Mali, Mauritania, and Niger.

Congressionally mandated coordination between the State Department and DOD was reportedly uneven in the early exercise of the new 1206 and 1207 authorities but has more recently been resolved. Although Secretary of State Condoleezza Rice supported granting additional authorities to DOD, misgivings have persisted in different parts of the administration, in Congress, and within the broader developmental and nongovernmental community over a perceived erosion of civilian control over assistance programs. Critics have warned of a "militarization" of overall U.S. policy toward Africa if a progressively larger percentage of U.S. programs, including nonmilitary ones, are funded by or executed by DOD. Further, some are concerned that aid will increasingly be pressed to fit into preset counterterrorism templates, thus flattening out and obscuring the true complexity of Africa's security problems. Another complaint is that the U.S. military is in fact less well suited than the relevant U.S. civilian agencies to provide nonmilitary security assistance (such as training for police, immigration, or customs officials) to African countries.

THE COMBINED JOINT TASK FORCE–HORN OF AFRICA AND AFRICOM

In early 2003 the Bush administration established a new military presence in Djibouti as a hedge against a possible surge of extremist or terrorist activity in the Red Sea and Horn of Africa. Combined Joint Task Force–Horn of Africa (CJTF-HOA) eventually numbered about 1,600 personnel.

Despite the heavy investment in this force, including steep rents negotiated by the government of Djibouti, CJTF-HOA appeared on the scene in 2003 without a well-defined mission. Early suggestions that the force might disrupt the activities of "transnational terrorist movements" were discarded when targets could not be readily identified. Over time, CJTF-HOA's writ evolved into a mixture of intelligence gathering, civic action operations, and host country training exercises, activities CJTF-HOA coordinated with U.S. embassies in the region. CJTF-HOA's limited firepower—a single rifle company was often the extent of its resident "kinetic" capability—may actually have been an advantage. With little need or means to fight, CJTF-HOA instead concentrated on understanding and working with other U.S. agencies and host governments to try to address the root causes of violent extremism.

Judged purely in military terms, CJTF-HOA might seem an expensive and unproductive venture. Its annual operating budget is an estimated $330 million, almost as much as the annual operating expenses for the AFRICOM headquarters in Stuttgart, Germany. In another sense, however, CJTF-HOA was a useful experiment, one that created a template of military-civilian cooperation and tested some of the premises on which a new unified command for all of Africa would be founded.

The launch of AFRICOM in early 2007 was the Bush administration's most important innovation with regard to security policy in Africa. From the outset, AFRICOM was envisioned as unique among the Pentagon's five regional combatant commands. It was intended to have a large contingent of civilians, drawn from other executive agencies, in senior supervisory positions. It would be less focused on "war fighting" than on anticipating and working to prevent conflicts. In early discussions of the new command's mission, some proposed that AFRICOM act to "integrate" not only the security-related activities of U.S. government agencies in individual African countries but also U.S. diplomatic and developmental activities that related to security issues.

The idea that AFRICOM might function as a supersized U.S. embassy, or as a cluster of regional centers with responsibilities to integrate official U.S. activities across a broadly defined spectrum of security interests, generated predictable resistance from the State Department and USAID, from Congress, and from other countries, most notably from within Africa. For some observers, DOD's ambitions with regard to AFRICOM appeared to confirm that a "militarization" of overall U.S. policy in Africa was under way. Sharp public debates in 2007 and early 2008 about the placement of an AFRICOM headquarters on the African continent highlighted African concerns about underlying U.S. motives and prompted some to reject outright a future relationship with the U.S. military through AFRICOM.

Overlooked in most of these early debates were the potential advantages to Africa of a new U.S. command dedicated solely to the continent. Often neglected was the prospect that AFRICOM could help African governments achieve more visibility in Washington, leverage resources that would otherwise be unavailable, achieve higher efficiencies and coherence, and gain new points of access and influence in the United States. After October 2007, when AFRICOM reached its initial operating status under its new commander General William "Kip" Ward, concerted efforts were undertaken to correct earlier miscues.

Discussion of the location of a future headquarters was shelved. AF-RICOM's purpose was more clearly defined as one of supporting and working in close coordination with U.S. civilian leadership.

For the next U.S. administration, deciding what to do with AFRI-COM—that is, how to use this powerful new tool of engagement—will be one of the first and most fundamental requirements of forging a new Africa policy. Chances of AFRICOM's gaining greater acceptance in Africa, among other donor states, in Congress, and elsewhere will greatly improve if AFRICOM resets its sights on core competencies. An approach that prioritizes scaled-up, improved, and sustained training and professionalization of African militaries, for example, would likely be welcomed across the board as a worthwhile new direction in U.S. policy.

MEETING THE NEW CHALLENGES

Traditional security assistance and counterterrorism programs do not adequately address many of Africa's emerging security challenges. Lawlessness and escalating crime, for example, are not security trends that U.S. or African militaries can be expected to resolve. Nor are there traditional security assistance solutions to the chronic instability that affects many parts of Africa due to persistent poverty, inequality, and governance failures. Within the U.S. government, the State Department's bureau of International Narcotics Control and Law Enforcement (INL) is charged with combating international drug trafficking and organized crime, money laundering, and human trafficking and with building the capacity of partner nations' law enforcement and criminal justice systems. Some two dozen U.S. departments and agencies work under INL's programmatic leadership around the globe.

Of INL's fiscal year 2008 requested budget of $1.24 billion for global operations, only $34 million, or less than 3 percent, was marked for Africa. Of that, $28 million was destined for just two countries—Sudan ($24 million) and Liberia ($4 million)—in both cases directed not at preventive or sustained capacity building but at high-profile post-conflict stabilization. The remaining funds were scattered in small programs in 12 other African states, and while they may have produced localized successes, these successes are clearly too small and episodic to qualify as a coherent program of nonmilitary capacity building.

Even when funds from other sources—for example, the Nonproliferation, Antiterrorism, De-mining and Related Programs account, which is programmed by several bureaus in the State Department—are added to the mix, the result is similar: a fragmented mosaic of loosely connected initiatives covering many countries and addressing many diverse issues in a generally superficial fashion. There appears to be no overarching or controlling doctrine to guide this diversified assistance effort, and it is nearly impossible to correlate these efforts with any durable improvements in African law enforcement or judicial capacity.

These limitations mirror a wider problem within the international community. For more than a decade, security and development experts alike have argued that creation of a secure environment is an absolute prerequisite not only for reconstructing war-torn countries but also for enabling development in societies that have not (or not yet) experienced widespread conflict. "Security first" is today a widely accepted mantra in both post- and preconflict settings. Yet no reliable formula exists whereby advanced states can deliver "security sector reform" to embattled or developing societies most in need of it. The closest the United States may have come to a workable formula of sustained capacity-building efforts in this area is with the operation of a chain of international law enforcement academies, including an Institute for Law Enforcement Academy (ILEA) based in Botswana, where the State Department has coordinated interagency programs to train African police forces across a wide range of disciplines since 2002. The ILEA effort is important but nonetheless needs to develop better post-training follow through and measurements of program effectiveness.

Overall U.S. government efforts to address nonmilitary security challenges in Africa are only slightly less coherent than actions by the UN, the Organization for Economic Cooperation and Development, the World Bank, and other governments (notably the UK and the Netherlands), all of which have invested significantly in trying to find holistic solutions to institutional weaknesses in the security sector. Bringing "whole of government" responses to bear on African vulnerabilities will remain a daunting but unavoidable challenge for the next administration.

FUTURE DIRECTIONS: RECOMMENDATIONS FOR POLICYMAKERS

While security gains are visible and encouraging across Africa, they are fragile. In many places, the underlying causes and drivers of conflict have not changed. Improvements in UN peacekeeping are encouraging, as is the AU's willingness to shoulder more responsibility. But a deficit of real African peacekeeping capacity remains, and serious uncertainty persists on Africa's capacity to respond to the next big crisis.

That international terrorism has not found a new home in sub-Saharan Africa is encouraging, but, as noted above, complacency would be mistaken. The worsening situation in Somalia will be of particular concern to U.S. planners in the months ahead.

Alongside these familiar vulnerabilities are the multiple dangers arising from persistent poverty and inequality, resource scarcity, uneven development, and governance failures. These are risk factors for state failure and will require innovative reponses from the United States and from other donor countries.

In this context, the new administration's security approach for Africa should rest on six priority actions:

1. Create an updated baseline assessment of U.S. security interests in Africa. Past administrations have veered between inflated claims of Africa's strategic value and offhand dismissals of its importance. During the Cold War, some strategists considered access to Rhodesia's and South Africa's mineral resources vital to U.S. interests. Today, some experts assign the same importance to West Africa's oil. After 9/11, Africa emerged as a potential hotbed of international terrorist activity. That perception has shifted significantly in recent years to a more focused and realistic appreciation of actual terrorist threats. At the same time, new nonconventional threats have proliferated, and UN peace operations and the aspirations of the African Union have become critical components of security in Africa.

Some argue that China's enormous commercial and diplomatic investment in Africa will inevitably set off a new scramble by outside powers for access and influence in sub-Saharan Africa and ignite a strategic rivalry with the United States. Many others see areas of convergence in U.S. and Chinese interests in Africa and argue for greater collaboration with China in enhancing African peacekeeping capacity, for example, or strengthening maritime security.

Above all, the new administration needs a clear-sighted consensus on the security stakes in Africa today, one that is realistic and that encompasses new threats and links between sub-Saharan Africa and North Africa. It should include an appraisal of UN and AU peace operations and multilateral strategies for easing their current overstretched condition. If one concludes that Africa's strategic importance in coming years will be linked less to the threats of war or terrorism than to questions of socioeconomic advancement and effective governance, then enhancing African security will inevitably be a more complex undertaking than in the past and will have major nonmilitary and developmental components.

2. Balance and integrate military and civilian initiatives in Africa under stronger White House direction. A striking feature of U.S. global engagement over the past eight years has been the steady growth of authority, responsibilities, and resources of the U.S. military as civilian diplomatic and development capacities have declined. Initial resistance to AFRICOM from African governments and development partners stemmed in part from the concern that a large and well-resourced AFRICOM would inevitably overshadow and "militarize" U.S. diplomatic and development programs across the continent. The new administration will need to address these fears and ensure that U.S. policy in Africa carefully balances defense, diplomacy, and development.

The administration will need a policy framework in which resources and capabilities across the U.S. government are identified and brought to bear in coordinated fashion. Complex security situations in individual countries and subregions are an emerging reality in Africa. It is not hard to envision a near future in which multiple African governments must cope simultaneously with crises as diverse as increased urban lawlessness, resource depletion, unrest in rural areas, the intrusions of international narcotics and organized crime syndicates, and chaotic refugee flows from neighboring conflict zones. In such circumstances, the United Sates cannot afford a dispersal of the authorities and resources needed to mount an effective response.

The new administration should place priority on developing such a framework through joint planning by State, DOD, and USAID at the regional level. Neither resources nor the attention of senior policymakers and members of Congress are infinite. A concerted interagency effort, under firm White House guidance, is needed to identify and pursue the highest regional priorities. Once a policy framework for regional engagement is decided at the Washington level, implementation should be assigned to the regional combatant command and the relevant country teams led by in-country U.S. ambassadors. Inevitably, it will be at the level of individual country teams that U.S.

security and development programs are integrated and executed. Since preparation of chiefs of mission to exercise such responsibilities is not routine, the State Department should undertake to ensure that all outgoing ambassadors are fully prepared to exercise whole-of-government authorities.

3. Develop a more coherent approach to combating terrorism in Africa. At present, the threat of international terrorists originating or operating in sub-Saharan Africa is limited. U.S. policies should acknowledge and reflect this reality rather than routinely depict sub-Saharan Africa as a zone of high risk and critical concern. Where active international terrorist threats do exist—as in the Horn—the most effective U.S. countermeasures will involve working closely with local partners who share U.S. strategic goals. Among the most common mistakes made by U.S. planners is to assume that a robust U.S. military presence is both a reassurance to friendly governments and a deterrent to extremists and potential terrorists. In fact, many friendly African governments regard a large and visible U.S. military presence as a handicap and potential magnet for both domestic political opponents and terrorists in search of high-value targets in an otherwise target-poor environment. Both DOD and State should devote more attention to calibrating correctly the size and visibility of the U.S. security presence in African host nations. In those few countries where international terrorists actually pose an active threat, priority should be given to clandestine operations conducted in close collaboration with partnering African governments and services. As a matter of policy, U.S. military operations to engage individual terrorists or small groups should be undertaken only when more discreet means fail.

Different rules may apply in North Africa where the international terrorist threat is entrenched and much more severe. Where North African states may be willing to share intelligence and operational information and collaborate on specific cases involving individuals or specific cells, they are highly unlikely to welcome direct U.S. participation in dealing with terrorist threats on their soil. Opportunities for U.S. military involvement in counterterrorist operations in North Africa are likely to be extremely limited, although North African militaries may be interested in opportunities to share information and to participate in joint training and exercises with U.S. forces in more traditional military-to-military modes.

The lack of a clear chain of command and control of counterterror plans and operations has been a persistent problem with U.S. counterterrorism policy in Africa. Among the highest priorities of the new administration should be to clarify the respective authorities of DOD and State and specifically of the regional combatant commander, other relevant combatant commands, and U.S. ambassadors in Africa with respect to theater counterterror policy and programs. As matters now stand, considerable uncertainty exists in the field, among civilian and military authorities alike, over respective responsibilities in this area.

4. Take a hard-nosed look at traditional military assistance programs. Despite years of effort and hundreds of millions of dollars in assistance from the United States, most African militaries today are marginally more professional and more capable of operating in peacekeeping roles than they were 10 years ago. Some militaries have regressed over the same period and are generally less capable than 10 years ago. The net effect is that while African states continue to contribute forces at a high rate to UN peacekeeping operations, these forces remain less well trained, equipped, and led than most U.S. observers had hoped when peacekeeping assistance programs began in earnest more than a decade ago. The AU is nowhere near is goal of security self-sufficiency.

Donor assistance has not always helped. Donors seldom effectively coordinate their security assistance to African states and often pitch it to meet their own localized security concerns rather than the longer-term needs of recipient states. U.S. training, for example, is sometimes driven by what the United States has available at the time and what it can conveniently offer in terms of particular units, schedules, and training modules. African militaries, which are starved for resources and training opportunities, will take what is on offer, even if does not correspond to long-term needs or requirements.

Building more professional, more capable militaries should remain a strategic priority of the United States in Africa. The new administration should acknowledge the mixed results to date of U.S. assistance programs and work to correct obvious deficiencies. A focal point of this effort should be the African Union and its new peace and security architecture. The Bush administration's appointment of an ambassadorial-level envoy to the AU was a good step and should be reinforced by an early offer by the new U.S. administration to review the effectiveness of existing assistance programs and make adjustments to them in line with AU needs and priorities.

Overall responsibility for security assistance programs should rest with the State Department, but AFRICOM should be brought into the planning process at the outset and given substantial responsibility for the codesign and implementation of military-to-military capacity building. More emphasis needs to be placed on strengthening institutions and capabilities in African militaries rather than simply imparting mission-specific skill sets. Better criteria should be developed for assessing the effectiveness of U.S. programs. Less use should be made of U.S. private sector contracts; priority should be attached to military-to-military interaction through AFRICOM. Finally, renewed efforts should be made to harmonize U.S. assistance with that of other major donors, notably the UK, France, and other EU states

5. Develop clear strategies to address the rapidly growing importance of nonmilitary security needs in Africa. Weak or nonexistent laws, inadequate police forces, shortages of trained prosecutors and judges, and pervasive corruption render many African states nearly defenseless against rising domestic and international crime. While African militaries are generally better organized and better resourced than civilian providers of security, placing responsibility for law enforcement with these militaries is not a viable strategy. A top priority of the next administration should be to develop a clear interagency consensus, under the shared leadership of the assistant secretaries for Africa and the State Department's INL, on priorities and modalities for delivering nonmilitary security assistance in a more predictable, measurable, and sustained manner.

U.S. support for building the capacity of law enforcement in Africa occurs mainly through INL programs administered by the State Department. They represent a small fraction of the budget devoted to traditional military-to-military assistance programs and lack strategic focus; these efforts are piecemeal, episodic, and chronically under-resourced.

6. Better define AFRICOM's mission and configuration. Despite significant progress in 2008 under General Ward's leadership, misgivings persist in Africa and elsewhere about AFRICOM's role. The new U.S. administration should:

- Determine (and emphasize publicly) that AFRICOM's core mission is cooperation with African partner states in traditional

areas of security assistance—and that AFRICOM's greatest comparative advantage will be to bring that cooperation to scale by
doing it in a more coherent, more effective, better resourced,
and more sustainable fashion than before. At the same time, the
administration should not downplay AFRICOM's status as a
combatant command. The likelihood of AFRICOM conducting
combat operations in Africa may be remote, but this capability
and potential role should not be dismissed or disguised.

- Single out maritime security cooperation as a special AFRICOM
  priority. The importance of offshore oil and gas production in
  West Africa is well known. Of increasing international concern
  are piracy, grand-scale oil theft schemes, narcotics shipments,
  human trafficking, and illegal immigration in Africa's mostly
  unpoliced coastal waters. Unchecked illegal fishing threatens the
  livelihoods of millions of Africans, as does severe environmental
  degradation in many maritime zones.

- African governments are beginning to confront these challenges, although maintaining navies and coast guards is still a low
  military priority for most of them. Many African states would
  welcome AFRICOM programs to help improve their maritime
  surveillance and enforcement capabilities. By helping restore
  physical security, AFRICOM could become an enabler of more
  broadly based "human security" initiatives in coastal Africa.

- Increase both budgetary and personnel support for State Department security assistance programs in Africa. Just as Secretary of
  Defenese Robert Gates has urged that more resources be made
  available to the State Department for stabilization and reconstruction missions worldwide, so too should AFRICOM call for
  a doubling of the roughly $250–300 million that the State De-
  partment now spends annually on security programs in Africa.
  Increases in Foreign Military Financing, the International Military and Education Training Program, and Peacekeeping Opera-
  tionsfunding should be used to support AFRICOM engagement
  initiatives. At the same time, the State Department's Africa Bureau will need at least a small increase in personnel to facilitate
  coordination with AFRICOM and to ensure faster processing of
  program and spending proposals.

- Connect AFRICOM's priorities more directly to UN and AU peacekeeping in Africa. With the UN present in virtually every corner of Africa, often in a security-building or peacekeeping activity, it will be impossible for AFRICOM to operate for long without intersecting in some way with UN activities. Whatever their operational shortcomings, the UN and its specialized agencies command respect and support from almost every African government and from all levels of African society. To the extent that AFRICOM is perceived as supportive of UN security and peacekeeping missions, international acceptance of AFRICOM will grow. Conversely, few things are as likely to undermine AFRICOM's effectiveness or its welcome in Africa as a perception that AFRICOM is working at cross-purposes with the UN.

NOTES

1. J. Stephen Morrison and Jennifer Cooke, eds., *Africa Policy in the Clinton Years: Critical Choices for the Bush Administration* (Washington, D.C.: CSIS Press, 2001).

2. Chapter 7 of the UN Charter permits the UN Security Council to authorize the use of force to carry out its mandate.

3

THE BIG U.S. LEAP ON HIV/AIDS IN AFRICA: WHAT IS THE NEXT ACT?

PHILLIP NIEBURG AND J. STEPHEN MORRISON

A surprising legacy of the George W. Bush era is the radical, sustained expansion of U.S. engagement in African public health from 2001 through 2008. Its pivot has been an unprecedented foreign policy commitment to bring life-extending AIDS treatment to a very large number of Africans, for the rest of their lives, for a disease for which no cure or vaccine is in sight. The commitment rested on dual imperatives: responding to a humanitarian emergency and addressing a rising transnational threat to security. Action flowed from the President's Emergency Plan for AIDS Relief (PEPFAR), which in its first five-year phase (fiscal years 2004–2008) expended nearly $19 billion, the majority of which was targeted at a dozen sub-Saharan African countries.[1] More than half of these resources went toward the provision of antiretroviral treatment (ART) and other AIDS-related care to an estimated 2 million Africans living with HIV/AIDS. Other major elements of the expansive U.S. approach to health in Africa include the President's Malaria Initiative, a three-year $1.2 billion program; an enlarged program based in the U.S. Agency for International Development (USAID) to address neglected tropical diseases; and substantial financial and diplomatic support to the Global Fund to Fight AIDS, Tuberculosis, and Malaria, the promising global health financing instrument established in 2002.

The "soft power" success of treating such large numbers of people for AIDS, increasingly manifest from 2005 forward, overcame domestic and international skepticism about the feasibility of such an endeavor, built considerable good will in Africa toward the United States, and helped sustain early bipartisan support within Congress for this expensive and uncertain grand experiment.

Sustained progress in AIDS care and treatment has been heavily reliant on White House leadership, strong day-to-day direction from the Office of the Global AIDS Coordinator, sustained bipartisan support, concrete performance targets, reliance on existing U.S. implementing agencies, and a broad U.S. constituency. Demonstrable progress also facilitated action on African HIV/AIDS that transcended what was an otherwise worsening partisan polarization in Washington on most other foreign and domestic policy matters. Momentum soon built upon itself: bold action on AIDS opened the space for a subsequent, wider, and more ambitious engagement in malaria, tuberculosis, and the strengthening of African health systems.

This momentum has not been free of controversy. Requirements that one-third of all monies allocated to prevention of HIV transmission be devoted to abstinence-until-marriage and fidelity programs and that recipients of U.S. government HIV/AIDS funds pledge to oppose prostitution overtly have caused considerable tension. There has also been resistance to integrating HIV/AIDS activities in any serious way into reproductive health and family-planning programs. In addition, although limited data suggest that providing HIV/AIDS–related investments can strengthen non-AIDS programs and overall health systems, criticism that U.S. HIV/AIDS commitments are increasingly weakening budgetary and other commitments in other key health areas such as child survival, reproductive health, and water and sanitation has intensified. A parallel concern is that these same HIV/AIDS commitments are crowding out U.S. foreign assistance for long-term basic nonhealth needs such as education and agriculture. By this same logic, U.S. commitments to the long-term delivery of mass ART in Africa may have created a de facto foreign aid entitlement with substantial and progressively mounting cost implications that, over the longer term, could further distort U.S. foreign assistance approaches and limit subsequent policy options.[2]

Passage of the Tom Lantos and Henry J. Hyde United States Global Leadership against HIV/AIDS, Tuberculosis, and Malaria Reauthorization Act of 2008[3] provided a politically euphoric moment in late summer 2008, shortly before the U.S. economic downturn and broader global economic crisis began to accelerate. President Bush signed the bill into law on July 30, 2008. Senators Barack Obama, Joe Biden, Hillary Clinton, and John McCain all voted in favor of the bill, which lays out a framework on global health that the Obama administration is likely to adopt, in some modified form, in Africa and elsewhere. The bill authorizes $48 billion for the second five-year phase (FY 2009–2013) of PEPFAR, allocating $37 billion to HIV/AIDS, a combined $9 billion to tuberculosis (TB) and malaria, and $2 billion to the Global Fund, which addresses all three diseases. Given the current U.S. and global economic crises, what monies will actually be appropriated and in what time frame remain unknown.

The bill broadens the parameters of the U.S. policy approach to HIV/AIDS to give greater emphasis to prevention of new HIV infections (relative to AIDS care and treatment) and a higher priority to issues such as gender inequity, malnutrition and food insecurity, and the training and retention of skilled health workers. It softens previously rigid spending requirements for HIV prevention, treatment, and care and allows slightly more flexibility in devising implementation strategies at the country level. It keeps in place the prostitution pledge requirement, and, as another apparent de facto cost of maintaining the fragile coalition that drove the legislation to a successful conclusion, it makes no change in the earlier bill's silence on the integration of reproductive health and family-planning activities with various aspects of PEPFAR. The sheer scale of these commitments and the broadening of policy approaches suggest that public health in general—and HIV/AIDS in particular—will remain prominent features of U.S. foreign policy in Africa.

The next U.S. act on health in Africa will confront a tough domestic economic crisis and a global economic recession that is likely to increase malnutrition, poverty, and instability among the poorest countries. Especially hard hit will be Africa, including those countries where the United States has made a substantial investment in HIV/AIDS programs. As the Obama administration seeks to advance U.S. policy approaches on health in Africa, White House leadership, especially visible attention from the president himself, will be key to preserving existing programmatic gains, preserving the fragile bipartisan coalition, and sustaining support for global health programs from a U.S. citizenry experiencing uncertainty and personal insecurity. At this historic moment, the U.S. government is being called upon to spend unprecedented sums to rescue the financial, automotive, and other sectors; underwrite a massive stimulus program; and pursue wide-ranging reform of health, energy, and infrastructure, while continuing with two costly overseas wars.

Taxes may be cut significantly as national deficits balloon. Under these circumstances, if U.S. engagement in health in Africa is to be sustained and protected, it will be essential that the president and those around him reaffirm the centrality of global health as an effective and affordable instrument of U.S. "soft power" that advances U.S. moral, economic, and stability interests. No less critical is that the president signal that the United States will seek special measures to mitigate worsening instability and promote economic recovery and development in Africa as a key dimension of its evolving health strategy.

It is essential in this delicate crisis period that incoming senior policymakers are seen as pragmatic, compassionate, realistic, and flexible. Foremost, the overarching rationale for U.S. investments in health in Africa and for U.S. policy approaches in general will need to be revised to take full account of the genuine threat to progress on public health that the new economic crisis poses. That means strengthening the economic and security case for health investments in Africa and clearly identifying core global health priorities that will need special protection: for example, continuing ART for the 2 million persons already on this life-sustaining therapy and enhancing HIV prevention efforts in eastern and southern Africa. It means intensifying efforts to better measure program outcomes and more credibly making the case that existing investments are indeed generating substantial gains. It means making special efforts to achieve higher efficiencies in the use of ongoing resources. And it means making any cutbacks in a rational and just way, while reaffirming the key goals laid out in the PEPFAR reauthorization and the hope to achieve them in a five-year or longer time frame.

The next U.S. act on health in Africa also requires an intensified effort to address five key challenges:

- tackling head-on Africa's health infrastructure deficits, including its massive shortages of health workers

- strengthening U.S. links and coordination with key multilateral and other non-U.S. institutions

- better integrating U.S. government HIV/AIDS goals with other health and development objectives

- ■ advancing a more strategic approach to HIV prevention

- ■ continuing to update HIV, TB, and malaria treatment and prevention approaches to better address the evolving characteristics of these pandemics, including the complex issues of co-infection and drug resistance

Despite the current economic crisis, there remains considerable promise for U.S. policy innovation on health in Africa. Within American society, nongovernmental groups engaged in the support for and promotion of public health activities in Africa have dramatically proliferated. This proliferation now includes global health programs in over 60 American universities, powerful new foundations, a more active corporate sector, religious groups, celebrities, operational nongovernmental organizations (NGOs), and successful new advocacy groups like The One campaign. This evolution has significantly enriched U.S. society, built a complex new web of ties between Americans and Africans, and forged within the United States a new global public health constituency for the long term. It has created new global health centers of excellence across the United States in key urban settings, which are generating knowledge, skills, employment, and complex new partnerships in Africa and elsewhere. It is generating well over $1 billion annually in private charitable commitments to health in Africa. In sum, this diverse community has a voice and influence that can and should be called upon systematically to sustain U.S. engagement in health in Africa. The recent Intelligence Community Assessment of global health issues from the National Intelligence Council (NIC) provides a detailed and thoughtful analysis of the reasons for U.S. policymakers to be concerned with global health issues.[4] In addition, the recent report from the Institute of Medicine (IOM) on the U.S. commitment to global health provides excellent additional guidance on ways for policymakers to move forward.[5]

U.S. HEALTH ACCOMPLISHMENTS IN AFRICA, 2001–2008

The increasing U.S. attention to global health issues that began in the 1990s accelerated in the early years of the George W. Bush administration. In an unclassified 2000 report, the NIC had identified a number of specific infectious diseases as possible threats to the United States.[6] Although many diseases were mentioned in that NIC report, it was the growing awareness of the impact of global HIV/AIDS that caught the attention of Washington. Moreover, since the general health situation is worse in sub-Saharan Africa than in other geographic areas and because the impact of HIV/AIDS was—and remains—greater in sub-Saharan Africa than elsewhere, health quickly came to the forefront as a concern in U.S. policy approaches to Africa, far more than in any other region.[7]

HIV/AIDS IN AFRICA DURING THE BUSH ADMINISTRATION

In retrospect, it was not at all clear at the beginning of the Bush administration that health in Africa was—or would become—a U.S. foreign policy priority. In the intervening years, a few key factors have become more widely known through conversation and reporting: that President Bush entered office with a strong personal interest in HIV/AIDS in Africa; that key White House officials (Gary Edson, Josh Bolton, Joseph O'Neil) shared that interest; and that in 2002 the president mandated these individuals, together with Anthony Fauci and Mark Dybul of the National Institutes of Health, to assemble, quietly and with little if any interagency deliberation, a plan of action on a bold scale. That plan is what ultimately resulted in the $15 billion President's Emergency Plan for AIDS Relief (PEPFAR) that was announced at the January 29, 2003, State of the Union address.

Since 2000, HIV/AIDS has continued to dominate health concerns in and about Africa, as it had begun to during the late 1990s. The statistics remain grim. The most recent global HIV/AIDS data from UN-AIDS indicate that sub-Saharan Africa is home to about 22 million (67 percent) of the world's 33 million adults and children living with HIV and approximately 1.5 million (75 percent) of the world's 2 million annual AIDS deaths.[8] Sub-Saharan Africa has about 90 percent of all children (younger than 15 years) living with HIV and nearly 90 percent of children newly infected with HIV in 2007. Sub-Saharan Africa's overall adult HIV prevalence is estimated at 5.0 percent, while the next highest regional prevalence is in the Caribbean, at 1.1 percent. No other geographic area's HIV prevalence exceeds 0.8 percent. To make matters worse, the global TB pandemic is increasingly linked to the global (and African) HIV/AIDS pandemic. Greater numbers of people in Africa (and elsewhere) are being found to be co-infected with both HIV and TB, a combination that is more difficult to treat than either infection alone. In addition, some HIV-infected people are co-infected with a variant of the TB bacillus that is resistant to the usual TB treatment drugs and is thus associated with higher mortality rates.

In May 2001, just after taking office, the president named Secretary of Health and Human Services Tommy Thompson and Secretary of State Colin Powell to cochair a government-wide task force on global HIV/AIDS. In 2002, after discussions with Kofi Annan and many others, the Bush administration joined in the creation (and initial funding) of the groundbreaking organization, the Global Fund to Fight AIDS, TB, and Malaria (the Global Fund).[9]

In October 2002, the NIC issued a second infectious diseases report, this time focusing on HIV/AIDS and on five populous "second wave countries" that had the potential to be heavily affected by rising rates of HIV/AIDS. [10] That report came close on the heels of the September 2002 White House National Security Strategy, which identified infectious diseases and health inequities as major causes of global instability and outlined a strategy that explicitly addressed the need for better approaches to help control global HIV/AIDS, TB, and malaria.[11]

Adding to the sea change in attitudes about global health and HIV/AIDS, cabinet and subcabinet officials, members of Congress, and other prominent Americans returning from field trips to Africa began reporting in great detail the horrendous impact of HIV/AIDS on individual Africans, on their families and communities, and on the already weak health systems that were supposed to care for them. Soon after the 2002 NIC recommendation, extensive behind-the-scenes discussions began, involving the White House, the Department of State, the Department of Health and Human Services, USAID, and prominent Republican Senators Jesse Helms and Bill Frist. These discussions culminated in an initial $500 million plan to address prevention of mother-to-child transmission of HIV (PMTCT) in a relatively small number of countries in which the United States already had ongoing HIV/AIDS programs of various kinds run by USAID or the Centers for Disease Control and Prevention (CDC).[12]

The ink was hardly dry on the PMTCT plan before the far more ambitious PEPFAR plan, to address intensively the population-level HIV/AIDS issues in a limited number of heavily affected "focus countries," began to take shape in the administration. After PEPFAR was announced in the president's January 2003 State of the Union address, the bill that became its authorizing legislation was introduced into Congress by Senators John Kerry and Bill Frist and was eventually passed as the Leadership Act of 2003, becoming Public Law 108-25 and covering fiscal years 2004–2008.[13] PEPFAR is directed and coordinated by an ambassadorial rank global AIDS coordinator who reports directly to the secretary of state and the president and who is housed in the Office of the Global AIDS Coordinator, a newly created management structure within the Department of State.[14] That coordinator and office have authority over all official U.S. funding streams and programs that address the global HIV/AIDS pandemic.

PEPFAR'S AIDS TREATMENT AND CARE ACCOMPLISHMENTS IN FY 2004–2008

PEPFAR began with a legislative authorization of $15 billion over its initial five fiscal years (2004–2008), although several congressional actions adding funds for specific additional tasks brought the final five-year tally to $18.8 billion.[15]

During its first phase, PEPFAR's focus was on provision of care and access to ART to people with AIDS; provision of care for other HIV-infected and -affected individuals, including AIDS orphans; prevention of new HIV infections; and strengthening of health systems.

During those five years, PEPFAR achieved some remarkable treatment and care successes. Through September 2008, more than 2.1 million people with AIDS had received ART in programs supported wholly or in part by PEPFAR. Nearly 2 million of these people reside in sub-Saharan Africa.[16] Although ART does not cure HIV/AIDS, and although it must be taken for the rest of a patient's life, it does allow most treated people to resume normal activities, some for many years. The ART support was projected to save 3.2 million adult years of life through September 2008.

PEPFAR has also supported more than 30 million HIV testing and counseling sessions and helped provide care to more than 6 million HIV-infected and -affected people, including AIDS orphans. In addition, PEPFAR had provided antiretroviral drugs to HIV-infected women for PMTCT in more than a million pregnancies by March 2008 and was estimated to have prevented nearly 200,000 HIV infections in their infants. However, data on the coverage of the PMTCT program vary widely, with extremely low coverage in some countries. Recent South African data, for instance, indicate that 70 percent of pregnant women in that country still did not have access to PMTCT programs.

SHORTCOMINGS IN THE U.S. APPROACH TO
HIV PREVENTION

Despite impressive care and treatment gains for infected individuals fortunate enough to have access to ART in PEPFAR's focus countries, new HIV infections have continued to occur, other AIDS patients unable to receive ART continue to fill many hospital beds, and life expectancy has continued well below pre-AIDS levels in a number of PEPFAR's focus countries. While PEPFAR has been highly successful in providing access to ART and other lifesaving treatment and care programs, PEPFAR's ability to prevent previously uninfected people in its focus countries from becoming infected—thus slowing the spread of HIV—appears inadequate so far. The major concern is that an enduring performance gap between AIDS care and treatment on one side and prevention of new HIV transmission on the other will create over time an innate vulnerability for sustained U.S. and other donor support. For example, the most recent global data indicate that, for each person placed on life-sustaining treatment, two to three others, previously uninfected, are becoming newly infected with HIV.[17] Persistence of this scenario, with steadily rising numbers of infected people yet to begin receiving AIDS treatment, poses considerable risk of donor fatigue.[18]

Recent setbacks in research into both HIV vaccines and HIV microbicides[19] and the slow pace of scaling up of adult male circumcision programs[20] are shifting the programmatic focus back to basics—to high-level leadership, to the need for structural change, and to behavioral interventions that can effectively reduce multiple concurrent sexual partnerships and change other norms of sexual and drug-using behavior.[21, 22]

Several fundamental obstacles to effective HIV prevention are internal to at least some of the focus countries themselves, including

- lack of sustained high-level national leadership and a strategic national approach to HIV prevention

- shortages of facilities and staff with the expertise and ability to implement effective prevention programs

- inadequate local data to use for rational program planning and implementation

- the stigma attached to at least some of the behaviors leading to HIV/AIDS risk

- the inability of society to successfully confront gender bias and the many other difficult structural issues that can result in high-risk behavior

On the U.S. side, the obstacles include various policy and funding decisions that have limited PEPFAR's ability to support use of known effective HIV interventions in certain circumstances.

For example, PEPFAR has been relatively unsuccessful to date in systematically integrating its activities with reproductive health and family planning (RH-FP) programs. This gap is important because, in many places, RH-FP programs are the only contacts that many women and older adolescent girls in focus countries have with formal health systems. Although the HIV/AIDS consequences of these missed prevention opportunities (for example, for AIDS education, for HIV counseling and testing, and for implementing PMTCT and other prevention programs) have not been quantified, they are likely to be substantial. This gap in PEPFAR's past approach to addressing HIV/AIDS in a reproductive health context was one of the reasons that the PEPFAR reauthorizing legislation refers more frequently to "gender" issues, including the greater HIV/AIDS vulnerability of women and girls, and places specific emphasis on the need (and accountability) for PEPFAR-funded programs to reach women and girls. However, the recent reauthorizing legislation did *not* set specific goals or targets for integration of HIV prevention activities with RH-FP programs.[23] Assessment of PEPFAR's compliance with this additional emphasis on protecting women and girls has been mandated for inclusion in the next Institute of Medicine evaluation.

In terms of program outputs, as of March 31, 2008, PEPFAR-supported programs to prevent sexual transmission of HIV, including the A-B-C approach of <u>A</u>bstinence-<u>B</u>e faithful-<u>C</u>ondom use, were said to have reached nearly 58 million people. While the U.S. government supplied nearly 2 billion male condoms to developing countries during this period, more than all other industrialized countries combined, the major policy focus of PEPFAR's approach to preventing sexual transmission of HIV was the A and B components of A-B-C.[24] No estimate of the numbers of HIV infections prevented through this combination of approaches has yet been made public.

Enthusiasm over PEPFAR's widely hailed treatment and care successes are thus tempered by the conclusions of the congressionally mandated formal PEPFAR assessments undertaken by the IOM[25] and the U.S. Government Accountability Office (GAO).[26]

The IOM study was conducted too early in PEPFAR's operational life to be able to focus on program outcomes; it thus concentrated on concepts of program targeting and sustainability. Members of the IOM committee were clearly concerned that PEPFAR had not given sufficient programmatic emphasis to prevention of new HIV infections nor to the factors leading to the greater HIV/AIDS vulnerability of women and girls. In addition, the committee felt that harmonization of PEPFAR's prevention programs with the programs of other donors and with local needs as determined by local surveillance data had not yet received sufficient attention. An additional IOM concern was an unmet need to emphasize capacity development in PEPFAR focus countries, including better integration of services to meet comprehensively the health needs of people living with AIDS. Finally, the IOM committee noted an opportunity, largely missed to that point, for PEPFAR programs to formalize learning from their experiences and to share those experiences widely around the globe with others involved in HIV/AIDS control activities.

The GAO report on PEPFAR's spending mandates pointed out that the requirements needed to meet rigid earmarks for various aspects of A-B-C programs had presented challenges for some of the PEPFAR country teams because of the difficulty of responding effectively to local HIV/AIDS disease and transmission patterns. Particularly disturbing was the observation by the GAO team that to meet their spending requirements for abstinence and faithfulness (A-B) programs, some PEPFAR country teams had to reduce their spending on other HIV prevention activities.

A number of the concerns identified in the IOM and GAO reports have been addressed, some through changes in collaboration among agencies, others by modifications of the Office of the Global AIDS Coordinator's policy for PEPFAR teams, and still others by changes in the recently passed reauthorizing legislation.[27]

PEPFAR has helped focus broader attention on several critical areas of HIV/AIDS control. First, PEPFAR has clearly helped highlight the need for specific programs to address the phenomenon of HIV-discordant sexual partnerships, in which one regular sexual partner is HIV infected and the other is not. These partnerships are high-risk settings for HIV transmission that are at the same time—provided the partners are aware of their infection status—highly susceptible to interventions. A second PEPFAR focus is an expansion of "prevention-for-positives" programs, in which people who are already infected but not yet medically eligible to receive ART receive condoms and counseling on how to avoid infecting their sexual partners. (Unfortunately, such HIV prevention programs are not yet consistently applied to participants receiving ART in PEPFAR-supported programs.) [28] Third, PEPFAR is moving to encourage the wide adoption of adult male circumcision in settings where the procedure is accepted and can safely be performed.[29] Another example of PEPFAR's program integration activities, although not directly related to HIV prevention, is movement toward an HIV/AIDS care and treatment model that integrates at least some previously separate health programs (for example, nutritional assessment and, when necessary, supplementary feeding) into a more comprehensive care and treatment system.[30] Finally, again not directly related to HIV prevention, the close collaboration in several countries between PEPFAR programs and programs supported by the President's Malaria Initiative (PMI) has helped facilitate malaria prevention through distribution of thousands of insecticide-treated bed nets (ITN) within PEPFAR-supported distribution systems. In some places, this ITN collaboration has focused on people living with AIDS, and in other places, the target group has been the larger general population at risk of malaria.

Several other examples of constructive integration of programs and spin-offs of PEPFAR have been cited as evidence of its positive impact on health systems in general. Resource and policy support provided for increasing collaboration between TB and HIV/AIDS programs is an example of PEPFAR's positive spin-off effects. PEPFAR resources have also been used to help a large number of countries, including some that are not specific PEPFAR focus countries, improve their disease survey and surveillance processes (data collection, management, and analysis) necessary to understand the circulation of HIV in their populations. Elsewhere, preliminary evidence suggests that providing PEPFAR-funded HIV/AIDS care in primary health care facilities can have a beneficial effect on the delivery of non-HIV care in the same facilities.[31] Another important PEPFAR success has been the creation of supply and logistics systems in focus countries that are adequate to purchase, transport, and store the enormous quantities of antiretroviral drugs, HIV test kits, laboratory supplies, and other items needed to run an effective HIV/AIDS program.

Finally, of the various factors limiting expansion of coverage of African health programs (including HIV/AIDS programs), the lack of access to adequate health facilities staffed by sufficient numbers of well-trained health workers is the most critical. PEPFAR-supported programs have been attempting to address this human resources gap in several ways: by supporting increases in preservice (basic) training to raise the numbers of health workers of various types; by shifting of job responsibilities from more specialized to less specialized health workers, carried out in conjunction with in-service training to upgrade skills of existing health workers; and by directly supporting the salaries for indigenous health workers. The long-term impact of this mix of support has yet to be measured.

Despite these examples of PEPFAR's positive spin-off effects, concerns continue to be expressed that PEPFAR and other externally funded HIV/AIDS programs are likely to undermine existing primary health care systems by drawing attention, staff, and other local resources from less well funded health programs. How these opposing effects will balance out over the longer term remains to be seen.

BEYOND HIV/AIDS

Although HIV/AIDS clearly received the most attention among global health issues in the Bush administration, it was not the only health issue important to Africa that garnered U.S. attention. In addition to its central role in the creation of the Global Fund, the administration also created special White House–sponsored programs in malaria and "neglected tropical diseases" and through PEPFAR, USAID, and CDC has provided additional funding and technical support for global TB control activities to the Stop TB Department of the World Health Organization[32] and to its TB control partner, the Global STOP TB Program.[33]

The President's Malaria Initiative is a five-year $1.2 billion program created in 2006 to focus attention and resources on falciparum malaria, a disease that each year kills over 880,000 people, mostly young children and pregnant women in Africa.[34] Falciparum malaria resisted an earlier global effort at control, from 1955 to the early 1970s,[35] but the recent addition to the antimalarial armamentarium of both the highly effective malaria treatment drug artemisinin and widespread access to inexpensive insecticide-treated bed nets that reduce night-time mosquito biting has again raised the possibility of effective malaria control. Prior to this initiative, malaria control efforts had been almost an afterthought in U.S. government global health activities, with most program activity carried out by the U.S. military, concerned about protecting troops working in locations of high malaria infection risk.[36] PMI, on the other hand, has moved well beyond that military focus, with a goal of reducing malaria deaths by at least 50 percent in the 15 PMI focus countries by 2010. PMI activities are managed primarily through offices located within USAID, with technical and logistic support from CDC's Malaria Branch. Country programs involve an integrated package of proven interventions (for example, ITNs and indoor spraying of insecticides); the strengthening of indigenous health systems, especially maternal and child health services; a commitment to strengthening national malaria control programs; and, finally, close coordination with international and in-country partners, including indigenous, U.S., and other international NGOs. The major international partner of PMI is the Roll Back Malaria Initiative,[37] a partnership among WHO, UNICEF, the World Bank, the UN Development Program (UNDP), the Gates Foundation, and others, which is focused heavily on African countries.

In February 2008, the White House announced a new initiative on neglected tropical diseases, funded through USAID.[38] Under this initiative, funding for these diseases is slated to increase from $15 million expended in 10 countries in FY 2008 to $350 million in 30 countries from FY 2009 to FY 2013.

The global measles control program, which receives strong U.S. technical and logistic support through CDC, has achieved notable success in the past decade, reducing the estimated global measles mortality numbers by more than 60 percent, from an estimated 873,000 deaths in 1999 to an estimated 345,000 deaths in 2005, the last year for which data are available.[39] The greatest proportion of these ongoing measles deaths, as well as much of the reduction achieved in mortality, occurred in Africa.

Despite a failure to achieve the original global goal of eradicating poliovirus by 2000, USAID and the U.S. Departments of State and Health and Human Services have continued their ongoing support for the Global Polio Eradication Program. That program has made some recent progress in reestablishing control of polio in the more than 20 countries affected by importations of poliovirus from Nigeria after that country failed to maintain its polio vaccination program in 2002–2004,[40] but polio problem areas remained as of late 2008 in Nigeria as well as in several non-African countries (Afghanistan, India, and Pakistan).[41]

The Department of Defense (DOD) has long been involved in research and other efforts to control diseases of public health importance (including cholera, malaria, and HIV/AIDS) in Africa and elsewhere. In fact, a number of specific military-to-military programs have provided direct U.S. support for HIV/AIDS control to several African militaries. With PEPFAR support, the Defense HIV/AIDS Prevention Program commits over $45 million annually in military-to-military HIV prevention efforts in Africa. More recently, the October 2008 launch of the U.S. Africa Command (AFRICOM) is an opportunity to involve DOD health personnel, laboratory assets, and special logistics capacities more extensively in improving health conditions in Africa. In the coming two years, it is expected that AFRICOM will develop a longer-term vision of its health strategy in Africa and of how that strategy can be integrated into the larger U.S. national strategy.

AFRICAN LEADERSHIP

Since 2001, many Africans—from political leaders to scientists to non-governmental activists—have worked harder and more explicitly on their countries' behalf to address the HIV pandemic. African heads of state met in Abuja, Nigeria, in April 2001 to discuss the impacts and responses to HIV/AIDS, TB, and malaria. The resulting Abuja Declaration on HIV/AIDS, Tuberculosis, and Other Related Infectious Diseases[42] makes it clear that the heads of state who attended were generally cognizant of the key issues; they pledged to spend at least 15 percent of their national budgets on health issues. This pledge was reaffirmed and slightly extended by the recently formed African Union in its 2003 Maputo Declaration.[43] However, subsequent activities on these issues in many of these countries have been spotty.

Nevertheless, several individual African leaders have demonstrated particularly strong leadership on HIV/AIDS issues. President Yoweri Museveni of Uganda, for example, had given unstinting support to open discussion of HIV/AIDS early in Uganda's epidemic (in the 1980s and early 1990s), which is now thought to have been responsible for the early decrease in new HIV infection rates noted in that country.[44]

Former President Festus Mogae of Botswana was highly effective in mobilizing significant government resources to complement external HIV/AIDS funding provided for testing and treatment; he has also been outspoken about both the need for broadly implemented HIV testing and the issue of male responsibility for HIV transmission.

Indigenous health-focused NGOs such as the African Council for Sustainable Health Development have helped keep health system improvements on the agenda of African governments.[45] The African Broadcast Media Partnership against HIV/AIDS, a coalition of African broadcast companies, has committed to providing public service airtime to help coordinate a public education campaign on HIV/AIDS.

Finally, a number of South African NGOs have been particularly outspoken about their own government's delays in providing access to ART for the millions of South Africans living with AIDS. The changeover in 2008 from President Thabo Mbeki to interim President Kgalema Motlanthe, coupled with a change of health minister, has raised hopes that South Africa's past dysfunction on HIV/AIDS has ended and that its future leadership in African health issues could be considerable.

Global philanthropic involvement in HIV/AIDS activities also accelerated early in this decade. Although many foundations have eventually become involved, the Ford and Rockefeller Foundations and the Bill and Melinda Gates Foundation were early leaders in this regard. In Botswana, for example, a pioneering collaboration between the Gates Foundation, the Merck Company Foundation, BroadReach (a small U.S. health management NGO), and the government of Botswana created and managed the African Comprehensive HIV/AIDS Partnership, a program that achieved notable success in providing large-scale access to AIDS treatment with ART for poor people in that heavily affected country.[46] Later, the William J. Clinton Foundation began what were ultimately successful negotiations with international organizations, pharmaceutical companies, and national governments on ways to reduce the costs of antiretroviral drugs to make them more broadly available in many countries. (More recently, in July 2008, that same foundation announced a similar program to reduce costs of the highly effective antimalarial drug artemisinin in developing countries.)

Notable health successes against other African health problems are being achieved through public-private partnerships, some, but not all, of which involve U.S. government agencies. For example, the highly successful program to eradicate guinea worm (dracunculiasis) is a collaboration among many groups, including the Carter Presidential Center, the CDC, the World Health Organization, and UNICEF. Several of the research training programs that the National Institutes of Health's Fogarty International Center supports to train African health scientists are being conducted in partnership with consortia of U.S. and African universities. The blinding parasitic disease onchocerciasis (river blindness) is under successful attack in Africa by the African Program for Onchocerciasis Control, a partnership of the World Bank, Helen Keller International, WHO, UNDP, the UN Food and Agriculture Organization (FAO), the Gates Foundation, the Merck Foundation and others. The Merck Company provides this latter program with the onchocerciasis treatment drug mectizan free of charge.

MOVING FORWARD FROM 2008

While the new PEPFAR reauthorizing legislation for FY 2009–2013 lays out a broad, integrated framework for action, the legislation was not devised with a U.S. or global recession in mind. Implementation awaits clarification of the policy priorities of the Barack Obama administration and congressional action in appropriations. A brief overview of the key elements is nonetheless valuable.

The reauthorization calls for a large increase in funds for HIV/AIDS to about $37 billion, up from the nearly $19 billion that was eventually appropriated in 2004–2008. In addition, the new bill explicitly adds $4 billion for TB control activities and $5 billion for malaria control.[47] Several earmarks remain from the earlier legislation, although they appear a bit more flexible than before. For example, the requirement that 33 percent of HIV prevention funds be spent on abstinence-until–marriage programs was replaced by a requirement that various prevention activities be funded in an equitable way and that Congress be notified if less than 50 percent of prevention funds dedicated to generalized epidemics in any particular country go to programs promoting abstinence, delayed sexual debut, monogamy, fidelity, and partner reduction. Finally, the prostitution pledge issue also remains, requiring that funded organizations have a policy explicitly opposing prostitution and sex trafficking.

Program targets and goals are modestly increased over those of 2004–2008. The new prevention goal adds 5 million additional infections prevented over the next five years, for a 10-year total of 12 million. The care goal is increased from 10 million people in 2004–2008 to 12 million overall by 2013 and now explicitly includes 5 million orphans and vulnerable children. The ART goal has been expanded from 2 million people in 2004–2008 to a new number to be determined by the funding amounts appropriated for AIDS treatment in any given year compared to the FY 2008 amount and any decrease achieved in PEPFAR's per capita AIDS treatment costs. A new goal of training 140,000 health workers has been added, as have specific targets for prevention of mother-to-child HIV transmission.

The legislation also adds explicit food and nutrition goals, including a provision that allows use of food as a component of AIDS treatment. Significantly, nutritional assessments of program participants will now be required in all HIV/AIDS treatment and care programs.

Funding allocations for the Global Fund are doubled in the authorizing legislation to $2 billion for FY 2009 (up from $1 billion in 2004–2008) with additional sums "as are necessary" for subsequent years.[48] The prior requirement of a U.S. cap of one-third of total Global Fund contributions is retained.

Notably, the 1993 statutory ban against allowing entry of HIV-infected visitors and immigrants into the United States was stricken by the bill[49] and the responsibility for decisions about whether HIV infection should be considered a "communicable disease of public health significance" (and therefore grounds for automatic exclusion of non-citizens from the United States) has been returned from Congress to the Department of Health and Human Services, as is the case for all other diseases. Once this transition is completed, it should again be possible for the United States to host the biennial International AIDS Conference, which has not been held on U.S. soil since the entry ban was put into place in 1990.

CONCLUSIONS AND RECOMMENDATIONS

In the Obama administration, the next U.S. act on health in Africa will rest on clear White House leadership and strong bipartisan congressional support. Those elements, the *sine qua non* of the Bush era's success in this arena, will not change. They will be the keys to achieving robust annual appropriations, systematically holding together the coalition that for the past seven years has stood behind these historic U.S. global health commitments in Africa and elsewhere, and reassuring the American people that these investments are achieving concrete results. However, because of the looming domestic and global recession, the next act will also require a special effort to successfully market continued high-level engagement in African health to an American people living with greater uncertainty and insecurity. It will also require adequate reassurance for African partners who will fear a reversal of commitments and an inward turn by the United States and other Western powers, at the same time that conditions may be worsening in much of Africa.

Incoming senior policymakers are likely to have a very different mind-set from the era of euphoric expansion in the funding of African health activities that occurred during the Bush era. There will be a premium on realism, pragmatism, compassion, and flexibility. To demonstrate that existing investments are delivering concrete results and to improve the efficiencies of ongoing programs, outcome evaluation programs will need to be strengthened. Balanced, judicious reductions in short-term plans will be likely. However, it will be essential to make those adjustments in a way that maintains critical core investments (including continuing support for those whose lives are already being extended through PEPFAR-supported antiretroviral treatment and care programs), while still allowing significant expansion of effective HIV prevention programs. It will be no less critical to reaffirm the commitment over the medium and long term to the goals set forth in the 2008 PEPFAR reauthorization.

Success of the next U.S. act on health in Africa will also rest on meeting five key policy challenges:

1. *There is no choice but to tackle head-on the weaknesses in Africa's health infrastructure, particularly its human skills deficit.* To expand and sustain HIV/AIDS, TB, and malaria programs on the prodigious scale envisioned in the PEPFAR reauthorization, while at the same time clearly identifying and responding adequately to other important African health issues, will require a strategic approach to Africa's health infrastructure weaknesses: its shortage of adequate health care facilities, its severe shortage of health workers at all levels, and the weakness of its disease surveillance systems that must provide the local data needed for rational policymaking. In many African countries, deficits in the health workforce in particular stem from a combination of weak health systems, poor national policies and planning, and global market demand that recruits scarce trained health personnel

out of poorer countries and into wealthier ones (including the United States), both inside and outside of Africa. Changing that scenario will require a well-considered, long-term, multilateral educational and diplomatic effort that simultaneously focuses on enlarging the global pool of skilled health personnel, strengthening incentives for their local retention, and finding effective offsets to global market forces.

2. *The Obama administration will need to strengthen U.S. government policy links to key partners, including the African Union, the European Union (and its component countries), fellow G-8 member states, and multilateral agencies that deal in global health. In the midst of a global economic downturn, the United States needs to be seen as leading on the multilateral stage to find common feasible solutions.* The new administration is likely to be far more successful if it proactively seeks to combine bilateral and multilateral approaches to Africa's health problems. To that end, it will be essential to sustain strong political and financial support to the Global Fund to Fight AIDS, TB, and Malaria; engage at a far higher level within the G-8 and with the World Health Organization and the African Union to put their core strengths on a firmer, long-term footing; coordinate global health policy development and program implementation with the European Union; ensure the continued strong leadership of other UN agencies (UNAIDS, UNICEF, the UN Population Fund, UNDP, the Word Food Program, and FAO, for example) that directly address public health issues; and expand support to African nongovernmental organizations involved in the health sector.

3. *The Obama administration should give a high priority to the need for integrating U.S. approaches to HIV/AIDS with other health and development priorities.* U.S. HIV/AIDS efforts in Africa are likely to be more successful if the rising tensions around HIV/AIDS programs are acknowledged and addressed systematically. Special care is needed to minimize unhelpful zero-sum battles by ensuring that, to the maximum extent possible, resource investments in HIV/AIDS also benefit programs to address other health issues such as other infectious diseases, child survival, reproductive health and family planning, food security, and basic needs for water and sanitation. Other U.S. government

programs such as PMI and the Neglected Tropical Diseases Initiative and the U.S.-supported STOP TB Program can also help address concerns about this set of issues. Even if U.S. resources cannot quickly be allocated to other serious health and development problems in Africa, however, every opportunity should be taken to continue to raise the profile of these problems for policymakers in the United States, the European Union, and other donor states.

4. *It will be essential for the United States to adopt a more strategic approach to HIV prevention that focuses on interventions of demonstrated effectiveness in reducing the risks of HIV transmission.* Early in its tenure, the Obama administration should join with congressional leadership to lay down the parameters of a robust new approach to HIV prevention, establish new partnerships with African leaders and international organizations, and set concrete numerical targets for reducing HIV prevalence and incidence rates, especially in southern and eastern Africa. In particular, PEPFAR should set clear and aggressive targets for accelerating the delivery of safe male circumcision services. Increases in overall PEPFAR funding for individual focus countries during FY 2010–2013 should be made contingent on countries' achieving measurable successes in reaching the numerical HIV prevention targets set for their PEPFAR-supported programs.

Because PEPFAR's laudable recent successes in providing access to AIDS treatment and care in its focus countries are not yet close to being matched by successes in preventing new HIV infections, a new approach to prevention programming is critical particularly in southern and eastern Africa.[50] Prevention of HIV transmission through transactional sex, other heterosexual sex, sex between men, and injection drug use are controversial, divisive, and politically uncomfortable issues in many settings, pitting those with a focus on evidence-based public health against others wanting to emphasize abstinence. It is now widely recognized both that achieving and sustaining major behavior change on a population basis is more complex than anticipated earlier and that evaluating the outcomes of programs to change sexual and drug-using behaviors can be difficult. Yet, as pointed out recently by both the IOM[51] and the Global HIV Prevention

Working Group,[52] these tasks are achievable. Because there are no biological magic bullets in sight for HIV prevention, there is little choice but to tackle these two challenges head-on by having U.S. resources, in concert with others, support behavior-based HIV prevention programs that can be demonstrated to be effective in reducing the numbers of people who become infected with HIV.

5. *It will be essential to refine and update treatment and prevention approaches continually for global HIV/AIDS, TB, and malaria to address better the evolving characteristics of these related pandemics, with particular attention to issues of drug resistance and co-morbidity.* Special attention and programs will be needed to address the increasing number of people in developing countries who are infected with drug-resistant forms of HIV.[53] As has been proven to be the case with TB, second-line antiretroviral drugs needed to treat drug-resistant HIV are likely to be much costlier than current first-line drugs and much more associated with adverse effects.[54] In addition, special efforts will be needed to identify and manage the increasing numbers of drug-resistant TB infections as well as the rising rates of co-infection with TB and HIV. For malaria, different control strategies may be required as cases become less common. As these epidemiologic and economic shifts occur, their magnitude and budgetary consequences need to be well understood by U.S. policymakers so that appropriate responses can be incorporated into both short- and long-term U.S. policies and strategies.

In closing, despite the growing complexity of the health agenda in Africa, the proliferating financial, managerial, and technical challenges, and the worsening global economy, there is much reason to be hopeful and proud of U.S. leadership in promoting better health within Africa. The commitments made in this decade have improved the lives of millions, changed perceptions, and proven to be very effective instruments of U.S. "smart power." A vision has been set and embedded in legislative action for carrying forward U.S. leadership that will deepen partnerships in Africa, adapt to new demands, and advance African and U.S. interests.

NOTES

The authors would like to thank the following people for helpful comments on various drafts of this chapter: Suzanne Brundage, Joanne Carter, Jennifer Cooke, Daryl Edwards, Janet Fleischman, Jim Herrington, Kate Hofler, Jennifer Kates, Judith Kauffman, Kyle Kinner, Mauro de Lorenzo, Princeton Lyman, Allen Moore, Ronald J. Waldman, and Lauren Weeth.

1. PEPFAR's initial 14 focus countries, 12 of which are in Africa, included Botswana, Côte d'Ivoire, Ethiopia, Guyana, Haiti, Kenya, Mozambique, Namibia, Nigeria, Rwanda, South Africa, Tanzania, Uganda, and Zambia. Vietnam was added in 2005 as a fifteenth country—and the only Asian focus country.

2. Mead Over, "Prevention Failure: The Ballooning Entitlement Burden of Global AIDS Treatment Spending and What to Do about It" (Working Paper 144, Center for Global Development, Washington, D.C., 2008), http://www.cgdev.org/content/publications/detail/15973\.

3. H.R 5501, which became Public Law 110-293.

4. National Intelligence Council, *Strategic Implications of Global Health*, publication ICA 2008-10D (Washington, D.C.: National Intelligence Council, 2008), http://www.state.gov/documents/organization/113592.pdf.

5. Institute of Medicine, *The U.S. Commitment to Global Health: Recommendations for the New Administration* (Washington, D.C.: National Academies, 2008), http://www.iom.edu/CMS/3783/51303/60714.aspx. The IOM document differs slightly from the NIC report in that it does not directly address some related issues such as water and sanitation, climate change, and food security.

6. National Intelligence Council, *The Global Infectious Disease Threat and Its Implications for the United States*, publication NIE-99-17D (Washington, D.C.: National Intelligence Council, 2000), http://www.dni.gov/nic/special_global-infectious.html. Some of the diseases discussed in this report have received even greater attention in the post-9/11 era than has HIV/AIDS.

7. UNICEF, *Child Survival: The State of the World's Children 2008* (New York: UNICEF, 2008). See statistical tables on pages 109 ff.

8. UNAIDS, *Report on the Global AIDS Epidemic* (Geneva: UNAIDS, 2008), http://www.unaids.org/en/KnowledgeCentre/HIVData/EpiUpdate/EpiUpdArchive/2007/default.asp. These data are based on UNAIDS's 2007 HIV/AIDS estimates.

9. The Global Fund was created as an independent international organization, located in Geneva, that solicits funds from national governments and other sources and distributes these funds to countries that meet certain economic and management criteria, including convening and empowering a participatory decisionmaking body known as a country coordinating mechanism. Eligible countries submit proposals that are judged on a competitive basis for funding of HIV/AIDS, TB, or malaria programs. Sir Richard Feachem (UK), the first executive director of the Global Fund, was succeeded in 2006 by Prof.

Michel Kazatchkine (France). U.S. DHHS Secretary Tommy Thompson was the first chair of the Global Fund board; the current chair is Rajat Gupta, affiliated with McKinsey and Company, a U.S. nongovernmental organization. As of April 2008, the Global Fund had approved proposals totaling $11.6 billion for programs in 136 countries; 61 percent of this amount was allocated for programs involving HIV/AIDS, 25 percent for malaria, and 14 percent for tuberculosis; 58 percent of the approved $11.6 billion total went to programs in sub-Saharan Africa. The Global Fund, "Distribution of funding after 7 rounds," The Global Fund, http://www.theglobalfund.org/en/funds_raised/distribution.

10. National Intelligence Council, *The Next Wave of HIV/AIDS: Nigeria, Ethiopia, Russia, India, and China* (Washington, D.C.: National Intelligence Council, 2002), http://www.fas.org/irp/nic/hiv-aids.html.

11. The White House, *The National Security Strategy of the United States of America* (Washington, D.C.: The White House, 2002), http://www.globalsecurity.org/military/library/policy/national/nss-020920.pdf. The public health stance in this 2002 strategy was reaffirmed in the next iteration of the strategy, issued in March 2006.

12. CDC is a component agency of the U.S. Department of Health and Human Services.

13. H.R. 1298, "United States Leadership against HIV/AIDS, Tuberculosis, and Malaria Act of 2003," May 2003, http://www.govtrack.us/congress/bill.xpd?bill=h108-1298.

14. The Department of State was chosen as a focus for the bureaucratic infrastructure both because the government's global HIV/AIDS activities were housed in multiple departments and agencies and because of a widely acknowledged inability of USAID and CDC to coordinate their HIV/AIDS programs and activities consistently. Secretary of State Colin Powell had also been an eloquent champion of the need for effective U.S. government HIV/AIDS control activities on a global level. The first U.S. global AIDS coordinator, Amb. Randall Tobias, was succeeded in 2006 by Amb. Mark Dybul.

15. Most of the following statistics are from PEPFAR, *The Power of Partnerships: Fourth Annual Report to Congress on PEPFAR* (Washington, D.C.: PEPFAR, 2008), http://www.pepfar.gov/press/fourth_annual_report/.

16. PEPFAR, "Latest Results" http://www.pepfar.gov/about/c19785.htm. When PEPFAR was announced in late 2003, only about 50,000 people in sub-Saharan Africa were estimated to be receiving ART for HIV/AIDS.

17. UN Secretary General Ban Ki Moon, "Declaration of Commitment on HIV/AIDS and Political Declaration on HIV/AIDS: Midway to the Millennium Development Goals" (presented at the U.N General Assembly, 62nd Session, Agenda Item 44, New York, April 1, 2008), http://www.stoptb.org/events/hivtbleaders/assets/documents/Secretary%20General%20Progress%20Rerport.pdf.

18. The newly reauthorized PEPFAR legislation is intended to add only approximately another 1 million people to treatment rolls over the next five years, while 1.9 million people in sub-Saharan Africa became infected with HIV in 2007 alone.

19. Recently completed research studies of HIV vaccines and vaginal microbicides have either demonstrated no efficacy of the experimental interventions or, in at least one vaccine and one microbicide study each, have shown higher HIV transmission rates among the group receiving the experimental interventions than among the control group receiving placebos. Thus, there is little likelihood in the near term of an effective biomedical method to prevent adult HIV infection on a population basis.

20. The data on the HIV prevention efficacy of adult male circumcision are strong and consistent, with each of three randomized studies completed in 2006 and 2007 showing more than 60 percent efficacy in reducing new HIV infection rates. However, programs to provide this intervention to men at risk are lagging badly. See David Wilson and Daniel T. Halperin, "'Know Your Epidemic, Know Your Response: A Useful Approach If We Get It Right," *The Lancet* 372, no. 9637 (2008): 423–26.

21. Global HIV Prevention Working Group, *Behavior Change and HIV Prevention, (Re)considerations for the 21st Century,* 2008, http://www.kff.org/hivaids/upload/pwg080508fullreport.pdf.

22. Although there has been increasing discussion about the potential utility of preventing HIV transmission through widespread use of antiretroviral drugs, either prior to HIV exposure or soon after HIV infection, the value of either of these approaches as public health tools remains to be demonstrated.

23. The absence of systematic programs for reaching women and girls may be one of the reasons that success rates in PMTCT programs were unexpectedly low. Given the increased attention and space in the recent reauthorizing legislation devoted to the issue of reaching women and girls, its lack of specific guidance or goals for the Office of the Global AIDS Coordinator about the importance of integration of HIV/AIDS activities with those of reproductive health and family planning programs is a striking omission. The reluctance to address this issue legislatively may rest at least in part on a concern that the program might thereby inadvertently fund abortion services.

24. See note 15. Although a number of scientific studies have been done in both industrialized and developing countries of the effect of abstinence programs on HIV transmission, none has found any reduction in HIV risk.

25. U.S. Institute of Medicine, *PEPFAR Implementation: Progress and Promise* (Washington, D.C.: National Academy of Sciences, 2007). The work of this IOM committee began in 2005.

26. General Accountability Office, *Spending Requirement Presents Challenges for Allocating Prevention Funding under the President's Emergency Plan for AIDS Relief,* Report No. GAO-06-305 (Washington, D.C.: GAO, 2006).

27. For example, on the treatment side, use of generic antiretroviral drugs, initially restricted because most were not FDA approved, has been expanded through a collaborative multiagency drug approval process. This particular change has allowed use of less expensive generic drugs, in turn permitting a larger number of patients to be treated in PEPFAR programs for the same cost.

28. See "Prevention Rapporteur Presentation," slide no. 60 (presented at the 2007 HIV/AIDS Implementers' Meeting, held in Kigali, Rwanda, June 16–19, 2007), http://www.hivimplementers.org/2007/summary.htm.

29. Adult male circumcision has been shown in several controlled studies to lead to a more than 60 percent reduction in men's risk of becoming infected with HIV. Men who benefit from circumcision in this way are obviously unlikely to infect their sexual partners with HIV. Unfortunately, the male circumcision procedure is being adopted very slowly in many countries, in part because of a lack of trained personnel.

30. In FY 2007, PEPFAR programs provided nutritional supplementation to approximately 50,000 pregnant and lactating women and to more than 300,000 orphans and vulnerable children.

31. PEPFAR, *The Power of Partnerships: Fourth Annual Report to Congress on PEPFAR* (Washington, D.C.: PEPFAR, 2008), http://www.pepfar.gov/press/fourth_annual_report/. See figure 11 and p. 22.

32. See WHO's Stop TB Department Web site, http://www.who.int/tb/about/en/.

33. See the Stop TB Partnership Web site, http://www.stoptb.org .

34. As of December 2008, PMI operates in 15 African countries: Angola, Benin, Ethiopia, Ghana, Kenya Liberia, Madagascar, Malawi, Mali, Mozambique, Rwanda, Senegal, Tanzania, Uganda, and Zambia. See PMI program description at http://www.fightingmalaria.gov/about/index.html.

35. The WHO-sponsored Global Malaria Eradication Campaign, which began in 1955 and ended in the mid-1970s, specifically did not include any countries in sub-Saharan Africa. See CDC, "The History of Malaria, an Ancient Disease," http://www.cdc.gov/malaria/history/index.htm#eradicationworldwide.

36. CDC, which began its existence as a malaria control organization in the 1940s, has always had a small malaria program, which in the past has focused on providing technical support directly to ministries of health and to WHO.

37. Roll Back Malaria Project Web site, http://www.rbm.who.int/. See also WHO Global Malaria Programme, "*World Malaria Report 2008*," WHO, http://www.who.int/malaria/wmr2008; and Susan Okie, "A New Attack on Malaria," *New England Journal of Medicine*, 358, no. 23 (2008): 2425–28.

38. Office of the White House Press Secretary, "Fighting Neglected Tropical Diseases around the World." The White House, http://www.whitehouse.gov/news/releases/2008/02/20080220.html. The seven diseases referred to include lymphatic filariasis (elephantiasis), schistosomiasis, trachoma, onchocerciasis ("river blindness"), and three soil-transmitted parasites (hookworm, whipworm, and roundworm). See also Peter Hotez et al., "Control of Neglected Tropical Diseases," *New England Journal of Medicine*, 357, no. 10 (2007): 1018–27.

39. CDC, "Progress in Global Measles Control and Mortality Reduction, 2000–2006," *Mortality and Morbidity Weekly Report* 56, no. 47 (2007): 1237–41, http://www.cdc.gov/mmwr/preview/mmwrhtml/mm5647a3.htm.

40. Recovering control of polio in the other 22 previously polio-free countries cost an additional $450 million between 2003 and 2006. See, for example, Leslie Roberts, "Polio: No Cheap Way Out," *Science* 316, no. 5823 (2007): 362–63.

41. A new and ongoing polio epidemic explicitly linked to failure to immunize has been reported from northern Nigeria in 2008. See CDC, "Progress toward Poliomyelitis Eradication—Nigeria, January 2007–August 12, 2008," *Mortality and Morbidity Weekly Report,* 357, no. 34 (2008): 942–46. http://www.cdc.gov/mmwr/preview/mmwrhtml/mm5734a4.htm. The Nigerian problems are not the only political obstacles being faced by the global polio eradication program. Persistent circulation of the poliovirus in a few other countries (for example, Afghanistan, India and Pakistan) is felt to be related to political instability in some higher polio risk areas in those countries.

42. Abuja Summit to Endorse ADF 2000 Consensus on Fighting HIV/AIDS, "Abuja Declaration on HIV/AIDS, Tuberculosis and Other Related Infectious Diseases," African Development Forum 2000, http://www.uneca.org/adf2000/abuja%20declaration.htm.

43. Assembly of the African Union, "Declarations" (adopted at the Second Ordinary Session, Maputo, Mozambique, July 10–12, 2003), http://www.africa-union.org/Official_documents/Decisions_Declarations/Assembly%20final/Assembly%20%20DECLARATIONS%20%20-%20Maputo%20-%20FINAL5%2008-08-03.pdf.

44. President Museveni is no longer a strong supporter of condom use in Uganda; HIV rates have been rising recently in that country.

45. Zoë Mullan, "Lola Dare: Creating African Solutions for Better Health," *Lancet* 372, no. 9637 (2008): 439.

46. Of note, two important lessons from that early effort were (1) that a specific effort was required to increase uptake of HIV testing to identify infected people early enough for them to receive the full benefit of highly active antiretroviral therapy (HAART), that is, before their HIV disease had progressed to full-blown AIDS; and (2) that without specific attention to HIV prevention programs, providing effective HAART to large numbers of people was not sufficient to reduce the continuing spread of HIV in the population.

47. The reauthorization language also includes a provision requiring development of five-year control strategies for both malaria and for tuberculosis.

48. As of this writing, only $1 million has been included in the nominal 2009 budget for the Global Fund.

49. See Phillip Nieburg, Helene Gayle, J. Stephen Morrison, and Kate Hofler, *Moving Beyond the U.S. Government Policy of Inadmissibility of HIV-infected Noncitizens* (Washington, D.C.: Center for Strategic and International Studies, 2007), http://www.csis.org/media/csis/pubs/movingbeyondinadmissibility.pdf.

50. U.S. Institute of Medicine, *PEPFAR Implementation: Progress and Promise* (Washington, D.C.: National Academy of Sciences, 2007).

51. Clara Cohen, Michele Orza, and Deepali Patel, *Design Considerations for Evaluating the Impact of PEPFAR: Workshop Summary* (Washington, D.C.: National Academies Press, 2008).

52. Global HIV Prevention Working Group, "Behavior Change and HIV Prevention: (Re)Considerations for the 21st Century," Global HIV Prevention, http://www.globalhivprevention.org/pdfs/PWG_behavior%20report_FINAL.pdf.

53. Some HIV-infected people have a drug-resistant virus because they adhered poorly to their ART regimen; however, even people who are fully compliant with ART can develop a drug-resistant virus, although at much lower rates. Finally, a third group includes those people infected with an HIV strain that was already drug-resistant when they initially became infected.

54. Over, "Prevention Failure." The issues of concern for malaria treatment bear some resemblance to concerns about AIDS and TB, although adverse effects of drugs currently used for malaria treatment are less common and less severe than with the other two diseases. In addition, current malaria control programs have a relatively greater focus on the prevention of new infections than do TB and AIDS programs.

4

PURSUING U.S. ENERGY SECURITY
INTERESTS IN AFRICA

DAVID L. GOLDWYN

Africa plays a strategic role in U.S. and global energy security. It is a critical supplier of new-source production to global and U.S. oil supply. It is a natural gas supplier, with enormous potential to meet increased future demand in a carbon-constrained world. Africa remains open to foreign investment and is one of the few continents that has not dramatically reduced access to investment in recent years. If the continent meets its potential, it may increase its production substantially over the next two decades, serving as a pillar of global energy security by providing a major source of diverse oil and gas supply. The risk of instability in many of Africa's key energy producers is high and rising, posing a threat to the stability of these nations and their neighbors, as well as to U.S. investment and the global economy.

While the Bush administration identified Africa's rising potential and associated escalating risks early in its first year of office, transparency and governance were low-priority issues, diplomatic engagement with energy producers atrophied, and no significant sums of new resources were deployed to address the challenges associated with rising revenues and eroding capacity of governments to manage them.[1] In the meantime, there have been significant changes in the global energy market since 2001—an explosion in global demand, led by developing Asia; a 340 percent increase in nominal prices,[2] followed by a sharp downturn in the fourth quarter of 2008 with the potential to trigger sudden budgetary contractions within African producing countries; a vast increase in the number of African countries undergoing hydrocarbon exploration and development activities; and a historic intensification of competition for access among China, India, Russia, and other emerging energy powers, with extensive help in many cases from their governments.

High oil prices have led to resource nationalism in several African countries with reduced access and harsher terms for the access that remains. Exploration has steadily moved further offshore, which has removed investment from land-based capital but left thinly protected offshore platforms exposed to maritime risk at a time of dramatically worsening piracy in the Gulf of Guinea. Angola, which has grown considerably as a producer, has joined the Organization of the Petroleum Exporting Countries (OPEC). Nigeria's production has risen, but it has also produced one of the global economy's greatest supply shocks: an average of 550 million barrels per day (bpd) were shut-in in 2008, with shut-ins reaching nearly 1 million bpd at times as compared with 2006 production levels due to violence in the Niger Delta.[3] Equatorial Guinea has become a major oil and methanol producer and is a provider of liquefied natural gas (LNG). Despite conflict and sanctions, Sudan's production has grown since 2001 to 466,000 bpd; Chad's has grown as well from zero production in 2002 to 156,000 bpd in 2006.[4]

These striking changes in the global energy market have occurred in a period when U.S. influence in the region has diminished, accompanied by an erosion in the U.S. ability to promote good governance, conflict resolution, and environmental standards and to reduce corruption. This shift notwithstanding, many companies and governments now accept in principle that good governance, respect for human rights, and transparency are the cornerstones of political stability, a level playing field for commercial competition and long-term security of investment and energy supply. The World Bank has begun to engage countries systematically on reforming the process of energy production—how acreage is allocated, how products are sold, how refineries are supplied—both to help them preserve value and to reduce corruption. In recent years, the United States, which at one time led the promotion of voluntary standards on environmental protection and respect for human rights in security protection, has become a marginal player in the international promotion of good governance and transparency in the extractive industries.

On critical energy sector issues, U.S. engagement with the continent has been drastically reduced over the past eight years. A continental

U.S.-Africa Energy Ministers Partnership begun in the late 1990s expired in this decade. Binational commissions and policy dialogues with Angola and Nigeria have similarly lapsed. Engagement on the Niger Delta has been episodic and ineffectual. Engagement of China and Europe—the other two largest investors in and consumers of energy in Africa—on the impact of instability and insecurity on global energy markets has been negligible. The United States contributed to the international Extractive Industry Transparency Initiative (EITI) only when forced to do so by a 2007 congressional earmark.

The grave energy-related risks of instability in Africa, acknowledged in 2001 and foreseeable for new energy producers, have not been treated through any serious or systematic policy approach. The conflict in the Niger Delta has grown in intensity and lethality. Angola does not engage with the United States on governance and transparency. Contact with Algeria, Chad, Equatorial Guinea, and Libya, which was negligible or nonexistent in early 2001, has advanced significantly, but serious engagement on bilateral or energy issues is still very modest for countries that constitute four of the top five suppliers of energy on the African continent. The potential risk to Africa's growing list of new energy producers of managing potentially enormous revenue flows has not yet been considered. At present the United States has no policy mechanism for systematically engaging Africa's leading or emerging energy producers. Although the lack of a coherent policy toward producing states in Africa may have been tolerable in the past, global energy interdependence has deepened this decade, and high, volatile prices have raised the stakes. The issues at hand—stability, good governance, economic development, and security—will remain vital to U.S. interests in Africa, even if a global financial slowdown suppresses the price of oil and natural gas. That downturn, in fact, may open a window for testing renewed efforts to engage African energy-producing countries in governance reform.

Several reasons account for the marginalization of U.S. engagement with Africa on energy during this period of rapid expansion in production. The Bush administration believed that the market would provide for energy supply without U.S. government engagement. In addition, crises in the Horn of Africa, Kenya, the Democratic Republic of Congo (DRC), Somalia, and Sudan absorbed a significant share of diplomatic attention. Massive new investments in public health, especially HIV/AIDS, superseded significant attention to governance. Counterterrorism was a priority focus as opposed to political and economic development. The conflicts in Iraq and Afghanistan drew diplomats out of the area, leaving scarce human resources for sustained engagement in places like Nigeria, or noncrisis countries like Angola. But more than anything else, the failure to engage strategically stemmed from structural deficiencies in the U.S. government. The many government agencies that engage on energy-related issues (State, Energy, Commerce, the U.S. Trade and Development Agency, the U.S. Agency for International Development, Defense, Treasury) were not formally integrated, leading to a disconnect between energy and national security policies and the absence of a central bureaucratic locus of oversight and coordination that was capable of identifying the connection between mismanaged oil and gas revenues and instability.

Achieving a coherent, interagency policy approach on Africa's energy sector is a core challenge before the new administration. If the United States sees stability in Africa as a national security priority for multiple reasons—reduction of conflict, counterterrorism, combating grand crime, eradicating disease, and promoting economic prosperity in Africa and at home—a strategic policy on energy security in Africa will be essential. Such a policy would identify U.S. energy security interests in Africa, take account of the emerging trends in the region and the role of other actors, consider what policies have and have not worked over the past eight years, identify the serious impediments to U.S. interests that loom ahead, and deploy the human and financial resources to meet this challenge.

This chapter will review Africa's role in U.S. energy security, emergent trends in the global energy market and on the continent, the Bush administration's policy record in this area, and the core challenges facing a new U.S. administration. It will conclude with a set of priority recommendations.

AFRICA'S ROLE IN U.S. ENERGY SECURITY

U.S. energy security depends on diverse sources of oil and, increasingly, natural gas supply. For the United States to maintain a diversified energy portfolio, there needs to be a free, global market for the trade of crude oil and petroleum products where international and indigenous companies produce in response to market signals.

International and national oil companies need sufficient access to exploration acreage in countries with stable commercial and political climates. In countries that welcome foreign investment, U.S. energy security depends on corruption-free access to reserves so that U.S. firms compete on a level playing field. In all countries where oil companies invest, improved rule of law and respect for the sanctity of contract are needed to ensure the security of investments and the fair and amicable resolution of disputes. Moreover, the commercial environment must enable private firms to earn a return on investments that will satisfy shareholders and validate the investment as a prudent use of shareholder funds. U.S. energy security also depends on the safe transportation of energy resources, free from piracy, theft, and violence.

In a global market, U.S. energy security is influenced by global demand and supply for oil and gas. Supply disruptions and demand shocks have an immediate impact on U.S. fuel prices and protection of personnel. Even as the United States and other nations move to a less carbon-intensive economy, nearly every respected international economic agency predicts that oil and natural gas will remain the dominant sources of total global energy demand over the next two decades.

Africa plays a strategic role in meeting global and U.S. energy security. African producers supply light sweet crude to U.S., European, and Asian markets. Africa's role in energy security has risen dramatically since 2001. Sub-Saharan Africa's share of global oil production rose from 5 percent in 2001 to 7 percent in 2007,[5] while production in the North Sea and other areas of the Organization for Economic Cooperation and Development (OECD) has declined. This growth has come from the marked increase in offshore, especially deepwater, oil production. In sub-Saharan Africa today, the key oil producers are Angola, Gabon, the Republic of Congo (Congo-Brazzaville), Equatorial Guinea, and Nigeria (see figure 4.1). Sub-Saharan Africa holds 6 percent of global reserves and 3 percent of global gas reserves.[6] By 2020, 95 percent of regional oil production will be offshore, and 85 percent of this production will come from Angola and Nigeria.[7] Of the 12 top producers of oil on the African continent, four are members of OPEC (Algeria, Angola, Libya, and Nigeria), but all welcome foreign investment.

Africa's share of U.S. imports of oil has risen from 15 percent to 24 percent, providing a key source of diversification of U.S. supplies (see figure 4.2). Nineteen percent of U.S. oil imports from Africa came from sub-Saharan countries in 2007.[8] U.S. imports of natural gas from Africa have increased ninefold since 2000 (see figure 4.3), from 13 tril-

Figure 4.1. Oil-Producing and Frontier Countries in Africa

■ Active Exploration & Production

▨ Frontier Exploration

Source: Monica Enfield, PFC Energy.

lion cubic feet (tcf) to 113 tcf.[9] The vast majority of shipments of LNG to the United States from sub-Sahara Africa are from Nigeria, while most imports from North Africa originate from Algeria and Egypt.

Africa is also an important source of oil and natural gas for U.S. allies in Europe. European states, which historically have relied on Russia for natural gas, are increasingly concerned about supply disruptions. Russia's rhetoric about diverting natural gas to Asian markets and its actions toward neighboring transit states have prompted the European countries to look as far as Nigeria for new sources of piped gas. While a trans-Sahara pipeline is considered economically infeasible at this time, there may eventually be a compelling geopolitical rationale for it, especially if Russian-European competition for control of gas flows to European consumers intensifies. The European Union Energy Commissioner has offered to help Nigeria develop plans. North African producers, including Libya and Algeria, already provide Europe with pipeline gas. Europe, too, receives shipments of LNG from Africa.

Figure 4.2. U.S. Imports of Oil from Africa as a Percentage of Total Imports, 2000–2007

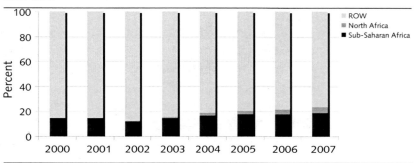

Source: Sheila Moynihan, Goldwyn International Strategies, using data from the Energy Information Agency and PFC Energy..

Figure 4.3. U.S. Imports of Liquefied Natural Gas from Africa as a Percentage of Total Imports, 2000–2007

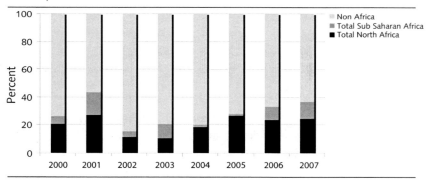

Source: Sheila Moynihan, Goldwyn International Strategies, using data from the Energy Information Agency and PFC Energy..

EMERGENT TRENDS ON THE CONTINENT

The global oil market has undergone dramatic changes in the past eight years, and the impact on Africa has been significant. The rise in oil prices, from an average of $26 per barrel WTI[10] in 2001 to an average of $109.64 a barrel for the first 10 months of 2008, has changed the terms of producing oil.[11] Many global producers, for instance, have been less willing to expand production. Governments of producing countries have increased demand for majority control of operations or a larger share of profits and have come to expect higher earnings from resource rents. Escalated prices have also led to a rush of new market entrants competing for access as well as a sharp increase in the cost of production as demand for steel rigs and skilled workers has risen steeply. While the higher price of oil has also made relatively expensive exploration and production projects economically feasible, continued capital expenditure on high-cost projects is dependent on sustained high prices. A slowdown in the global economy, which has the effect of dampening oil prices, could result in reduced funding for more expensive projects.

Africa has been affected both positively and negatively by changes in the global energy market. The amount of investment and the profile of investors have expanded, revenue has increased, the number of producers has grown, and the continent's infrastructure for transporting energy has improved. New international voluntary standards for addressing revenue management, security, and environmental protection have evolved. But alongside these promising trends have emerged troubling developments. Unrealized expectations of the transformation oil wealth should bring has fostered discontentment. A failure to address the security implications of moving gas and oil production offshore has left workers and equipment in Nigeria vulnerable to attacks. Host governments are torn between the lure of nonmarket entrants like China that offer turnkey infrastructure solutions and traditional bids for new acreage. The result is an opaque and inconsistent investment environment.

RISING INVESTMENT

In a global market where access is increasingly restricted, Africa is a uniquely open market (see figure 4.4): nearly 50 percent of African production came from international companies in 2005.[12] In 2007, the continent received record foreign direct investment (FDI) inflows of $53 billion.[13] Because of the commodity price boom, the rate of return provided by FDI was higher in Africa than in any other developing region in 2006 and 2007.[14] Nearly every country in Africa with a coast has licensed some acreage for exploration.

While Nigeria and Angola, traditional large producers, have grown, new major players have also emerged: Equatorial Guinea, which produced just 168,000 bpd in 2000, is now the third-largest producer in sub-Saharan Africa.[15] Exploration has moved from West Africa to East Africa, with new discoveries in Uganda and Tanzania. Exploration is under way in Madagascar, and licensing or exploration is being con-

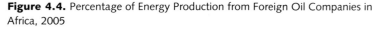

Figure 4.4. Percentage of Energy Production from Foreign Oil Companies in Africa, 2005

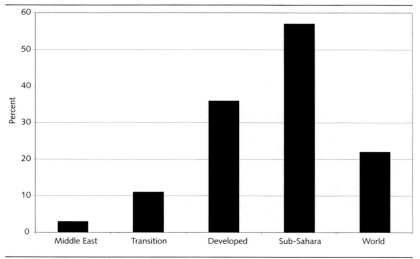

Source: Willy Olsen, Revenue Watch Institute Governing Board, using data from the United Nations Conference on Trade and Development (UNCTAD), Part Two: Transnational Corporations, Extractive Industries and Development, *World Investment Report 2007* (New York: UNCTAD, 2007).

ducted in Côte d'Ivoire, Gambia, Guinea, Liberia, Mali, Niger, Rwanda, and the Puntland region of Somalia. New infrastructure is emerging, from the West Africa gas pipeline (which will take Nigerian gas across Benin and Togo to Ghana) to development of major LNG facilities in Algeria, Angola, Equatorial Guinea, and Nigeria.

Investment levels are rising and moving offshore. According to PFC Energy, an energy consulting group, 95 percent of all regional production will be offshore, with 85 percent of total production coming from Nigeria and Angola by 2012–2015. Firms may invest as much as $485 billion in regional exploration and production between 2005 and 2030.[16] Forty-five percent of the gross amount of capital expenditures for deepwater oil development worldwide is likely to be spent in West Africa. Gross deepwater capital expenditure in West Africa between 2008 and 2015 will exceed that spent in Latin America, the Gulf of Mexico, the North Atlantic, and the Asia-Pacific. These investments, however, may be slowed by a tightening of credit markets.

Africa's natural gas sector is positioned to expand in the coming years, particularly through the increase in LNG capabilities and facilities. Advancements in LNG will enable the continent to serve as a welcome alternative supplier of gas to Europe, the United States, and the Asia-Pacific region and will also help countries meet their goals of reducing gas flaring. Africa has 211 tcf of natural gas reserves. Equatorial Guinea is seeking to become a major regional LNG hub. Investments in LNG have been made in Algeria, Angola, Egypt, Equatorial Guinea, Libya, and Nigeria, and LNG projects have been proposed for Algeria, Egypt, Equatorial Guinea, Gabon, Libya, and Nigeria, although multiple delays to proposed projects are expected because of cost increases, security, social and environmental concerns, feedstock uncertainty, rising domestic demand for natural gas, and negotiations over project terms.

NEW INVESTORS

As global demand for oil and gas has grown, competition in Africa's energy sector has expanded from U.S. and European firms to new competitors, including firms from Brazil, China, India, Korea, Malaysia, and African countries. Russia, which had disengaged from the continent, has returned with hopes of securing natural gas. Africa is no longer the province of major international oil companies; literally hundreds of smaller companies, mostly private, are exploring the new energy-frontier nations and taking over mature properties in other countries.

In the current global economic slowdown with the resulting softening of crude prices, some of the more costly exploration and production projects may fail to generate sufficient revenue to justify investment. Frontier states and new investors with limited experience will be more vulnerable to price drops than experienced actors more familiar with the cyclical nature of commodity prices. Western companies, which have tended to be conservative in their investment decisions, will be in a better position to weather an international financial crisis than small firms backed by hedge funds or those that cannot access credit to fund projects. Similarly, producing countries like Nigeria that premised their national budget on a price of less than $60 per barrel are less likely to experience financial hardships than countries depending on higher oil prices to fund their government.

THE ASIAN PRESENCE

The presence of Asian investors and energy companies on the continent has risen considerably, in tandem with rapidly growing demand for oil and gas in developing Asia. The major Chinese national oil companies—China National Offshore Oil Corporation (CNOOC), China National Petroleum Corporation (CNPC), and Sinopec—Malaysia's Petronas, and India's Oil and Natural Gas Corporation (ONGC) have all purchased equity shares and bid for new licenses in Africa. Geographically, Asian national oil companies (NOCs) have expanded their presence on the continent significantly. In the 1990s, China's involvement in Africa's energy sector began with rogue states such as Sudan. As U.S. companies were barred from operating in Sudan, and other companies such as Canada's Talisman withdrew under shareholder pressure, Asian NOCs such as India's ONGC stepped in to purchase their shares. Next, Asian NOCs began to explore stranded basins in Mali and Nigeria that were exited by international oil companies for commercial reasons. By 2005, Asian NOCs had expanded their operations into traditional producing countries like Algeria, Libya, Mauritania, and Nigeria through aggressively overbidding for acreage. Operationally, Africa now contributes a significant share of the international equity production portfolio for CNPC (40 percent), Sinopec (22.6 percent), CNOOC (45 percent), ONGC (54 percent), and Petronas (76 percent).[17]

It is important to keep the new Asian presence in perspective. On an economic level, fear of Asia's domination of the African energy sector is highly premature. First, while Asian NOCs are exploring in many African countries, the Asian share of oil production in Africa remains modest. Even though the equity stake is high, African oil production constitutes a minor share of the total domestic and international hydrocarbon production for CNPC (6.7 percent), Sinopec (3.4 percent), ONGC (6.7 percent), and Petronas (24 percent).[18] Second, while Asian NOCs have acquired a number of exploration blocks, it is unclear whether they are economical or technically viable to develop. China does not at present have the capability of developing offshore blocks where most African oil is found. Asian NOCs aggressively overbid for blocks in traditional producing countries, and it remains to be seen whether they will be able to produce from these blocks at the level needed to justify investment. If governments do not see results from their NOCs, the flow of Asian investment into Africa could be reversed. The resulting slowdown of foreign investment could significantly affect the political stability of many African regimes. From an energy security perspective, Africa is important to China because it is a source of procured oil. In 2005, 31 percent of China's total crude imports came from

Africa, up from 11 percent in 1995. Moreover, resource-rich countries in Africa provide Chinese NOCs a venue for developing exploration and production skills while securing exploration acreage that could translate into increased production in the future.[19]

The real concern over the rise of Asian NOCs, therefore, stems primarily from anxiety over business practices that negatively affect competition and the long-term stability of producing countries. So far, Asian NOCs have tended to place commercial considerations over humanitarian concerns and have failed to incorporate into the norms of their overseas operation the long-term risks of disregarding governance, environmental, and human rights concerns. These investments have enabled Sudan to grow its production, enjoy substantial oil revenues, and withstand robust international pressure to end the genocide in Darfur and fulfill its obligations under the north-south peace accords.

Western companies also find the way Chinese NOCs compete distressing. The ability of the Chinese to draw on nonmarket tools such as government funds to finance acquisitions and to offer package deals involving construction of roads, soccer stadiums, or railways as a sweetener makes competition for acreage unfair from a Western point of view. Moreover, infrastructure projects in Africa funded by China's Export-Import Bank are required to have Chinese nationals make up 70 percent of the workforce. As a result, the value added to the local community during the construction phase is minimized because there are fewer local citizens employed and developing skills.

A related concern is the fact that no Asian NOC yet participates in any of the voluntary standards created by Western governments to foster improved governance, consideration of environmental impacts, and respect for human rights in oil and gas investments. When companies are able to acquire acreage without a tender that meets international standards, the nascent trend toward enforcing those standards in countries like Nigeria and Congo-Brazzaville is undermined. Moreover, the ability of other nations, such as Angola, to decline to participate in those standards and maintain opaque financial practices is reinforced. From the perspective of U.S. interests, the need for these standards is fundamental to the long-term security of those nations and to energy security as well. These concerns should be of as much interest to China as they are to the United States.

NORTH AFRICA ON THE RISE

Another major shift from 2000 is the change in relations between the United States and North African producers. While relations with Egypt have been strong for many years, the United States is on dramatically new footing with both Algeria and Libya. Following September 11, 2001, the United States formed a close counterterrorism partnership with Algeria. While Algeria has been a long-time producer of LNG, the United States began engaging Algeria bilaterally (although episodically) on energy. Algeria itself underwent a period of reform, offering natural gas exploration through open tenders and expanding opportunity in oil as well. As prices have risen Algeria has retrenched, seeking majority control of new projects and demanding swaps of acreage overseas to sustain its perhaps peaking oil reserves base. Nevertheless, Algeria has sustained its receptivity to LNG investment.

Relations with Libya have moved from sanctions to engagement, as the United States and Libya resolved bitter and long-standing issues. After Libya agreed to dismantle its weapons of mass destruction and renounce terrorism in 2003, the United States dropped bilateral sanctions in 2004 and subsequently removed Libya from the list of state sponsors of terrorism in 2006. In 2008, Libya and the United States began the path to full normalization when they reached a global settlement of outstanding private claims by creating a fund to compensate the victims of Libya's actions with respect to Pan Am 103 and the Labelle discothèque bombing, as well as Libyan victims of the 1986 U.S. retaliatory bombing for the Labelle attack. By October 2008, the United States had received the full $1.5 billion for the families of U.S. victims. In November, Gene Cretz was confirmed by the Senate to be the first U.S. ambassador to Libya since 1972. Libya and Algeria have both embraced the use of public tenders for allotting conventional oil and gas exploration acreage, enabling them to reap high bonuses and large government shares of production in a manner that is a model of transparency. In contrast to their sub-Saharan neighbors, neither Libya nor Algeria has opaque local content requirements or vague weighting factors that could invite mischief. Not coincidentally, production in Libya and Algeria is growing fast, with combined production from both countries rising from 3 million bpd to 4 million bpd from 2001 to 2008.[20]

EMERGENT RISKS

With the prospects of enormous investment, production, and revenue come major risks. In oil-rich countries in Africa, the emerging and largely unaddressed risks originate from unattainable expectations, rent seeking, corruption, the erosion of nascent good governance efforts, security threats to operations, rising resource nationalism, and political instability.

With the promise of high oil and gas revenues comes rising expectations of poverty reduction and prosperity. In frontier countries, these expectations are almost always unfulfilled, as eight years or more can elapse between the first exploration agreement and a profit return to the government when hydrocarbon production commences. In cases like São Tomé and Principe—where prospects for production attracted enormous press attention, one major coup attempt, and a robust program of bilateral advice on revenue management—actual exploration produced disappointing results. Mauritania also seemed promising in 2006, but complex geology and ineffective reservoir management led to unmet expectations. Mauritania's government, which had come to power in a coup but had enjoyed an unprecedented phase of civil society development and transparency, was felled by another coup in 2008. This instability raises a flag of caution for countries like Ghana, whose offshore Jubilee field discovery recently raised hopes of transforming the economy. The recurrent issues of whether the field will deliver and whether the government will put revenue management measures in place before the revenue comes in will inevitably surface in Ghana and as well as in other frontier states unless these issues are properly addressed.

For established players like Angola, Equatorial Guinea, Gabon, and Congo-Brazzaville, and Nigeria, the question is whether the flood of revenues will be put to good use or whether rent seeking by members of the government will foster corruption and kill even nascent efforts to improve governance. In Nigeria, trends are rapidly heading downward. Even in the waning days of the reformist Obasanjo administration, which introduced landmark reforms in revenue transparency, procurement, and civil service, questionable licensing rounds were offered where technically unqualified bidders won access to acreage. Blatant defects in sector management, from the failure to meter oil to the failure to measure the match between refinery inputs and outputs, were left unaddressed. Under President Umaru Yar'Adua, the Nigerian government did not constitute the Nigeria Extractive Industry Transparency Initiative (NEITI) Board, as required by the country's NEITI law, until January 2008, and it has already failed to comply with the legal requirements to audit 2006 and 2007 extractive industry revenues.

Equatorial Guinea is taking some initial steps in constituting an EITI program and obtaining outside help for identifying social investment projects. It has also been cooperating with the International Monetary Fund (IMF) and publishing results of its annual IMF article IV reports. Time will tell whether Equatorial Guinea will move from candidate to compliant status under EITI, whether social investment projects will be implemented, and whether efforts to foster a civil society in Equatorial Guinea capable of participating in governance efforts will evolve.

Angola is a mixed case. While Angola does not participate in voluntary initiatives, driven by its motivation to access international capital markets, Angola's state oil company, Sonangol, publishes its production with regularity. The Angolan finance ministry has accepted a program with the IMF to monitor and manage oil revenues, and Angola's tender system is viewed as transparent and fair. But the Angolan model raises concerns for the future. As Angola grows its own private sector oil services and other related enterprises, credible reports indicate that many companies are owned by current members of the Angolan government or Sonangol, creating worries for U.S. companies under the Foreign Corrupt Practices Act.

As a result of the global financial slowdown, sustained low prices could usher in new challenges in resource-rich countries in Africa. Countries that budgeted for higher oil prices will face greater risk of domestic instability and reduced international influence as tighter coffers cause them to rein in spending. Countries reliant on international aid risk serious setbacks as development institutions in the industrialized world curb their support. A prolonged tightening of credit or slowdown in the global economy will have serious repercussions, including possible unrest, if there is a contraction in FDI.

Security risks are on the rise as well. The most acute and obvious case is Nigeria. The continued failure of Nigerian governments to effectively address the Niger Delta crisis has led to an unprecedented lethality and disruption. Nigeria produced only 1.8 million bpd of its 2.2 million bpd quota as of summer 2008. Attacks on offshore facilities, thought to be beyond the range of the Niger Delta militants, took place in June 2008. Kidnappings and murder of hydrocarbon sector personnel continue. Equatorial Guinea has had bank heists and at least three coup attempts in five years. While investment is moving offshore, none of the littoral states has effective navies or coast guards with which they can even identify, much less deter or repel, pirates or attackers.

Rising resource nationalism—as evidenced by Nigeria's plans to renegotiate production contracts, Algeria's introduction of heavier taxes on oil profits, and Angola's joining of OPEC—also heightens risks that investments will be below expectations and that revenues will fall as a result. Governments historically respond to high prices with demands for a greater share of the economic rent and in some cases insistence on majority control of projects. Even attempts to sell acreage to the highest bidder by tender, without careful screening to ensure bidders are all technically capable of delivering on their bids, can defer investment and production. In other cases, governments try to create value at home by local-content requirements or by mandating that a percentage of the oil or gas production be sold at subsidized prices to the domestic economy, rather than purchased at market prices.

While the nations' motives are understandable, they can produce unwelcome results. Uncertainty about how gas will be priced, how much will be retained, and how it will be regulated has delayed Nigeria's LNG development for many years. Moreover, attempts to define local content by who owns a local service company, rather than by how much value is created locally, have led to shell companies of mysterious ownership that transfer their service obligations to other companies or simply do not perform the work.

The broader risk is the instability that the confluence of the above factors can produce. Even with unprecedented oil and gas prices, revenues across the continent have not yet produced the investments in physical capital (roads, power stations, schools, and hospitals) or human capital (primary and secondary education, vocational training, enterprise management, and development of civil society) that will be required for social peace. Some countries like Equatorial Guinea, Ghana, and Libya are at the beginning of major investment programs. Their progress will be measured soon. But more mature producers like Algeria, Angola, Chad, Congo-Brazzaville, Gabon, and Nigeria face impatient populations with expectations of better results, thus opening the door to external adventurism, as we now see with al Qaeda of the Islamic Maghreb (AQIM) in Algeria and internal conflict in Chad,

Mauritania, and Nigeria. The risk to the newest producers across East and Central Africa is that they will repeat the errors of their predecessors.

THE BUSH ADMINISTRATION'S POLICY

The Bush administration, through its National Energy Strategy, identified the importance of Africa as a strategic supplier, the risks of poor governance and corruption, and the need for engagement.[21] The key metrics for assessing energy policy are policy engagement with suppliers, technical and other assistance on energy policy itself as well as related issues of transparency and governance, and a policy response to emerging threats to U.S. investment and personnel.

DIPLOMATIC ENGAGEMENT

The Bush record on engagement is mixed. As part of a general dismantlement and minimization of standing bilateral policy dialogues, the United States retreated from engagement with most suppliers. The U.S.-Africa Energy Ministers Partnership—which was the only forum that brought together all energy producers on the continent to address energy security, investment security, and sustainable development—lapsed after a single meeting because little political effort was expended to sustain it. During the past eight years, head-of state-level China-Africa, European Union–Africa, and Latin America–Africa annual policy dialogues were launched. Bilateral commissions with Angola, Nigeria, and South Africa lapsed. The United States engaged Nigeria on regional issues, ranging from Liberia to Sierra Leone to Darfur but only episodically on the internal crisis in the Niger Delta and only rhetorically on the theft of oil or the positive steps taken in the extractive industry revenue area. Engagement with the new Nigerian government has been tentative, given the nature of the election and the challenge that the government has in mustering a policy consensus. The first visit of the assistant secretary of state for Africa to Angola during Bush's second term was in 2007. Engagement with European countries (whose aggregate energy investment in Africa exceeds that of the United States) or of China (the major new player in Africa) was negligible until 2008. Remarkably, both U.S. and Chinese sources confirmed that President Bush and Chinese President Hu Jintao barely discussed energy during Hu's 2006 visit to Washington.

On the positive side, the United States recognized that the emergence of Equatorial Guinea, with nearly $10 billion in U.S. investment, required engagement and a diplomatic presence. It opened a special embassy post and eventually a U.S. embassy in Malabo, where it now engages on human rights, transparency, social investment, and fiscal management.

In the period from 2001 to 2008, many voluntary initiatives to improve transparency and governance emerged: the implementation of the U.S.-UK led Voluntary Principles on Human Rights and Security; the development of the Equator Principles, which require assessment of the environmental impact of lending; and the internationalization of the UK-initiated EITI. The United States took a surprisingly distant approach to all these efforts. The U.S. executive branch first opposed, and eventually tolerated, the EITI but contributed funding to this effort only when Congress earmarked its contributions to the World Bank Trust Fund. The United States recognized the importance of these efforts in several G-8 summit communiqués, including the U.S.-led Sea Isle Summit in 2004 but insisted on its own G-8 compacts on corruption and transparency, which have little discernable follow-up.

Several reasons explain this relative disengagement on energy issues. First was a shift in focus. After 9/11, the White House emphasis was on counterterrorism, with little attention on political and economic development. The role of underdevelopment in potentially creating ungoverned spaces where terror might emerge was not identified or acted upon as a priority. A second reason was that the White House and State Department saw that the market provided for energy supply despite internal problems in Africa and concluded therefore that no energy market-related policy was required.

A third rationale was the absence of responsibility. The Bureau of African Affairs at the State Department saw its duties primarily as crisis management. Sudan and Darfur, in particular, along with the DRC, Kenya, and Somalia, took most of the time of senior diplomats. Nigeria's crisis in the delta—despite implications for financing crime, spreading violence to neighboring countries, and destabilizing Nigeria's democracy—did not make the cut for top priority. The State Department's Bureau of Economic and Business Affairs follows business interests generally but has no funds or mandate to address internal energy developments in producing countries. The Energy and Commerce Departments are technical agencies with no funds or mandate to engage producing countries. No one at the White House had the mandate to pull together a strategy for preventive diplomacy in a place like Angola or conflict management in the Niger Delta, much less to consider the potential impact of conflict-driven disruption—such as a shut-in of nearly 1million bpd of production in Nigeria—on U.S. economic interests.

Finally, there was a lack of strategic vision. A consensus is growing among companies, nongovernmental organizations, and many African countries that among energy-producing countries, good governance, sound revenue management, curbs on corruption, and provision of development needs can ultimately contribute to global energy security and avoid the human and economic depredations suffered by Nigeria, Sudan, and other "resource-cursed" countries. A partner country can help advance energy security by engaging nations on simply improving their own economy and governance. This view, which would require a coordinated multiagency approach, did not appear to figure in Bush administration calculations. Indeed, several in and close to the administration remarked that transparency will never be a top priority.[22]

DEVELOPMENT ASSISTANCE
U.S. policy on development assistance was highly creative in many sectors but did not invest significantly in improved governance in energy-producing countries. The Millennium Challenge Corporation (MCC), while innovative and useful, sets a participation standard that most energy-producing countries do not meet. MCC has no reason to change its standards, but it does exclude the countries most in need of improved governance. USAID invested heavily in health in Nigeria and Angola but has not invested in technical assistance to countries that sought to improve their revenue management, either through the EITI (like Nigeria) or on its own agenda (like Angola).

SECURITY ASSISTANCE
The United States, through the European Command, saw the importance of maritime security in the Gulf of Guinea early on. Prior security arrangements such as the Gulf of Guinea Guard recognized that the sea lanes through which oil traveled and the offshore installations themselves merited protection. U.S. defense officials understood that most countries lack a competent navy or coast guard and that indigenous capacity needed to be improved for the benefit of the host countries as well as for the protection of U.S. interests. According to current policy, African nations that wish to work together on U.S. terms—that

is, improving policy, establishing doctrine, purchasing equipment to improve the visibility of the maritime environment—will be welcome in a regional partnership. One visible demonstration of this policy is the African Partnership Station—a floating multinational, multiagency platform deploying a rotation of U.S. naval ships for policy engagement, training, and improvement of goodwill. Congress has been willing at times to allow U.S. providers of security training to help improve the police, the coast guard, and eventually the military of countries like Equatorial Guinea. This outreach enables countries to purchase security training with a human rights component rather than purchase services without that component elsewhere.

CHALLENGES FOR A NEW ADMINISTRATION

The new administration will face several challenges in the Africa energy arena: the crisis of corruption in Nigeria, escalating conflict in the Niger Delta, diminished U.S. leverage over energy-producing countries, the need to secure U.S. investment in the offshore areas, intensifying global competition over investment values and standards with new investors in Africa, the absence of a strategic vision for the region, and the lack of U.S. diplomatic and financial resources to address these challenges.

NIGERIA

The most critical challenge for U.S. policy will be how to engage Nigeria. Nigeria's size, its role as an energy producer of global stature, its cultural ties, and its potential to be the economic engine of West Africa should put it at the top tier of U.S. foreign policy priorities. Multiple issues must be addressed. The Niger Delta conflict poses physical risk to U.S. and Nigerian citizens in the delta. The militants are well armed and are reportedly exporting weapons and crime to neighboring countries like Cameroon, Côte d'Ivoire, and Equatorial Guinea. If Nigeria's shut-in oil production were restored, it could add up to 550 million bpd of oil to the global market. Nigeria could be a major source of LNG supply to Europe, Asia, and the United States. But unaddressed, the Niger Delta conflict will lead to sustained shutting-in of onshore production and a slowdown of further investment as companies decline to risk the lives of their employees for the onshore support of offshore production and the growing risk of attack on offshore facilities. The deep corruption in Nigeria overall must be addressed as well. Investment will fall in Nigeria, as it appears that every aspect of the energy procurement process—from the leasing of acreage, to local-content mandates, to the sale of crude —risks engagement with Nigerian government officials. The United States needs a realistic strategy for addressing the issue of the delta that acknowledges the complexity and severity of the instability—especially in the absence of a credible government counterpart with whom the United States and its allies can engage.

DECLINING U.S. INFLUENCE

If the United States is to influence the development path of current producers like Angola, Chad, Equatorial Guinea, and Nigeria and emerging producers like Ghana and Madagascar, it must make a special effort to restore a respected voice in those countries. In many of these countries, the United States has left the field completely, and in countries where the United States does not seriously engage, it pays little attention to those countries' own economic agenda. Odds will be low that the United States will be heard on the issues of investing resource revenues in physical and human capital or avoiding mismanagement of economies inundated by unprecedented influxes of cash, if relationships of respect are missing. U.S. advocacy for access to acreage, conducted at the head-of-state level by most U.S. competitors but rarely a priority for U.S. administrations, is best effected not by a demand for access but by a relationship of mutuality between the United States and the host country.

Traditionally, the United States and international institutions have effectively used their financial clout to compel developing countries to implement policies aimed at sustainability and stability. But new centers of wealth in Asia and the Middle East, combined with unprecedented windfall profits in producing countries, have diminished the influence of loans and foreign aid, as most recently evidenced by the World Bank's pullout of the Chad-Cameroon pipeline project. The 620-mile pipeline, one of the Bank's biggest investments on the continent, was intended to generate wealth that would be spent by the government on local communities, health, and education. Chad failed to deliver on its promise to spend 70 percent of revenues on programs for the poor, and in 2006 the World Bank halted lending. Bolstered by high revenues, Chad continued to disregard the World Bank's request that it spend revenues on development and instead increased its military expenditures. By 2008, Chad had generated enough revenue to pre-pay its outstanding balance of $65.7 million, and the Bank withdrew from the project. The failure of the Chad-Cameroon pipeline suggests that the United States should be cautious about providing financing to countries not ready to manage risk and make a political commitment to the project. It also suggests that the United States will need a more nuanced approach to engagement, since resource-rich countries now have ample funding on their own or through unconditional loans from China.

SECURITY OF THE OFFSHORE

If 95 percent of all energy production in West Africa will be offshore by 2010, the United States will need to monitor international waters, and countries will need to provide the wherewithal to see who is in their water, to interdict pirates and criminals, and to deter attacks on facilities and protect the lives of workers. Nigeria has surpassed Indonesia as the "number one hot spot" for piracy in the world. In the first quarter of 2008, 10 of the 49 attacks registered worldwide occurred off the coast of Nigeria.[23] An investment of both time and revenues will be required to bring together those countries that can create security forces with respect for human rights.

THE COMPETITION FOR VALUES

The United States will compete with China for influence in Africa. U.S. companies will come with a package of values attached to their operations: compliance with anticorruption laws; participation in voluntary standards on human rights, security, and transparency; and investment in health, safety, and environmental practice. The Chinese competition may not share those values or impose such conditions on their investments. Indeed, the great challenge that China poses to U.S. and European investment in Africa is not domination of acreage (its share remains minimal) but the refusal thus far to participate in international standards, a stance that erodes the incorporation of these standards into host-country practice. Protection of those values will require engaging China, India, Malaysia, and others on both the need for such standards and their contribution to global energy security. The United States will also need to engage Africa on those issues and make clear that it is a priority of the U.S. government to advocate those values and, where it is welcome, to provide assistance to countries adopting and implementing them.

THE NEED FOR A STRATEGIC VISION

The United States cannot get where it wants to go—a stable, prosperous Africa that contributes to global energy security and uses its wealth to develop its nations—unless it has a vision of how to get there. A challenge for the new administration will be deciding whether and how to integrate energy policy, development initiatives, security assistance, and bilateral diplomacy into a coherent policy.

DEPLOYING RESOURCES

The two components needed to implement an effective policy are people and money. The United States needs people at the White House charged with a focus on a strategic energy policy for Africa and a greatly enhanced diplomatic capacity. The United States needs more diplomats on the ground in developing countries, more eyes and ears in the producing regions, and more high-level diplomats focused on energy issues. It needs to put money on the table in Africa. The prudent use of development aid to help with the redesign of procurement systems, with the audit of national and international oil companies, or with the creation of systems for metering production should be supported.

ASYMMETRIC ENGAGEMENT

The United States should take a holistic approach to improving stability and development, with an indirect benefit being increased energy security. Efforts to promote economic development, democracy, human rights, public health, and security will create an environment favorable to achieving energy security goals. Asymmetric engagement will help the United States enhance relations with African states, develop a stronger presence on the continent, and support other vital areas of U.S. interest. While the driver for overall improvement in the quality of diplomatic exchanges may be energy, such an approach will provide additional dividends. Energy-producing states in Africa are important to the United States for reasons beyond their natural hydrocarbon resources. Following 9/11, Africa became strategically important to U.S. counterterror efforts. The fight against HIV/AIDS has drawn U.S. resources to the continent out of concern for public health. The genocide in Darfur has warranted U.S. attention for humanitarian reasons. U.S. efforts in these areas could indirectly increase U.S. energy security, just as U.S. efforts to increase energy security could support these other causes.

RECOMMENDATIONS FOR THE NEW ADMINISTRATION
Below are 10 priority recommendations for addressing the challenges discussed above:

1. *Issue a policy decision directive on African energy security.* A policy directive should come from the president that explicates U.S. interests and priorities and directs agencies to coordinate and support it. This policy should include the role of diplomacy, security assistance, governance and transparency promotion, human rights, and development assistance. While the new administration may indeed look at energy security or Africa in a broader context, the very challenge of getting economic, security, and diplomatic agencies to address Africa in a coordinated way warrants an African energy–specific policy committee and directive.

2. *Provide White House leadership.* The coordination of energy security policy should come from the White House to muster the disparate agencies behind the policy, under the leadership of one individual. While this person might usefully coordinate energy security policy in other regions as well, that person should have the rank, status, and mission to ensure the implementation of the president's policy. In addition, most African energy producers either manage or reform energy policy at the head-of-state level. The United States needs a counterpart level of engagement.

3. *Apply State Department diplomatic resources and leadership to energy security.* The State Department should play a key role in engaging countries both on access and on reform. While major companies do not always request advocacy from the U.S. government, in today's market, heads of state of their competitors advocate vigorously. Small and midsize U.S. companies would welcome a restoration of the U.S. government's role as commercial advocate where appropriate. Engagement on reform should be at high levels and with multiple ministries. U.S. diplomatic resources must be applied both at a senior level to engage other ministers and at the bureau level to provide programmatic support.

   Historically, the Department of State denotes this priority by appointment of a special ambassador, as it has for the Caspian region, or by directing an undersecretary to place a priority on promotion of a policy. The undersecretary of state for economic, business, and agricultural affairs may be best positioned to serve this role. In today's world, the undersecretary for political affairs will be consumed with a broad range of security issues. The economic, business, and agriculture undersecretary can address a number of economic issues of interest to counterparts, while carrying the governance and energy promotion agenda at the same time. An issue like energy security is better addressed by officials whose mission is to promote the policy in all relevant agencies than by changes in the State Department's organizational structure; but with respect to energy security policy, one of these options should be considered. In addition, the department needs to collect more data on energy developments, as well as on political developments, in producing areas.

4. *Give governance and transparency policy a bureaucratic home.* At this time, no office has dedicated responsibility for the promotion of good governance and transparency in energy-producing countries. The Democracy and Human Rights Bureau owns some policies, such as the voluntary principles on energy and security. The Economics and Business Bureau has at times staffed the EITI at a junior level but so has the Policy Planning Office. In the spirit of integrating economic and governance issues rather than stove-piping them, this responsibility could be placed in the Economics and Business Bureau.

5. *Engage Africa on its own energy and economic agenda, not just on that of the United States.* The best way to enhance U.S. influence with Africa's energy producers, and to promote U.S. interests in both access and governance, is to engage governments on what interests them, not just on what interests the United States. Most producers want to create jobs, promote economic development, and enjoy a respectful, mutual relationship with the United States. Nearly every country tries to find ways to increase power generation and distribution in an affordable sustainable way. Many of them struggle with ways to target subsidies for fuel or power for the poor rather than the entire economy.

The United States could use a range of tools to engage different countries, depending on U.S. interests and partner country needs. These could include reviving the U.S.-Africa Energy Ministers

Partnership; reviving or creating bilateral multiagency economic working groups with Algeria, Angola, Libya, and Nigeria; and creating an electric power policy partnership—"power for the people"—to engage countries on power pooling and smart policies. It could also include technical assistance programs designed to build local human capacity, particularly in countries that have local-content requirements. The U.S. government should allocate sufficient funds to support proposed assistance and development programs. It should be mindful that citizens of countries with recent resource discoveries will likely have unrealistically high expectations. And it should strive to support economic and energy projects that are realistically achievable.

6. *Focus development and technical assistance on governance.* U.S. investment in governance in general, and energy governance in particular, is modest. USAID, in coordination with the World Bank and other development agencies, should be directed to promote EITI in countries that are receptive; should consider assisting countries interested in reforming the governance of their energy sector, from procurement to local content to regulation; and should support the efforts of civil society groups and their media to understand the extractive industries and participate in indigenous reform efforts. This mandate should be funded appropriately.

7. *Sustain efforts to promote maritime security.* Led by U.S. Naval Forces/Europe (NAVEUR), one of the most successful efforts of the Bush administration has been the engagement of African nations in enhancing their own capacity to identify ships in their waters and police them for the protection of their fisheries, to deter crime, and to protect investment in their waters. That success, though, has been tempered by a requirement that countries be willing to engage on NAVEUR's terms, which are the improvement of policy, not unconditional security assistance. This effort can be the key to securing energy investment abroad. If Nigeria reaches a point where it will seriously engage on this issue, it could lead to the containment of oil theft as well. The United States should be prepared to engage with African countries on maritime security when the government in question demonstrates it is ready by developing a strategy in advance, raising the issue during diplomatic exchanges, and seeking allied support.

8. *Engage Europe and Asia on African issues.* Europe and Asia have as great a stake in African development, stability, and energy security as does the United States. The United States needs a strategy for engaging Europe and Asia on the security and energy fronts in the context of declining U.S. influence. It should work in a multilateral context to address the crisis and should revive conversations on these issues in general through a transatlantic dialogue and high level U.S.-China and Asia Pacific cooperation.

9. *Procure a National Intelligence Estimate on African energy security.* U.S. policymakers rarely see the links among energy production, instability, conflict, and stability of supply. A National Intelligence Estimate of African energy would identify those links and provide a common understanding of the potential for conflict that rising prices (or sharply falling prices) and new exploration might pose for the continent.

10. *Engage on the Niger Delta.* The United States, the European Union, and China must engage Nigeria on the crisis in the delta. Central to the crisis is the lack of political legitimacy of the leadership in Nigeria itself. But as a friend and partner of the leaders in Nigeria, the United States must make clear that the conflict has become an international as well as an internal crisis: crime is spreading to neighboring states, and Nigeria's democracy is under attack. Money is not the core of the problem, as there are ample funds at the federal and state level for a development plan. But without a serious political dialogue, perhaps supported quietly by external partners, no progress will be made, and no serious political progress is possible unless corruption is addressed. To date, Nigeria has taken greater steps on transparency and reform than any other African nation. But if it does not fulfill its basic commitments, efforts to get smaller countries to adhere to stricter standards are destined to fail.

NOTES

The author acknowledges Sheila Moynihan for providing editorial and research assistance and Monica Enfield of PFC Energy for providing many of the tables and charts that illustrate the chapter.

1. National Energy Policy Development Group, *Reliable, Affordable, and Environmentally Sound Energy for America's Future* (Washington, D.C.: U.S.

Government Printing Office, 2001), 162. The NEPD Group recommends that the president direct the secretaries of state, energy, and commerce to reinvigorate the U.S.-Africa Trade and Economic Cooperation Forum and the U.S.-African Energy Ministerial process; deepen bilateral and multilateral engagement to promote a more receptive environment for U.S. oil and gas trade, investment, and operations; and promote geographic diversification of energy supplies, addressing such issues as transparency, sanctity of contracts, and security. The NEPD Group recommends that the president direct the secretaries of state, commerce, and energy to support more transparent, accountable, and responsible use of oil resources in African producer countries to enhance the stability and security of trade and investment environments.

2. Calculated based on Energy Information Agency prices for Cushing, OK WTI Spot Prices FOB (dollars per barrel), by Goldwyn International Strategies, an energy consulting firm.

3. "Shut-in" refers to the deferred production from a site that is capable of producing oil. A shut-in occurs when a property, known to be capable of producing a given quantity of oil, is forced to produce less because of extenuating circumstances. The quantity of oil "shut in" is measured by the difference between the site's normal production level and its temporarily reduced level of output.

4. Energy Information Administration (EIA), "World Production of Crude Oil, NGPL, and Other Liquids, and Refinery Processing Gain, Most Recent Annual Estimates, 1980–2007," EIA, http://www.eia.doe.gov/emeu/international/oilproduction.html.

5. Ibid.

6. Unpublished 2008 estimate by PFC Energy, an energy consulting group.

7. Ibid.

8. Ibid.

9. EIA, "International Natural Gas and Liquefied Natural Gas (LNG) Imports and Exports," EIA, http://www.eia.doe.gov/emeu/international/gastrade.html.

10. WTI refers to West Texas Intermediate (WTI) crude oil. WTI is a very high quality crude oil and is used as the major benchmark of crude in the United States. Because of its high quality, WTI is normally priced at a premium to Brent crude and the OPEC basket.

11. EIA, "Petroleum Navigator Cushing, OK WTI Spot Price (FOB)," EIA, http://tonto.eia.doe.gov/dnav/pet/hist/rwtcm.htm.

12. United Nations Conference On Trade And Development (UNCTAD), 2007 World Investment Report 2007, as quoted in Willy H. Olsen, "The African Oil and Gas Scene" (PowerPoint presented at the Center for Strategic and International Studies Africa Program, Washington, D.C., June 20, 2008).

13. UNCTAD, "FDI in Africa Hits Record, and Continent Has Highest Return on Investment of All Developing Regions," UNCTAD, http://www.unctad.org/Templates/webflyer.asp?docid=10499&intItemID=1634&lang=1.

14. Ibid.

15. EIA, "World Production of Crude Oil, NGPL, and Other Liquids, and Refinery Processing Gain, Most Recent Annual Estimates, 1980–2007," EIA, http://www.eia.doe.gov/emeu/international/oilproduction.html.

16. International Energy Agency (IEA), *World Energy Outlook 2006* (Paris: IEA, 2006), 77.

17. Unpublished 2008 estimate by PFC Energy, an energy consulting group.

18. Ibid.

19. In August 2008 CNOOC sold most of its 35 percent shares in one of its smaller Nigerian oil stakes. CNPC also eliminated some of its assets in Sudan by parking them in a new independent entity.

20. EIA, "Recent Total Oil Supply Barrels Per Day," EIA, http://www.eia.doe.gov/emeu/international/oilproduction.html.

21. National Energy Policy Development Group, *Reliable, Affordable, and Environmentally Sound Energy for America's Future*, 162.

22. Interviews conducted by the Center for Strategic and International Studies Africa Program's Energy Security Working Group for the Bush Africa Policy Review.

23. International Maritime Bureau.

5

ADVANCING DEMOCRATIZATION IN AFRICA

JOEL D. BARKAN

The advancement of democracy worldwide has been a continuous and defining theme of U.S. statecraft since the presidency of Woodrow Wilson nearly a century ago. At the same time, promotion of democracy has invariably competed with and been trumped by the advancement of other foreign policy objectives, particularly U.S. security and economic interests. U.S. efforts to support democratization across sub-Saharan Africa are thus best understood within this broader and changing dynamic of U.S. foreign policy. That dynamic was especially evident during the Bush administration, which after 9/11 increasingly defined its foreign policy in terms of the "Global War on Terror," which it often pursued unilaterally basis.

The Obama administration faces similar trade-offs in developing its Africa policy. The diversity of conditions across Africa's 48 states argues strongly against a one-size-fits-all approach to democracy promotion on the continent. Advancing democracy and good governance in Africa, however, is arguably more important in this region than in any other. Further, every U.S. interest in Africa—from security and counterterrorism to economic development, trade, health, and energy—will depend on participatory, capable, and accountable governments with which the United States can partner. Marked by poor governance, failed states, and chronic instability from the mid-1960s through the mid-1990s, Africa has achieved remarkable advances in recent years that were unimaginable a decade or two ago. Much work needs to be done, but there is today a solid platform of achievement on which the new administration can build. A more nuanced and sophisticated approach will also be required to foster the democratic institutions that are the essence of good governance on the continent. The need for the United States to use both its "smart power" and its "soft power" is nowhere greater than in this area.

DEMOCRATIZATION AND AMERICAN FOREIGN POLICY

U.S. efforts to promote democracy in Africa and their juxtaposition with other foreign policy goals can be traced back to the 1950s when African nationalist movements sought independence during the height of the Cold War. Although the United States was reluctant to part company with its European allies, it supported nationalist aspirations, provided nationalist leaders did not ally themselves with the Soviet Union .While the United States supported self-rule because it was consistent with democratic principles, it became cautious when one African country after another lapsed into one-party or military rule during the first decade of independence. Many questioned whether conditions in Africa, especially the mix of widespread poverty, uneven development and ethnic diversity, could sustain democracy.

U.S. interest in democratization soon took a back seat to U.S. security interests for the remainder of the Cold War, from the mid-1960s through the 1980s. During this period, the United States worked closely with authoritarian regimes across Africa to contain Soviet expansionism, including those in the Democratic Republic of Congo (the former Zaire), Ethiopia (prior to the takeover by a military junta in 1974), Kenya, Nigeria, and Somalia. The United States likewise embraced the apartheid regime in South Africa until the passage of the U.S. Comprehensive Anti-Apartheid Act over President Reagan's veto in 1986.

The end of the Cold War, including the winding down of wars between Cold War proxies in the early 1990s,[1] enabled the United States to return to the Wilsonian goal of promoting democracy abroad. During the administration of President George H.W. Bush, and continuing through the Clinton administration, the United States mounted an aggressive and extensive program to support democratization across Africa and in other world regions. The release of Nelson Mandela from prison in South Africa in 1990 and the onset of negotiations to end apartheid and transition to democratic rule in that country accelerated U.S. support for expanding political space for civil society, the press, and opposition political parties; the holding of free and fair elections;

and the building of democratic institutions. During this period, the spread and deepening of democracy worldwide was viewed as a long-term project pursued mainly for its own sake because it embodied a core American value but also because it served the national interest. Democracy promotion also enabled the United States to present its best face to the world as an example of American "soft power."

Though facilitated by the end of the Cold War, democracy promotion was also a U.S. response to the demands posed by the "third wave of democratization"—the historic series of transitions from authoritarian to democratic rule that swept the world during the last quarter of the twentieth century. These transitions began in southern Europe in the mid-1970s, and spread across Latin America and Eastern Europe during the 1980s. The "Third Wave" finally hit Africa at the beginning of the 1990s.[2]

During the 1990s, the United States became the most important bilateral player in this new combination of diplomacy and technical assistance. Together with Canada, Germany, the Netherlands, the Scandinavian countries, and the UK, the United States was more active than it had ever been in promoting democratic governance in Africa. In 1994, the U. S. Agency for International Development (USAID) established the Center (later Office) for Democracy and Governance and deployed advisers to most countries where USAID had missions on the continent. By the end of the decade and the beginning of the Bush administration in 2001, all but five of Africa's 48 countries had held multiparty elections. Many, including Benin, Ghana, Kenya, South Africa, and Zambia, had held two. Some—Benin, Ghana, Senegal, South Africa, Tanzania, and Zambia—experienced peaceful transfers of power through the ballot box.

Dramatic changes had also occurred in the pattern of governance across the continent. Most countries were arguably "more democratic" than they had been in 1990. In addition to elections, there was now space for civil society. The press and broadcast media were noticeably freer and no longer a state or party monopoly in many countries. But as the United States and other countries engaged in democracy promotion soon learned, the holding of multiparty elections alone does not make a democracy. Multiparty elections are a necessary but insufficient requisite for democratic rule. Authoritarian leaders are often able to retain power despite the holding of such elections. Progress at democratization was uneven, especially the development of key state institutions such as the legislature and judiciary. The bottom line was that Africa was marked by a greater diversity of regimes than a decade earlier. These included a small number of failed states and a somewhat larger number of liberal democracies, with two-thirds of sub-Saharan Africa's 48 countries falling somewhere in between—countries whose transitions from authoritarian to democratic rule had stalled or remained incomplete.

DEMOCRATIZATION IN AFRICA, 2000–2008

Three broad trends characterized African democratization during the period of the Bush administration.

First, even after two decades of significant progress, Africa, as a whole, remains the least democratic region in the world except the Middle East (see table 5.1). Further, data compiled by Freedom House suggest that progress toward democratization in Africa, as in other regions, has leveled off or slowed in recent years when compared with the 1990s. Most experts now conclude that the "Third Wave" is over and that the principal challenge is to consolidate what has been achieved by minimizing the rollback of democracy that has followed previous periods when democratic rule has been extended to many new countries.

Second, progress toward democratization across Africa has been highly uneven, resulting in a wide diversity of regimes (see table 5.2). Indeed, Africa today arguably has the most diverse mix of regimes of any world region. Stated simply, *there is no single "Africa" with respect to democratization*; instead, there are several. This situation poses a major challenge to the United States both in how it promotes democracy on the continent and in how it pursues its foreign policy toward Africa generally. Both approaches must be better calibrated to account for this diversity than in the past, because one size does not fit all.

As indicated in table 5.3, the vast majority of countries (71 percent) are neither liberal democracies or closed political systems but fall in between the two extremes. These countries are themselves divided into two distinct groups. The first group is at the upper-middle range where significant opportunities for further democratization still exist are those countries labeled "aspiring democracies" and "ambiguous." It is within this group that the level of democracy improved in more countries (63 percent) than in any of the others. Below them, in a second group, are countries labeled as "competitive authoritarian" and "electoral authoritarian," regimes where elections are held but where

Table 5.1. Democracy and Freedom by Region, 1974, 2000, and 2008

Region	Number of Countries	Number (Percent) That Are Liberal Democracies FH score ≤ 2.0	Average Freedom Score for Region 1974 2000 2008
W. Europe, Canada and U.S.	27	26 (96%)	1.58 1.17 1.12
Latin America & Caribbean	33	18 (55%)	3.81 2.41 2.20
Eastern Europe and Former Soviet Union	27	11 (41%)	6.50 3.27 3.03
Asia (E, SE, and S)	26	6 (23%)	4.84 4.58 3.90
Pacific Island	12	8 (67%)	2.75 2.25 2.12
Africa (Sub-Sahara)	48	8 (17%)	5.51 4.44 4.20
Middle East- North Africa	20	1 (5%)	5.15 5.63 5.26
Total	193	78 (40%)	4.39 3.48 3.12

Note: Freedom House uses two scales to measure the extent of democracy and democratization in more than 180 countries worldwide—a political rights (PR) scale and a civil liberties (CL) scale. Each scale ranges from 1.0 to 7.0 with the *lowest* number indicating the greatest or highest level of democracy. Regional average scores were obtained by first computing the average of the PR score and the CL score for each country in the region and then computing the average of all country scores. Average scores for all countries were computed by adding up all average country scores and dividing by 193, the total number of countries rated by Freedom House.
Source: Freedom House, *Freedom in the World 2009: Setbacks and Resilience* (Washington, D.C.: Freedom House, January 2009), http://www.freedomhouse.org/template.cfm?page=445.

the prospects for an alternation of government by the ballot, and genuine democratization, are limited. Only 22 percent of these countries became more democratic between 2000 and 2008.

The range of African regimes and the pace at which democratization has occurred since 2000 raise two important questions for the new Obama administration. First, should the United States invest in the *consolidation* of democracy or in the *spread* of democracy? Second, how and through what combination of diplomacy and technical assistance should the United States pursue its policy goal? Specific recommendations with respect to these questions are provided in the last section of this essay.

Table 5.2. Measurement of Political Rights and Civil Liberties in African Regimes, End of 2008

Liberal Democracy	Aspiring Democracy	Ambiguous	Competitive Authoritarian	Electoral Authoritarian	Politically Closed
Benin (2,2)	Kenya (4,3)	Comoros (4,4)	Burkina Faso (5,3)	Angola (6,5)	Chad (7,6)
Botswana (2,2)	Lesotho (2,3)	Guinea-Bissau (4,4)	Burundi (4,5)	Cameroon (6,6)	Equatorial Guinea (7,7)
Cape Verde (1,1)	Liberia (3,4)	Malawi (4,4)	Central African Republic (5,5)	Congo, Democratic Rep. (6,6)	Eritrea (7,6)
Ghana (1,2)	Madagascar (4,3)	Nigeria (5,4)	Djibouti (5,5)	Congo, People's Republic (6,5)	Somalia (7,7)
Mauritius (1,2)	Mali (2,3)		Ethiopia (5,5)	Cote d'Ivoire (6,5)	Sudan (7,7)
Namibia (2,2)	Mozambique (3,3)		Gabon (6,4)	Guinea (7,5)	Zimbabwe (7,6)
Sao Tome & Principe (2,2)	Niger (3,4)		Gambia (5,4)	Mauritania (6,4)	
South Africa (2,2)	Senegal (3,3)		Togo (5,5)	Rwanda (6,5)	
	Seychelles (3,3)		Uganda (5,4)	Swaziland (7,5)	
	Sierra Leone (3,3)				
	Tanzania (4,3)				
	Zambia (3,3)				

Note: The numbers within parentheses are the political rights (PR) score and the civil liberties (CL) score for each country. The first number is the country's PR score; the second is its CL score. Labels for each category of countries by Larry Diamond.
Source: Freedom House, *Freedom in the World 2009* (see source for table 5.1).

Table 5.3. Improvement or Decline in Democratization in Africa, 1990–2008 (percent change)

	Democratization	1990–2008	1990–1995	1995–2000	2000–2008
All Africa	Improved	53	43	18	35
	No change	40	51	79	56
	Decline	6	6	6	8
	N	(47)	(47)	(48)	(48)
Liberal Democracy (FH 1.0-2.0)	Improved	62.5	75	13	37.5
	No change	37.5	25	87	62.5
	Decline	0	0	0	0
	N	(8)	(8)	(8)	(8)
Aspiring Democracies and Ambiguous (FH 3.0-4.0)	Improved	87.5	44	25	63
	No Change	12.5	44	75	31
	Decline	0	12	0	6
	N	(16)	(16)	(16)	(16)
Competitive and Electoral Authoritarian (FH 5.0-6.0)	Improved	33	41	12	22
	No Change	56	53	76	72
	Decline	11	6	24	6
	N	(18)	(18)	(18)	(18)
Closed (FH 7.0)	Improved	80	0	0	0
	No Change	0	100	86	67
	Decline	20	0	14	33
	N	5	6	7	6

Note: Prepared by Joel D. Barkan, Eric Kramon, Mathew Borman, and Robert Mylroie from Freedom and the World for 1990, 1995, 2000, and 2009. Percentages are for the number of countries within each category whose average Freedom House score improved or declined by 1.0 or more for the time period indicated.

N = number of countries.

DEMOCRACY PROMOTION DURING THE
BUSH ADMINISTRATION

Democracy promotion during the administration of George W. Bush is best understood within the context of the administration's overall foreign policy. In this regard, two considerations were paramount for the president and his advisers. First was the belief, especially during the administration's first term, that the U.S. national interest is most effectively served when the United States takes an unambiguous position on major issues and then pursues that policy regardless of whether other countries, including America's historical allies, endorse it. While unilateralism per se was not the basis of U.S. foreign policy, unilateral initiatives were regarded as necessary to advance the national interest. Second, and in response to the 9/11 attacks less than eight months after President Bush took office, was the decision to subordinate or rhetorically reinterpret nearly all foreign policy objectives to support for the Global War on Terror.

NEW RATIONALE FOR PROMOTING DEMOCRACY

Viewed through this prism, U.S. efforts to promote the spread of democracy, especially in the Middle East, took on new meanings. Rather than being pursued primarily as a long-term project for its intrinsic value, "democracy" and democracy promotion became instruments to advance other short-term goals, specifically the reestablishment of political authority in Iraq and Afghanistan and countering terrorism. In this context, the extension of democracy to new lands was important because democracies have never engaged in armed conflict with each other,[3] nor, historically, have democracies attacked other states unless attacked themselves. And, as stated by President Bush in its most basic form, democracy is desirable because democracies do not breed those who engage in terrorist acts against the United States.[4] It was a perspective on democracy and a rationale for democracy promotion that emphasized the *inter*state benefits of the process for the United States rather than the *intra*state nature of the process and the benefits accruing to the countries concerned.

The logic of this new perspective was clear. Democracy promotion meant the United States would proselytize for democratic rule to non-democratic states, including, if necessary, by forced regime change as in Afghanistan and Iraq. Unfortunately, this perspective failed to account for the fundamental nature of democratization in the post–Cold

War era and what the United States and other democratic members of the international community can *and cannot* do to accelerate the process. This constraint has proven especially true with respect to Africa. As demonstrated by several academic studies, democratic transitions in Africa (and elsewhere) are driven mainly by *internal* forces and local actors rather than by those outside the countries concerned.[5] That fundamental reality applies to nearly all Third Wave democratizers, African and non-African. The United States and other countries seeking to support the spread of democracy thus do so at the margins—as facilitators of a home-grown process and in partnership with local leaders committed to the realization of democracy. Without local democrats, no democracy. The United States can, however, accelerate the pace of democratization and ensure the success of local democratic movements by providing them with diplomatic support and appropriate technical assistance.

POLICY AMBIGUITY

Given these realities, and because most democratic transitions in Africa were already well under way when the Bush administration came into office, leaders of democratic movements across Africa met the administration's approach to democracy promotion with caution and, in some instances, suspicion. The war in Iraq, U.S. treatment of prisoners at Abu Ghraib and Guantanamo, and U.S. efforts to persuade African states to pass local versions of the U.S. Patriot Act, struck many of these leaders as inconsistent with U.S. democratic ideals and was an agenda that did not address their continuing internal struggles for democracy. U.S. pressure on democratically elected African governments (Kenya, for example) to either not ratify the treaty creating the International Criminal Court or pass legislation to exempt U.S. forces from prosecution of human rights violations under Article 98 of the treaty also evoked skepticism about U.S. commitment to democratic governance and the end to human rights abuse. To many, especially leaders of civil society organizations trying to advance democratization and commentators in Africa's emerging free press, the U.S. commitment to democratization was qualitatively different, if not less strong, than during the administrations of George H.W. Bush and Bill Clinton.

The Bush administration's approach to the issue of term limits also shaped perceptions of U.S. intentions. During the first term of the Bush administration, Secretary of State Colin Powell engaged in public diplomacy to urge incumbent African presidents to respect constitutional provisions that limited their tenure in office to two elected terms. By the end of the 1990s, nearly 30 African states had adopted such provisions to block the return of "big man" rule under the guise of democracy. The importance of term limits cannot be overstated if African states are to break with their authoritarian past. Respect for term limits contributes to good governance generally, because it prevents the entrenchment of executive power and the use of such power to loot the state and private sector as occurred in Africa through the mid-1990s.

Powell's diplomacy paid dividends in Kenya in 2002 when President Daniel arap Moi did not try for a third elected term. The U.S. message was also understood in Ghana, Malawi, Tanzania, and Zambia, where incumbent presidents retired, though not always willingly. U.S. efforts to sustain term limits, however, declined sharply during the Bush administration's second term and became an element of disagreement within the Africa Bureau at the Department of State. In Nigeria and Uganda, where Presidents Olesegun Obasanjo and Yoweri Museveni sought to extend their terms in office by amending the constitution, two U.S. ambassadors who publicly questioned these moves were instructed by Washington to lighten up on these U.S. allies. Given Nigeria's prominence as a major oil supplier to the United States and its assistance on a range of West African regional issues, Obasanjo was to be given a pass. His quest for a third term was ultimately blocked by the Nigerian National Assembly, but in Uganda, Museveni succeeded in repealing term limits with the predictable result. Having stood for and won a third term through repressive means, he has now indicated that he will be a candidate for a fourth. U.S. silence can be explained largely by Museveni's long-term support for the Sudan People's Liberation Army in southern Sudan and by his support for U.S. counterterror initiatives, including deployment of Ugandan troops to Somalia to defend the Transitional Federal Government against the Islamist insurgency in that country. Continued and strong U.S. support for regimes with questionable democratic credentials and poor human rights records in Ethiopia and Rwanda, including the elevation of the latter to threshold status under the Millennium Challenge Account, has also signaled a U.S. retreat from the principle of term limits and democratic rule.

By contrast, substantial U.S. support for elections in the Democratic Republic of Congo (DRC) and for the restoration of democracy in Li-

Figure 5.1. USAID Democracy and Governance Programs in Africa, 1990–2008

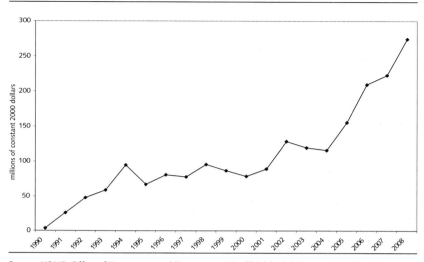

Source: USAID Office of Democracy and Governance. Unofficial final data completed by Andrew Green. Unpublished 2008.

Figure 5.2. USAID-Managed Democracy and Governance Programs by Subsector in Africa, 1990–2007

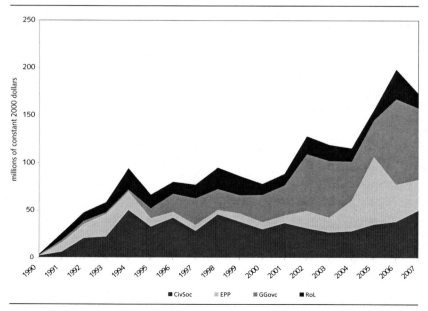

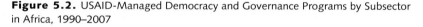

Note: CivSoc = civil society; EPP = elections and political processes; GGovc = good governance; RoL = rule of law.
Source: USAID Office of Democracy and Governance. Unofficial final data compiled by Andrew Green.

beria under the government of Ellen Johnson-Sirleaf in 2006 conveys a different image. Similarly in Kenya, where a bungled election and post-election violence threatened to undo substantial democratic gains that had been painstakingly won over a 15-year period, U.S. support for the mediation process to end the crisis in February 2008 was critical for the eventual power-sharing deal between the protagonists. President Bush's dispatch of Secretary of State Condoleezza Rice to Nairobi to move the negotiations forward, as well as her close monitoring of the talks and public statements after her visit, was arguably diplomacy for democracy at its best. Notwithstanding these examples, the overall picture is one of greater ambiguity with respect to U.S. intentions vis-à-vis democratization than in the past.

Ambiguity on the diplomatic side is mirrored by ambiguity in U.S. efforts to provide technical assistance to support democratization on the ground. On the positive side is the very large increase in annual funding for USAID's democracy and governance programs, the principal mechanism by which the United States supports democracy promotion both globally and in Africa. USAID expenditures for such programs in Africa more than doubled between FY 2001, the last budget of the Clinton administration, through 2008 (see figure 5.1). In 2008, the United States spent $274.4 million on democracy and governance programs in sub-Saharan Africa, up from $89.2 million (in constant 2000 dollars) in 2001.

FUNDING AND INSTITUTIONAL SUPPORT

Money spent on electoral assistance quintupled between 2001 and 2005 (see figure 5.2) and then moderated in 2006 and 2007. Expenditures on civil society remained fairly constant from 2001 to 2006 but received a substantial increase in 2007. Expenditures on rule of law spiked in 2006, but fell back to previous levels in 2007. Funds allocated to good governance fluctuated over the course of the decade.

As discussed above, a major lesson learned from early elections in Africa and elsewhere throughout the 1990s was that they often masked the continuation of authoritarian or semi-authoritarian regimes. Far more important for the sustained development of democracy over the long run is the establishment of institutions of countervailing power to contain executive authority. Such institutions are particularly important in Africa where presidents have long abused their powers to entrench themselves in office. Without such institutions—a strong and independent judiciary, a viable legislature that both represents societal interests and oversees the executive, a strong civil society, and an independent press—democracy will be neither consolidated nor sustained.

These institutions have been historically weak in Africa and are the principal reason democratization varies so greatly across the continent. Such was true in 2001 when the Bush administration came in office. Yet instead of strengthening these institutions—a priority appreciated by experts on democratization and by career civil servants at USAID's Office for Democracy and Governance—the administration devoted the bulk of its increased funding and programming to the spread of democracy to countries where the prospects for democratization are arguably the least promising. It was like pounding the proverbial square peg into the round hole.

During the course of the administration's tenure, USAID's democracy and governance programs in Africa also increasingly focused on a few countries. In 2007, USAID had such programs in 24 countries. Of these countries, five—Sudan ($55.6 million), Liberia ($22.2), Sierra Leone ($15.3), DRC ($14.6 million), and Somalia ($9.0 million)—consumed 60 percent of the total budget. All five had been wracked by civil wars. Only two, Liberia and Sierra Leone, could be called good prospects for democracy.[6] USAID's remaining democracy and governance programs in 19 countries were funded at an average level of $3.9 million each. Twelve of these programs, nearly all of which were mounted in countries classified as "liberal" or "aspiring" democracies (see table 5. 2), received less funding for democracy and governance programs in 2007 than they did in 2003.[7] By the end of the Bush administration, USAID's democracy and governance programs had morphed into programs for stabilizing postconflict societies and spreading democracy rather than for consolidating democracy.

The allocation of increased resources for democracy promotion to elections and the spread of democracy to postconflict societies reflected the Bush administration's reorientation of U.S. foreign policy generally. This reorientation, which included substantial budgetary increments to democracy and governance initiatives in the Middle East, especially Iraq and Afghanistan, was accompanied by several changes in the way U.S. development assistance, including democracy promotion, was directed in Washington. Within USAID, the Office for Democracy and Governance was shifted to a new bureau for Democracy, Conflict, and

Humanitarian Assistance, while the leadership of the new bureau had become increasingly politicized by 2006. That division limited the ability of career staff at the democracy and governance office (many of whom were trained social scientists or lawyers with a professional understanding of democratic processes) to pursue programs focused on strengthening institutions of countervailing power. The breakup of USAID's Bureau of Policy Planning and Coordination and the de facto merger of USAID into the Department of State by the creation of the "F" Bureau at State, cemented this policy shift.

These changes exacerbated—and were exacerbated by—the hollowing out of USAID's capacity to deliver aid generally, a process that was forced on the agency by Congress beginning early in the Clinton administration. During the 1990s, and continuing through the first term of the Bush administration, USAID's complement of career officers shrank by roughly half. One consequence has been USAID's increasing and excessive reliance on contractors outside the agency to design and implement its programs. Indeed, the reliance on contractors has become so great that USAID personnel are unable to satisfactorily guide and monitor programs that implement democracy and governance initiatives on the ground. A second, and particularly deleterious consequence, was the decline in USAID's capacity to mount innovative programs informed by state-of-the-art research. Monitoring and evaluation of programs to obtain lessons learned and adjust future interventions likewise declined.[8] Whereas the agency had once been one of the world's premier development assistance agencies, it has slowly atrophied to a shadow of its former self.

The Office of Democracy and Governance was also hamstrung by the widespread imposition of congressional earmarks on USAID, particularly with respect to democracy and governance programming in Africa. There, earmarks for humanitarian aid in combination with the President's Emergency Plan for Aids Relief (PEPFAR) crowded out funds available for democracy promotion.

THE MILLENNIUM CHALLENGE CORPORATION

Notwithstanding the shift in U.S. effort to promote democracy during the Bush administration and the decline of USAID's capacity to implement such programs, the establishment of the Millennium Challenge Corporation (MCC) in 2003 was a major innovation that deserves both praise and comment. MCC does not mount democracy assistance programs of its own, but countries cannot qualify for its large "compact" grants until they pass the test of "ruling justly" in respect to three measures of democratization—the Freedom House political rights and civil liberties scales and the World Bank Institute's "voice and accountability" scale. Three other measures, including the rule of law and control of corruption, round out the "ruling justly" evaluation. In addition to "ruling justly," countries must also achieve passing scores with respect to "encouraging economic freedom" and "investing in people."

In marked contrast to the shift in programming by USAID, MCC provides what is in essence a form of budget support to countries that have achieved a substantial measure of democratization. Put differently, it helps these countries consolidate democracy through substantial support for economic development. MCC also sends a powerful signal to other countries that the United States is serious about democratization beyond elections and will reward those countries that move in this direction. In this regard, it is noteworthy that of the 18 compacts announced by MCC to date, 10 or nearly two-thirds, totaling $3.8 billion, are in sub-Saharan Africa.[9] Most noteworthy is that all, with the exception of Burkina Faso, are classified by Freedom House as liberal democracies or aspiring democracies.

To increase the number of countries qualifying for compact status, MCC has also established a "threshold" program. The program provides assistance to countries that fall short of meeting the criteria for compact status, including any of the six measures of "ruling justly." The threshold grant program, by definition, thus directs assistance to questionable performers whose prospects for democracy are less. For example, MCC has made threshold grants to Rwanda and Uganda, two countries that have arguably become *less* rather than more democratic in recent years. On the other hand, Kenya, which easily passes the test of ruling justly except with respect to the control of corruption, has also recently received a threshold grant.

In contrast to its compact grants, MCC efforts to improve a country's performance under the threshold program include democracy and governance initiatives. Ironically, these initiatives are designed and implemented by USAID. It is too early to determine whether MCC's threshold program is in fact increasing the number of countries eligible for MCC compact grants, including raising their performance with respect to democracy and governance. It is also important to note that the bar for African countries to graduate from threshold to compact status is modest, as countries need only score above the median for all countries in their region. Moreover, once a country graduates to compact status, no support is provided to ensure that its level of democracy does not slip back to previous levels. Thus, while MCC addresses the challenge of democratic consolidation at the qualifying phase, it appears to retreat from the challenge after compact grants are made.

In sum, the lofty goals of spreading democracy articulated and funded by the Bush administration raised democracy promotion to a new pedestal but compromised the achievement of these same goals for the reasons discussed. The resulting picture is thus mixed. The administration's approach nonetheless offers several lessons for the incoming Obama administration and, more generally, for other countries seeking to promote democracy abroad.

THE WAY FORWARD

The new administration should develop a smarter and more effective program of democracy promotion in Africa that recognizes present realities on the continent. Above all, the future efforts of the United States to promote democracy will require decisions by President Obama and the new secretary of state that set the course and tone for the next four to eight years. Both must appreciate that efforts at democracy promotion remain an important tool of American soft power; that the United States has important opportunities in Africa; and that a combination of sustained efforts at institution building by USAID or a successor agency on the one hand and vigorous diplomacy on the other—particularly in key regional "anchor states"—can both consolidate and extend the significant, though uneven, progress toward African democratization to date. Now is not the time for the United States to turn away from the process on which the future prosperity of large parts, if not all, of Africa depends.

A new approach to democracy support must take account of the following realities:

1. *The Third Wave of democratization in Africa is largely over.* The continent is populated by a wide diversity of regimes within which a significant but limited number of fragile democracies are worthy candidates for democratic assistance in the near term.

2. *The principal challenge facing the United States is how to consolidate democracy across the continent rather than how to the spread*

it. Efforts to promote democracy must also be distinguished from—and not mortgaged to—programs that address the unique problems of governance in postconflict societies, as had been the tendency in Africa during the Bush administration.

3. *The United States must have viable partners with which to work before it mounts any program to promote democracy.* Because democratization is fundamentally an internally driven process, it cannot be advanced by the United States alone.

4. *The United States should address the challenge of democratic consolidation by targeting aspiring democracies and key anchor states in its democracy and governance assistance programs, including the 12 aspiring democracies listed in table 5.2 plus Nigeria, and possibly Ethiopia, Malawi, and Uganda.* Together with the 8 countries classified as "liberal democracies," roughly 24 of Africa's 48 countries appear to be viable candidates for smarter programs of democracy promotion that focus on building democratic institutions of countervailing power over the long term.[10] It is also particularly important to recognize that the challenge of consolidating democracy includes three regional "anchor states" critical to the peace and stability of the continent as a whole—Kenya, Nigeria, and South Africa. Each of these states presents its own unique challenge for achieving democratic consolidation, and U.S. efforts to meet those challenges must be carefully calibrated to the case.

5. *Future progress toward democratization in Africa is dependent on strengthening viable institutions of countervailing power, and U.S. programs to promote democracy must place greater emphasis on this task.* Such programs would include but not be limited to those that strengthen electoral systems (as contrasted to individual elections), national legislatures, the judiciary, local government, civil society, and the press. The good news is that these are all areas in which the United States has mounted successful programs in the past. But institution building and the programs to support it take time—usually 10 to 15 years, sometimes longer.[11] Strengthening institutions also requires more nuanced programming tailored to country conditions, especially the commitment of appropriate personnel on the ground.

6. *A smarter effort at democracy promotion will require the rehabilitation of the Office for Democracy and Governance at USAID and the reversal of the hollowing out of USAID generally.* The good news, given the current economic crisis and ballooning deficits, is that the shift to a smarter and more appropriate policy of democracy promotion can probably be obtained through a reallocation rather than a substantial increase in total funding Both will require more resources for what is, in essence, institution rebuilding at home. Both will also depend on the appointment of an appropriate administrator of USAID who understands the field of international development and the role of democratization in it. This is particularly true in Africa where *no* country under authoritarian rule has achieved a sustainable record of economic growth.

7. *A smarter and more appropriate policy of democracy promotion will also require a rethinking and possible reversal of the de facto merger of USAID into the State Department.* While some argue that democracy is best promoted as a component of development assistance and integrated into U.S. foreign policy, the experience and results of the past eight years suggest that this assumption may not be true. Instead, the case can be made that USAID and State have complementary, albeit different, roles to play and that promotion of democracy is stronger with some distance between the two entities. This separation could facilitate the type of institution-building efforts in appropriate countries backed by strong diplomatic support that only the Department of State can provide. Put differently, the tension that has sometimes existed between USAID and State, between specialists in development who can mount operations and diplomats who can provide political support, is a creative tension that also applies to the field of democracy promotion.

8. *An improved program of democracy promotion should include a continuation of the MCC and MCC compacts.* They are arguably the most innovative and useful legacy of the outgoing administration with respect to democracy promotion, because they have addressed the challenge of democracy consolidation. Future implementation of MCC's compact program, however, needs to be reviewed. The bar for inclusion in the compact

program needs to be raised, particularly with respect to ruling justly. MCC's threshold programs should be continued, but because they are implemented by USAID, their future success depends on the revitalization of USAID and greater coordination if not integration between MCC and USAID.

NOTES

The author would like to thank Mark Billera of the U.S. Agency for International Development, Chris Fomunyoh of the the National Democratic Institute, Gerald Hyman of the Center for Strategic and international Studies, and Richard Joseph of Northwestern University for their helpful comments on early drafts of this essay. However, the author is solely responsible for the final text.

1. In Angola and Mozambique, between Ethiopia and Somalia, and between Angola and South Africa.

2. For the best-known exposition of the "Third Wave" see Samuel P., Huntington, *The Third Wave: Democratization at the End of the Twentieth Century* (University of Oklahoma Press, 1991). The National Conference and historic multiparty election in Benin in 1990 and the election in Zambia the following year mark the beginning of the Third Wave in Africa.

3. See Bruce Russet, *Grasping the Democratic Peace Principles for a Post–Cold War World* (Yale University Press, 1993), for the best-known examination of this argument.

4. For the president's articulation of his view of democracy and democracy promotion, see his series of presentations made at the National Endowment for Democracy (September 2005), Freedom House (March 2006), and the United States Institute of Peace (Spring 2006).

5. For the best demonstration of the argument, see Michael Bratton and Nicolas van de Walle, *Democratic Experiments in Africa* (Cambridge University Press, 1997).

6. Both score moderately high on the Freedom House Scales and are classified as "Aspiring Democracies" in table 5.2. By contrast, the DRC, Somalia, and Sudan are at the very bottom of the scale.

7. These included Benin, Ghana, Madagascar, Malawi, Mali, Mozambique, Namibia (where USAID closed its program in 2008), Senegal, Sierra Leone, South Africa, Tanzania, and Zambia.

8. Once a hallmark of USAID, the ability of the agency to mount knowledge-based assistance declined as its partnerships with U.S. universities declined. A 2008 study by the National Research Council of USAID's democracy and governance programs reported that the decline of research-based interventions and of monitoring and evaluation threatened the viability of the programs. This was particularly true with respect to interventions to strengthen democratic institutions. See Committee on Evaluation of USAID Democracy Assistance Programs, *Improving Democracy Assistance: Building Knowledge through Evaluations and Research* (Washington, D.C.: NAP, 2008), http://www.nap.edu/catelog12164.html.

9. Benin, Burkina Faso, Cape Verde, Ghana, Lesotho, Madagascar, Mali, Mozambique, Namibia and Tanzania. MCC also includes its $697.5 million compact with Morocco as funding for Africa, but it is excluded here.

10. Some members of the CSIS working group on democracy promotion opined that this strategy would eliminate support to democratic forces, particularly civil society organizations, in small countries mired in authoritarian rule, for example, Equatorial Guinea. The author acknowledges this possibility but concludes than in a time of scares resources, USAID's democracy and governance programs cannot operate everywhere. Moreover, candidates for this type of assistance could still receive small grants from the National Endowment for Democracy and its constituent organizations, for example, the National Democratic Institute and the International Republican Institute.

11. One notable example of U.S. support for strengthening an institution of countervailing power is USAID's program of technical assistance to the Kenya National Assembly. Now in its eighth year and implemented by the State University of New York, the program has achieved remarkable results but must now solidify its gains. USAID rightly intends to extend the program another four years. The program is also notable for the fact that it has attracted co-funding from Britain's Department for International Development.

6

U.S. FOREIGN ASSISTANCE AND TRADE POLICIES IN AFRICA

PRINCETON N. LYMAN

Some the Bush administration's most well received achievements were in its aid and trade policies in Africa. Under President George W. Bush, aid to sub-Saharan Africa tripled from $2.3 billion in 2000 to $6.6 billion 2006, and the president pledged to increase it further to nearly $9 billion by 2010. President Bush's initiative on HIV/AIDS—that is, the President's Emergency Program for AIDS Relief (PEPFAR)—not only dramatically increased U.S. aid for combating this disease but also stimulated major increases from other donors. Other initiatives in Africa addressed malaria, education, debt relief, and multiyear commitments to well-governed countries through the Millennium Challenge Corporation (MCC). On trade, the Bush administration improved the conditions of the African Growth and Opportunities Act, helped African countries cope with strong competition from China and other textile producers, and strengthened trade capacity through infrastructure projects under the MCC and through hubs for regional trade assistance.

Pledges, like those of President Bush for 2010 and that of President Barack Obama during his 2008 campaign, to double foreign aid worldwide may nevertheless be circumscribed by the global financial and economic crisis that erupted in late 2008. This crisis will force a hard look at foreign aid priorities in general and perhaps strain the remarkable bipartisan support that has existed for more than a decade on behalf of increased aid and improved trade opportunities for Africa. It will be important that recent gains—especially the broad commitment to global health, the achievements in treating AIDS victims, and the lessons learned from the PEPFAR and MCC operational innovations—be preserved and built upon in undertaking any new directions. Most of all, the Obama administration will have to make clear to the American people and the Congress the importance of these past commitments and continued dedication to such international cooperation.

A new administration will also need to address the structural problems in the aid program, which have given rise to a plethora of calls for reform, as well as for changes in its future composition. The pattern whereby the Bush administration created new independent programs and institutions for its various initiatives has led to recommendations in Congress and by nongovernmental organizations for a major overhaul of the U.S. aid program, with greater consolidation and in most cases a higher priority for long-term development. Advocates for relatively neglected areas such as agriculture, health infrastructure, and family planning as well as closer coordination of aid and trade policy are all pressing for new programs, in some cases special new funds, and new White House coordinators for these fields. The new administration would do well, however, to avoid undertaking major organizational overhaul of the aid program: such a process would be time consuming, would be subject to intense bureaucratic and political infighting, and would keep the administration from quickly pursuing important initiatives of its own while preserving the substantial gains made in recent years. The same is true for bringing greater cohesion to U.S trade policies. New trade strategies do need to be developed for the resumption of the Doha round, for preserving special African preferences, and for finding new vehicles for building trade capacity. Better coordination of aid and trade is clearly desirable.

However, judicious use of an empowered coordinator, strongly backed by the president and secretary of state, could achieve much in the first two years in developing overall strategy and coordinating aid programs and could—and should—be charged with integrating aid and trade policies for Africa to the benefit of both Africa and the United States. A high-level commission should be established to examine the range of aid and trade issues that would impinge on any reorganization of these functions and provide a road map for any such reorganization later in the first term.

FOREIGN ASSISTANCE: ACCOMPLISHMENTS OF THE BUSH ADMINISTRATION

The increases in aid to Africa were particularly significant, constituting nearly a tripling of aid to Africa from 2000 to 2006. The signature global aid initiatives of the Bush administration, PEPFAR and the MCC, have been heavily focused on Africa. Much of the increase also came from debt relief for the poorest African countries, as well as for Nigeria and the Democratic Republic of Congo (DRC), in accord with actions of the G-8 and international financial institutions along the same lines.

The specific accomplishments of the Bush programs for Africa can be summarized as follows (figures are in disbursements):[1]

- U.S. development assistance to sub-Saharan Africa (in 2005 dollars) went from $2.3 billion in 2000 to $6.6 billion in 2006, a near-tripling as the Bush administration often indicated. Of the $6.6 billion, $5.4 billion was in bilateral assistance and $1.2 billion in multilateral aid.

- Debt relief was a substantial contributor to the figures for 2006, including relief for the DRC ($689 million), Nigeria ($597 million), and Zambia ($188 million).

- Excluding debt relief, the increase was still substantial, going from $2 billion in 2000 to over $5 billion in 2006.

- Humanitarian assistance was a significant part of the total: $1.7 billion in 2006, accounting for 31 percent of disbursements that year.

- PEPFAR was also an important contributor, accounting for approximately 25 percent of disbursements of nondebt aid in 2006.

- The MCC committed $3.1 billion to eight sub-Saharan African countries, based on their meeting 16 specific criteria of good governance, although disbursements by mid-2008 amounted to approximately $145 million. Three other countries are in line for compacts. President Bush initially proposed that MCC commitments globally should rise to $5 billion annually by 2010, although Congress cut his requests for the MCC each year since 2006. Other specific initiatives of the Bush administration included in the above figures are a $1.2 billion program to combat malaria, a three-year $350 million program for neglected tropical diseases, and an African education initiative expected to reach $245 million in 2008.

- On top of these achievements, at the 2005 G-8 Summit President Bush pledged that the United States would double its aid to sub-Saharan Africa by 2010 from the 2004 level of nearly $4.5 billion. While the aid level reached $6.6 billion in 2006, a 45 percent increase, much of this was in the form of one-time debt relief. To reach the 2010 goal will require further high levels of disbursement under PEPFAR and from the existing MCC grants as well as further development assistance. PEPFAR has strong bipartisan support; indeed, Congress has authorized an increase from $30 billion in the first five years to $48 billion for the coming cycle. And the backlog of existing commitments from MCC grants should allow for substantial outlays through 2010.

In his campaign, Obama promised to double aid overall. For Africa he proposed additional funding for malaria, education, agriculture, and health. However, with the burgeoning financial and economic crisis, the new administration will face severe budget problems as it and the new Congress wrestle with domestic stimulus packages, a backlog of domestic demands, increasing deficits, and other foreign affairs pressures. Thus, even if the Bush target is met in 2010, lack of strong support for follow-on commitments to programs such as the MCC could result in a decline after 2010, hardly what was intended by the G-8 pledge.

Disaggregating the Bush figures points to other challenges. First, despite the impressive rise, assistant still averages less than $9 per African per year, this for the poorest continent in the world. Second, the rise in humanitarian assistance—for example, to Sudan and Ethiopia, the two largest recipients of assistance in 2006, and the large amounts of debt relief to the DRC, Nigeria, and Zambia—meant that increases in broad development assistance to the bulk of the poorest countries were not great. This factor was influenced as well by the focus of PEPFAR, understandably enough, on countries where HIV/AIDS was most prominent, including middle-income South Africa, rather than on the basis of the poorest. As a result of these other priorities, the share going to the best-governed states dropped from 33 percent in 2000 to 11 percent in 2006, though this decrease should be redressed by steadily increased disbursements from the MCC.[2]

THE CALL FOR REFORM

The rapid rise in the Bush administration's assistance created structural problems as well as questions of distribution. Proliferation of special programs with different organizational leadership has complicated the coordination and focus of U.S. aid. The administration began with a feeling, fair or not, that USAID had by and large been ineffective. Large amounts of assistance to Africa in particular seemed to have produced few results. The MCC was thus established as a separate corporation, outside of USAID. PEPFAR was placed under the direction of the State Department rather than with USAID and even within State was established separately from the department's Office of International Health. Programs from other U.S. government agencies have proliferated, with Treasury, Health and Human Services, Energy, and other agencies operating in many countries, sometimes through USAID support but sometimes with their own resources. Another development has been the increased role of the Department of Defense. The establishment in October 2008 of the U.S. Africa Command has raised questions of how development and security considerations need to be managed, especially on a continent with many weak states and, at least in the Horn of Africa, with a significant terrorist presence. Whatever the rationales, the proliferation of responsibilities for assistance is clear. In 1998, USAID managed 64.3 percent of official development assistance: State, 12.9 percent; and DOD, only 3.3 percent. In 2006, USAID's share had dropped to 45 percent while DOD's had risen to 18 percent. Responsibility of agencies other than USAID, DOD, or State rose from 19.3 percent to 23.6 percent.[3]

The conviction that significant reorganization of U.S. assistance was needed came from within the Bush administration itself, when Secretary of State Condoleezza Rice asked the USAID administrator, who was then given a joint high-level appointment in State, to undertake a process of bringing greater coordination and an even closer relationship to State for those programs already under the direction of State and USAID. That process was slowed when shortly into his term USAID Administrator Randall Tobias resigned, and the reorganization did not fully address the relationships and coordination of programs outside

State control. Moreover, the process did not receive substantial support or authority from Congress for major reforms.

Even more forceful calls for reform have come now from Congress and from a host of experts, nongovernmental organizations (NGOs), and think tanks. House Foreign Affairs Committee Chairman Howard Berman, for example, has stated:

> It is painfully obvious to Congress, the administration, foreign aid experts, and NGOs alike, that our foreign assistance program is fragmented and broken and in critical need of overhaul. I strongly believe that America's foreign assistance program is not in need of some minor change, but, rather, it needs to be reinvented and re-tooled in order to respond to the significant challenges our country and the world face in the 21st century.[4]

The number of studies and recommendations for aid reform from the community of experts and NGOs is legion. (A sampling can be found in the appendix.) These studies all confirm the achievements of the Bush administration but argue the need for reform. Emphases vary. Most argue for higher-level influence within the administration on long-term development. They recommend keeping to the president's pledge to double aid to Africa but with more focus on relatively neglected sectors, for example, agriculture, education, democracy, family planning, and infrastructure. Some tension is growing between those calling for renewed emphasis on these neglected sectors, on the one hand, and the forward commitment to HIV/AIDS and attendant attention to global health, on the other, which may well occupy much of the room for increased assistance in the years ahead.

Some also want more aid to go to the poorest countries, while others argue for giving more attention to addressing weak and fragile states, like the DRC and Nigeria, and those where security considerations may be greatest such as in the Horn of Africa. Particular attention is paid to the need to reverse the decline in USAID staff over the past two decades, with the reliance on contractors instead of direct management responsibility for programs, and the consequent loss of in-house development expertise. Some nongovernmental organizations, for example, Oxfam, emphasize greater reliance on ideas, ownership, and leadership coming from within the recipient countries (a "bottom up" approach) and longer-term objectives.

Some worry about the growing role of DOD, but others (Morrison and Hicks, Adams), though wary of too great an emphasis on short-term "hearts and minds" programs, emphasize closer coordination of development and security objectives even while greatly strengthening civilian development capacities. Most of these studies call for greater coordination of aid and trade policy to meet African needs, though specifics on how to balance overseas and domestic interests are scarce.

Overall, these studies and papers provide a rich source of assessments, ideas, and recommendations on which a new administration can draw. But while pressure for reform is widespread, the new administration will face a number of difficult issues and challenges in accomplishing it.

COMPETING PROPOSALS FOR REORGANIZATION

Virtually every recent study of assistance programs urges greater unification of programs and much closer coordination. But the argument breaks down between those who argue that long-term economic development must be raised to a higher priority in U.S. policy vis-à-vis other foreign policy and security objectives and those who argue for closer coordination of assistance in relation to a broad range of foreign policy objectives, including security. Most studies that favor a development approach more clearly separated from shorter-term political and security objectives argue for one of two alternative structures:

- Creating a cabinet-level department of development, similar to DFID in the UK

- Bringing several of the current programs (USAID, MCC, and PEPFAR, in particular, but programs in other agencies as well) under a restructured and greatly strengthened USAID, which would nevertheless continue as an autonomous agency under the State Department[5]

A cabinet-level department is seen by many of the development experts as the ideal: it would raise the importance of economic development to equal that of diplomacy and security as a basic tool and objective of U.S. foreign policy; it would attract the needed expertise; it would give the development secretary input at home and abroad into related policies such as trade; and it would counter the increasing trend of shifting development-related programs to DOD. Nevertheless, many development advocates, even some who prefer a cabinet-level solution, believe that political support in the public and Congress is lacking for such a radical change and sees the second alternative as the more practical. In this scenario, USAID would regain the subject expertise it once had, as well as the responsibility for setting development policy, and would manage all but the most specific security-related development programs. Some studies that focus more exclusively on Africa argue for a separate budget for development assistance to Africa to shield it from pressures to devote significant amounts of development assistance to support DOD-led or other security-related programs and allow for a continental strategy that would better integrate development, trade, and governance activities.

Running almost in the opposite direction are studies by Stephen Morrison and Kathleen Hicks and by Gordon Adams, for example. They argue that the need for closer relationships between foreign assistance and foreign policy, including security policy, is a given in the present world, whether dealing with weak states and terrorist threats or supporting longer-term development as a foreign policy objective. These studies say less about how to restructure the aid programs per se but advocate more integration of strategy and budgetary planning for national security to include foreign assistance, covering both short- and longer-term objectives. Adams advocates closer operational cooperation among personnel from aid agencies, State, and DOD to create an "interagency national security culture." The Morrison and Hicks study argues specifically for elevating long-term development but as part of a broader security strategy. These approaches are not entirely incompatible with the ones cited earlier—the InterAction (see appendix) proposal, for example, tries to bridge some of this gap—but it will take some work to bring them closer together.

THE ARGUMENT AGAINST MAJOR REORGANIZATION

While the argument for organizational reform may be strong, the long and arduous process of reorganization may be well beyond what a new administration can accomplish in the face of so many other major foreign policy issues and crises. Bureaucratic rivalries will be intense in any major overhaul. As for the proposal to create a cabinet-level department of development, for example, it is worth recalling that all recent secretaries of state have sought greater, not less, control over the assistance program, including total integration with State (advocated, for example, by Madeleine Albright). This same predilection could well arise in the Obama administration. Congressional cooperation will also be essential. Most studies advocate a rewriting of the Foreign Assistance Act, with its 247 directives and 33 policy goals. Congress has indeed supplemented the basic Foreign Assistance Act with 20 separate pieces of related legislation. No single committee in Congress has sufficient mandate to address these matters alone (for example, the relation of trade and aid or even uses of food aid), and there would be resistance to doing so in any case. Any serious effort at reorganization also faces several critical questions.

HOW EXTENSIVE?

The wider the reach of reorganization—for example, if it is to include policy toward the international financial institutions, trade, the State Department's current postconflict reconstruction programs, domestic agency (Labor, Health and Human Services, and Interior, among others) programs, relations with AFRICOM—the more complex the reorganization would be, the more challenging politically and bureaucratically, and the more time required to complete it. What is the optimal degree of reorganization that does not inhibit ongoing programs and the relatively rapid introduction of new and better programs of a new administration?

HOW MUCH CONSOLIDATION?

While most analysts and advocates have a predilection toward consolidation of programs under one agency or department, with a national strategy for global development, keeping distinct entities to carry out diverse objectives of U.S. foreign policy has some merit. An MCC, for example, will be better able to reward truly well governed countries—without undue pressure for including more strategically important if less well governed countries—if it is not under a single agency closely integrated with other policy objectives. The programs needed in weak and fragile states, or more politically important but poorly governed ones, may themselves demand different direction, skills, and focus from those in the sights of the MCC.

Similarly, if PEPFAR were placed under USAID, as some consolidation proposals suggest, would the high funding levels and political salience of that program be so great as to occupy most of the time and attention of senior and staff to the detriment of the other sectors that USAID now serves? Finally, is a single agency like USAID likely to have all the staff expertise needed, say, for trade assistance or for fiscal and monetary policy reform, when other agencies are steeped in such issues? In other words, it may be better to let a number of flowers bloom within a well-planned garden rather than consolidate under a single organic structure.

CENTRAL POLICY DIRECTION VERSUS FIELD AND COUNTRY INPUT AND OWNERSHIP

The challenge is how to balance the nearly unanimous recommendations of development advocates for central policy direction and a national strategy for global development—focusing more attention on agriculture, climate change, and governance—with the need for greater flexibility at the country level, more ownership by recipient governments and local communities, and more diversity of programming, which many of the same studies advocate. It is hard to have it both ways.

THE NEW SECURITY REALITY

How can the advantages of staff presence in the field be balanced with today's security context? There are now some 900 unaccompanied (that is, no family members) State Foreign Service positions and over a thousand unaccompanied USAID positions worldwide, reflecting the greater insecurity overseas today. Many officers in these posts serve shortened tours. Nongovernmental organizations carrying out humanitarian programs face threats of attack in such places as Darfur and eastern DRC. The implications of heightened insecurity for implementing development programs need to be studied. It is one thing to expand USAID staffing and expertise, as almost all the studies cited above recommend, but another to have people on the ground long enough to carry out such programs with the sensitivity and time required. With all the advantages of a strong field presence, is, in fact, a new paradigm necessary?

THE SUBSTANTIVE ISSUES

Early on, any reorganization should also address issues relating to the purposes and role of foreign assistance within the development and security communities about. These may well determine the nature of any reorganization. Indeed, if these other issues are not addressed conceptually, any reorganization will be all bureaucratic bargaining and movement of chairs but will not necessarily provide real improvement in the foreign assistance program. These critical issues are discussed below.

DEVELOPMENT AND SECURITY

It is easy to say that in the age of terrorism foreign assistance policy should be more closely integrated with security policy. While most of the studies cited above agree, at least in principle, after that, the differences are significant.

Should there be an integrated *foreign assistance strategy* as some recommend (Lancaster, Radelet) or an integrated *national security strategy* that links foreign aid closer to U.S. security objectives (Morrison and Hicks, Adams)? The former approach emphasizes the importance of long-term development, with allocations based largely on economic need and linked to building institutions and capacities for economic growth and social progress. The latter approach emphasizes the importance of relating assistance more closely to problems with weak or failing states, advocating quicker on-the-ground results, and allocating of assistance more on the basis of strategic importance than on need.

How great a role should DOD play in foreign assistance? DOD today accounts for 21 percent of official U.S. development aid. Some believe the lessons from Iraq and Afghanistan, in particular the use of interagency provincial reconstruction teams, should be extended to other regions, including Africa. Others believe this is a dangerous idea, misconceiving the nature of development and threatening the role and credibility of development agencies and NGOs.

TARGETS OF DEVELOPMENT ASSISTANCE

Should development assistance focus on the poorest people or on countries with the greatest potential? With a possibly shrinking budget for foreign assistance, or one increasingly dominated by the commitment to HIV/AIDS, this question is more than academic. It pits those most concerned with poverty reduction and the Millennium Development Goals (MGDs) against those in the development community who emphasize the need for integrated subregional development, a strategy that requires strengthening the better-endowed anchor states in those subregions, among other things.

And should development aid focus mostly on achieving the MDGs or on promoting economic growth? The tendency of development advocates is to argue that the two are not inconsistent, that the social objectives of the MDGs—education, health, and so forth—empower people and undergird growth. But those concerned with growth argue for more investment in infrastructure, power, entrepreneurial development, and aid for trade, none of which is included in the MDGs. Efforts to close the gap by advocating it all (see, for example, the HELP Commission Report) only skirt the issue. Even if rising aid levels were posited to cover all these sectors, it is questionable that such a broad mandate would have the necessary political support and clarity of purpose that both Congress and the public often demand.

How important is building self-sufficiency and avoiding long-term dependency? The HELP Commission (and others) recommends avoiding long-term dependency by supporting growth strategies and programs. But the reality is that achieving the MDGs (which the HELP Commission and most other studies also advocate) in countries as poor as Mali or Burkina Faso, for example, can be done only by long-term (if not permanent) subsidization by donors.

What will be the impact of increased allocations to HIV/AIDS, already one of the largest U.S. commitments in Africa? Concern is growing that the new and larger authorization for PEPFAR, and the long-term G-8 commitment to providing AIDS treatment to all who need it, will crowd out other assistance needs. Even if AIDS treatment does not crowd out other priorities in the short term, the rising numbers and higher costs for treatment over time could well do so, in addition to creating a backlash in public and political support for this program, especially if new infections continue to outstrip the number of those who gain access to treatment.

Another question is whether the generous U.S. commitment to HIV/AIDS is serving America's political interests in Africa, where leaders may well have other priorities, or to put it more crudely, whether the United States is gaining influence from this program commensurate with its size. It can be argued that the United States will be unable to discontinue or even reduce what is becoming its major aid program in countries with which it has serious disagreements because the PEPFAR program is directly tied to keeping people alive. Ethiopia, which currently receives $350 million from PEPFAR and nearly twice that much in emergency relief, may already be exemplifying this dilemma as it flouts U.S. concerns over backsliding in democracy and human rights. (Phillip Nieburg and Stephen Morrison offer a fuller discussion of these issues in chapter 3.)

CORRUPTION

Almost none of the studies address in any depth the problem of corruption and how to operate development programs within societies where this problem is endemic. Even less well addressed is getting at the second side of corruption—that is, corruption carried out by multinational corporations, tolerated by export finance agencies and financial institutions, and prosecuted to only a limited degree by members of the Organization for Economic Cooperation and Development (OECD). A World Bank study reports that 60 percent of multinational corporations recently paid undocumented bribes in non-OECD countries. How valid are anticorruption programs in developing countries if this side of the problem is not addressed? How should a reorganized aid program relate to enforcement agencies and help raise priorities for prosecution both in the United States and in other members of the OECD? How central, as recommended in this chapter, should addressing corruption be as a theme of the Obama administration?

NEW ISSUES LESS WELL ADDRESSED

In addition, foreign assistance programs will need to turn attention to new issues beyond education, health, and infrastructure. (Michelle Gavin addresses some of these new issues in chapter 9 on Africa's "mega-challenges.") These new challenges may well demand not only new skills but also changes in priorities and perhaps major shifts in the way traditional programs have been conceived.

FOOD SECURITY

The recent rise in food prices, though abating, has raised anew the priority of agricultural investments. In response, the Bush administration rushed through an emergency $1.8 billion program in 2008 to help countries most affected. The Morrison and Tuttle report cited above calls for changes in emergency programs, biofuels policy, and trade policy and puts forward a number of other recommendations that go beyond just aid. Senator Lugar, following on that report, has proposed a five-year, $5 billion program for agricultural and rural development. While new emphasis on agriculture is welcome, serious policy questions raised by the recent crisis are not fully addressed even in these reports and recommendations. Surely developing countries will place more emphasis now on greater domestic food security rather than dependence on the world market. How will this emphasis affect aid policies on market development, privatization, subsidies, and trade? (Malawi boasts of having rejected virtually unanimous donor advice last year during a similar crisis when it provided free fertilizer to its farmers; this year it is a food exporter.) The importance of genetically modified foods will surely receive more attention in this context. What position will the U.S. aid program take on this matter, and how hard will the United States press the European Union (EU) on the issue?

CLIMATE CHANGE

Africa will be hit hard by climate change. The impact on development could be catastrophic. It could also have serious destabilizing effects and create added security threats. One estimate is that Africa's agricultural yields, already low by global standards, could be reduced by 50 percent.[6] This estimate goes well beyond the current food security crisis. Are any of the current or newly proposed U.S. development programs structured to address such a calamitous possibility? How much need is there to rethink overall aid and development strategies in regions where drought, floods, and disease will increase in major ways in the next few decades? Should foreign assistance agencies contemplate major changes in geographic investments, readying for major shifts in population? Where should such policy thinking be located, and how should this be factored in with Congress? On the positive side, Africa could benefit from renewed attention to climate change, with its vast forests and biodiversity. Several projects are already under way for protecting this diversity and stopping environmentally damaging deforestation. Other donors are even more engaged than the United States, and this area may also provide a valuable opportunity for collaboration.

MIGRATION

Migration is already a seriously destabilizing problem in several African countries (Côte d'Ivoire, Kenya, and South Africa, for example) and will surely become worse. One of the major projected impacts of climate change in Africa is massive movement of people, both within Africa and to Europe and the Americas. Much of this migration will be rural to urban, but current U.S. priorities are only indirectly related to urban development and many of the new emphases being advocated are specifically directed to the rural areas. Job creation, which no country in Africa has managed well, will become an even greater problem. No really new and more effective strategy for employment is evident in the development literature so far or in any of the several studies cited above.

POPULATION

Population growth is not a new concern, but it has been a badly neglected issue. Few studies give this subject high priority. Yet population growth in Africa is aggravating the problems of food security, environmental degradation, and migration. How should this issue be addressed within the health, education, and other programs that the new administration will implement? How high a priority should the administration make it with the new Congress, especially if majority support for such programs is insufficient?

NEW PLAYERS

The development field will become more complex as Brazil, China, India, and Russia increase their involvement on the continent. China is making the strongest impact, with very large loan commitments to countries like Angola, the DRC, and Nigeria and engagement in a wide number of infrastructure and other projects. (See chapter 7 in this volume by Ambassador David Shinn.) Multilateral cooperation has always been the bane of donors in Africa. Despite a myriad of agreements and commitments, donors continue to demand a multitude of distinctive management structures, reports, and attention to high-level visitors. In Mozambique, for instance, there are still nearly a thousand different donor activities, with an average value of $2 million. Some countries report hosting more than a thousand donor missions and providing as many as 2,400 quarterly progress reports.[7]

If the OECD countries are unable to coordinate effectively, the new players have few prospects for doing better. Yet, without closer coordination, at least on basic principles, donors could be working at cross-purposes in such areas as debt management, corruption, environmental protection, promotion of democracy, and governance. The new players, moreover, mix public and private commercial activities well beyond what is practiced or allowed under the OECD's Development Assistance Committee (DAC) rules, raising important questions of aid policy and corporate social responsibility. One of the arguments in favor of an enhanced assistance entity within the U.S. government is to provide a strong focal point for negotiating such issues with other donors, including such strategically important countries as China with which the United States has so many other issues demanding attention.

AVOIDING ORGANIZATIONAL BREAKDOWN AND KEEPING FOCUS

Given the differing approaches advocated by various important constituencies, the bureaucratic complexities, and the important substantive issues that need to be resolved, a major restructuring of the aid program in the beginning of the Obama administration could sap the energies of new administrators and actually slow preparation of new policies and implementation of new programs. The administration would be well advised instead to initiate a vigorous process of cross-cutting coordination mechanisms, that is, various forms of matrix management, in its first few years, while commissioning a high-level study with Congress of more comprehensive alternatives for reorganization that deal with both the substantive and the structural questions.

In its first years, the administration could appoint a high-level administrator, perhaps best in the National Security Council (rather than several new NSC coordinators for the various topic areas), backed by the president and secretary of state, and empowered to coordinate existing programs as needed, for example, PEPFAR and USAID on issues of health infrastructure; USAID and State on postconflict reconstruction programs; State, USAID, MCC, and others on food security; USAID, MCC, and the U.S. Trade Representative (USTR) on trade; USAID, the Environmental Protection Agency, and others on the implications of climate change. This approach would permit speedier initiation of new programs and ideas and the testing of new directions. Meanwhile, the high-level commission—including nongovernment stakeholders, administration officials, and members of Congress—could be charged with studying organization and prioritization. Subsequently, perhaps toward the middle or end of the first term, after building more consensus, the administration could undertake any needed major reorganization more quickly and with less disruption to ongoing programs.

TRADE

As with foreign assistance, the Bush administration established a solid record of support for sub-Saharan Africa on trade. The record was stronger on trade agreements such as the African Growth and Opportunity Act (AGOA) and on building trade capacity than it was on multilateral trade negotiations, in particular in the Doha round. Nevertheless, the United States is Africa's largest single-country export market, with 98 percent of AGOA-related exports entering the United States duty free. China is the largest single-country exporter to sub-Saharan Africa.

AGOA, which began during the Clinton administration as a bipartisan congressional initiative, was warmly supported and strengthened under the Bush administration. Legislative improvements were passed in 2002, 2004, and 2006, promoting better opportunities for African producers as well as diversification and competitiveness. Today, 40 African countries are AGOA-eligible, and 27 receive AGOA apparel benefits, with 18 of those receiving approval for hand-loomed and handmade articles.[8]

Recent increases in African exports to the United States are distorted to the extent that the very largest increases are in oil and related energy products. Of $67 billion in African exports to the United States in 2006, only $3.4 billion represent AGOA-related nonpetroleum products. Nevertheless, the nonpetroleum products are increasing. One of Africa's earliest successes under AGOA was in the growth of textiles and apparel products. Africa saw a drop of $300 million in these items in 2005 with the expiration of the restrictions on Chinese exports to the United States, but it is heartening that the fall was reversed in 2006, with apparel exports reaching $1.3 billion in 2007, compared with $359.4 million in 2001. In 2007, 21 African countries exported such products to the United States, with Kenya, Lesotho, Madagascar, Mauritius, and Swaziland being the top exporters in this field. Minerals, transportation equipment, chemicals, and related products were particular gainers in 2007, while agricultural exports declined. Overall, South Africa, with its highly diversified economy, is the single-greatest beneficiary of AGOA.

Increasing African diversity of exports and competitiveness has been a major focus of U.S. trade policy, in part to take the pressure off the politically sensitive area of textiles and apparel. The United States has provided $1.6 billion in trade capacity assistance to sub-Saharan Africa since 2001, with $505 million in fiscal year 2007. The largest source of that assistance is through the MCC, which has restored U.S. aid to infrastructure after a long hiatus. Infrastructure expenditures constitute a large component of MCC's contribution to trade capacity. USAID, through its Africa Global Competitiveness Initiative (AGCI), provides the bulk of U.S. technical assistance for trade capacity, with four regional trade hubs for global competitiveness, which help African countries improve procedures for transit and customs and other efficiency matters.[9] The Bush administration also promoted negotiation of six additional trade and investment frameworks agreements, including two with subregional African economic organizations, establishing policy frameworks and the bases for further cooperation in these areas. After efforts to negotiate a free trade agreement with the Southern Africa Customs Union collapsed, the administration signed a trade, investment, and development cooperation agreement with those countries in July 2008.

THE TRADE CHALLENGE

Despite recent economic growth in Africa, trade preference programs such as AGOA and the EU's "everything but arms," and indeed increases in African exports, Africa's share of world trade remains minuscule. In 2006, sub-Saharan Africa accounted for only 1.74 percent of world trade. Trade capacity, moreover, is highly concentrated in South Africa and Nigeria, the latter because of oil, which accounts for 50.7 percent of all sub-Saharan exports. If bringing Africa more into the global economy is essential for its long-term growth and stability, as many argue, then the task ahead is enormous. Although U.S. bilateral efforts are commendable and helpful, Africa's larger successes will rely first of all on its increased trade capacity and second on worldwide and regional trade agreements that enhance African opportunities. In this regard, failure to reach agreement so far in the Doha round, which was supposed to be directed specifically to helping developing countries, is a blow to such hopes, although sub-Saharan Africa did not necessarily stand to benefit from some of the proposals—even those coming from the developing countries.[10]

Nevertheless, with the lack of progress on Doha, Africa has become subject to the appeals of its trading partners for interim, subregional, or individual trading agreements that may further impede its competitiveness. Thus, the commitment at the G-20 summit in November 2008 to reinvigorate the Doha process is promising. But Africa will not benefit in the absence of some changes in the U.S and European negotiating positions and in those of sub-Saharan Africa as well.

POLICY REFORM PROPOSALS

Several recent studies and recommendations have addressed trade issues affecting Africa, although not as many as those dealing with the foreign assistance program. The trade studies have focused more on policy than on organizational changes. Conferences cosponsored by the Council on Foreign Relations and Realizing Rights: The Ethical Globalization Initiative and studies by Oxfam, the Institute for Agriculture and Trade Policy, and the American Enterprise Institute have focused for several years on African trade issues and U.S. trade policy, including negotiating strategies in the Doha round and the effect of farm subsidies. In 2008, the USTR documented the experience of AGOA and other Bush administration trade initiatives, as has USAID, and identified some of the issues the new administration will face. Manchester Trade has produced a number of reports and analyses on U.S. trade policy, the problems posed by European trade practices, and recommendations for the Obama administration. (Some of these publications can be found in the appendix.)

Almost all these studies point to the need for U.S. trade policy to support African development and recommend closer coordination between USTR trade policies and aid for trade and related programs of USAID and MCC. Yet trade issues are in many ways more complex than foreign assistance, because trade policy reflects and affects important U.S. domestic concerns. The farm bill passed in 2008 is a prime example, pitting U.S. domestic pressures for subsidies against obligations under the World Trade Organization (WTO) and negotiations in the Doha round to reduce them. Recent changes in the world may also require a rethinking of those positions advocated by both developed and developing countries in the recent Doha round.

TREATING AFRICA AS A WHOLE

One of the dangers for African development, in the mind of some experts, is the focus in recent trade discussions on the least-developed countries (LDCs). While quite a few countries in sub-Saharan Africa are LDCs, some critically important countries like Côte d'Ivoire, Ghana,

Kenya, Nigeria, and South Africa do not fall into that category. Proposals to provide duty free and quota free (DFQF) access to all LDCs, a position advocated by several international NGOs (for example, Oxfam) and, of course, by many LDCs, would in fact hurt much of Africa in several ways. First of all, large, better-organized LDCs like Bangladesh could very well take away precious gains, especially in textiles, that African LDCs have enjoyed under AGOA. Second, distinguishing between trade access for African LDCs and their relatively better off neighbors undermines plans and potential for African subregional free trade and customs union arrangements, which some analysts believe is one of the most important ways to develop African trade and trade capacity.[11]

The European Union's proposed economic partnership agreements (EPAs) have been criticized precisely on these grounds, as they establish separate trade liberalization and tariff schedules for countries in West Africa like Ghana and Côte d'Ivoire with potentially negative effects on the plans for the Economic Community of West Africa (ECOWAS), and similarly in East Africa through separate agreements with Burundi, Kenya, Rwanda, Tanzania, and Uganda, all members of the East Africa Community and of an expanding Common Market of Eastern and Southern Africa (COMESA).[12]

One way to counter this trend is to have the WTO agree to treat Africa as a single entity for trade purposes, without distinguishing between its LDCs and its relatively better off nations. At minimum, this approach would lend support and legitimacy to the subregional economic entities being developed in Africa and work against divisive trade agreements. Neither the United States, nor for that matter African nations, have advocated this policy at WTO. But the issue may be a valuable one for the United States and for Africa to champion. The United States should back this policy by greater support to subregional economic integration in Africa, including the development of mechanisms and funding lines for regional infrastructure projects and technical assistance to subregional organizations like COMESA, ECOWAS, the East Africa Community, and the Southern Africa Development Community.

AFRICAN PREFERENCE: HOW LONG?
AGOA has been a singular bipartisan success for both the Clinton and the Bush administrations. But, as noted earlier, with the end of the

multifiber agreement restricting Chinese exports, the early successes in textiles have given way to more challenging problems for African countries. While African manufacturers have recovered somewhat from that challenge, they still compete at fairly low levels of output. One issue, therefore, is how much to defend Africa's special preferences under AGOA against pressure for DFQF and other worldwide demands for preferences or freer trade. The challenges from other large developing countries like Bangladesh, whose capacity is farther advanced, along with Africa's still limited trade capacity, argue for continuing to extend AGOA and the special preferences therein to give Africa more time to develop capacity and attract more private investment. Extending the third-country fabric provision and making other improvements in AGOA, such as adding items now excluded (luggage, handbags, and hats and agricultural products like sugar, dairy, beef, groundnuts, cotton, and some chocolate), are ways the Obama administration could expand and sustain such preferential treatment.

On the other hand, some might argue that maintaining such preferences too long only perpetuates Africa's special status without necessarily providing the incentives for Africa to become more competitive. The United States may well face greater pressures from other regions and countries of more strategic importance for either similar preferences or for an end to Africa's special status. African countries would like to see AGOA made permanent, but this is unlikely and perhaps not in Africa's own interest. At what point, in other words, should policy shift toward helping Africa become more competitive in the global market place and away from protecting its special preferences?

MORE FREE TRADE AGREEMENTS?

A certain bifurcation in U.S. policy has led to promoting AGOA while at the same time seeking a free trade agreement with the Southern Africa Customs Union in place of the unilateral concessions of AGOA. The new administration may be faced with more such pressure to reexamine whether AGOA should continue to be an Africa-wide program, unilateral in its benefits—that is, without reciprocal concessions for U.S. exports—or at a minimum directed more narrowly to the poorer African countries. Moving in the latter direction would, like the EPAs, undermine some of Africa's subregional development and upset regional trade patterns. Another challenge for the United States in seeking free trade agreements is the most-favored nation clause in the EPAs, which gives Europe the benefit of any advantages that the United States might seek to negotiate in a post-AGOA phase. For example, one of the problems in the negotiations between the United States and the Southern Africa Customs Union was that any opening of the auto market to the United States, would, by dint of the EU's most-favored-nation clause in its agreement with the customs union, open the South African market to Europe as well. U.S. negotiations with the customs union also revealed the difficulty in applying the U.S. comprehensive template to Africa where some exceptions may make more sense. The United States might want to consider whether it can develop an "FTA lite" model for Africa that allows advancement of a more limited reciprocity.

THE DOHA ROUND

Neither the United States nor Africa should take any satisfaction from how the Doha negotiations nearly collapsed. The U.S. farm bill that passed in May 2008 ran counter to much of Bush administration policy for reducing agricultural subsidies, including the U.S. positions on this issue advocated within the Doha round. Despite the brave front of U.S. negotiators that such reductions were still on the table, the politics in the United States seemed to be running the other way. Possible retaliation could come from countries like Brazil, pointing to the fact that the bill violates WTO rulings. In Africa, the cotton-producing countries, including security-sensitive countries like those in the Sahel, will be negatively affected as well and may join in a WTO challenge.

African negotiating strategy at Doha, however, raises questions of its own. South Africa, in alliance with Brazil, India, and other middle-income countries, led Africa as a whole into supporting China's and India's resistance to liberalization of their markets, whether in agriculture or manufacturing and services. This is a nice position to take from a South-South perspective, but it does not necessarily serve most of Africa's purposes. Middle-income countries like Brazil, China, and India maintain tariff and nontariff barriers to African goods as high as or higher than those in the EU or United States. Moreover, U.S. concessions on cotton were more likely to be politically palatable in the United States as part of an overall agreement that opened markets to the United States in countries like Brazil and India. It is thus not clear what advantages most African countries get from supporting the positions of those countries, at least if not getting concessions from them on barriers to African exports. Yet, the United States was not able to break African unity in the negotiations. The new administration will need to ponder what its trade strategy with Africa could be and how it would change this lineup as the Doha round resumes.

FOOD SECURITY

As noted earlier, the recent crisis over rising food prices may lead to a major revision in approaching global agricultural policies, including subsidies and trade. First, one of the arguments against U.S. and EU subsidies—that they increase production and lower prices to the disadvantage of developing countries—may become moot if the objective is now to lower food prices. Lower subsidies, however, could lead to lower production of some key food grains in formerly subsidizing countries making the price impact neutral, or even lead to higher food prices with added hardship to food-importing countries. The outcome is thus not so clear.

Second, with more emphasis on national food security, developing countries will likely seek special exceptions to liberalization of agricultural trade. The whole issue of agricultural liberalization will thus be subject to new debate and review and likely considerable controversy. Here is where coordination of development assistance and trade policy is most needed but where divergent interests may make such coordination nearly impossible. The United States has recognized that assistance for agricultural research and productivity has been badly neglected in the past decade, and, as noted, several proposals recommend increased attention to the sector. But whether U.S. trade policy in the WTO will support greater protection for African agricultural development, or do so without reevaluation of other trade preferences such as those in AGOA, is uncertain.

TRADE CAPACITY ASSISTANCE

Africa has difficulty in many aspects of trade capacity, for example, in scaling up to meet large import opportunities, in overcoming border and transport costs, and in addressing quality control matters. The question is whether—and how—trade and aid strategy will be coordinated well enough in the new administration to make possible an informed decision on its priority and place in the various aid and trade structures. Much of trade capacity assistance to Africa has come through the MCC and the AGCI, the latter the source of some $200 million in technical assistance. The MCC, however, has not garnered strong support in Congress, as noted earlier in this chapter, and does not fund regional projects; it is also scheduled to reach only 11 of sub-Saharan Africa's 43 countries so far. AGCI legislation extends only to 2010. In a tight aid budget environment, trade capacity will thus be competing with many other demands. In 2007, Congressman Jim Mc-Dermott proposed that a special office be established in USAID for building trade capacity and that hundreds of millions of dollars be authorized each year for this purpose. That proposal, of course, competes with proposals by Senator Lugar for new funds to agriculture and rural development and would add to the proliferation of special line items in the aid budget.

BRINGING ABOUT COHESION

For all the reasons described above, the new administration will need to reexamine U.S. trade policy toward Africa more broadly, with a clearer long-term view on development and sustainability, and an understanding of how to balance the various cross-cutting pressures that it will confront worldwide. Given the strong domestic interests in U.S. trade policy, however, it is highly unlikely that any reorganization of foreign assistance will bring U.S. trade policy under the direction of a single overall development czar or agency. Coordination and trade-offs of interests will therefore require negotiation, sometimes at the cabinet level and sometimes at the level of the National Security Council. However the foreign assistance programs may be reorganized, there will be no substitute for broad policy direction, from either a strengthened and broadened State Department or from the National Security Council, or both. This author recommends both.

Certain policy improvements seem especially important in bringing about this coordination:

- Develop a comprehensive trade and development strategy that will appeal to African nations and allow for a more effective line-up of African votes and policies within the Doha negotiations.

- As part of this strategy, vigorously support designation of sub-Saharan Africa as a single trading entity, allowing Africa to compete more effectively under any DFQF agreements and to develop strong subregional trading entities.

- Provide strong support for strengthening Africa's subregional trading blocs through development of means and funding for

regional infrastructure projects and continued provision of assistance for trade capacity at least at current levels.

■ Engage the EU to support the designation of sub-Saharan Africa
as a single trading entity and postpone finalization of individual
EPAs already signed.

■ Negotiate new rules of the road with the EU, the "new players"
in Africa, and African governments that both support Africa's
trade capacity and avoid beggar-thy-neighbor trade practices
among donors.

CONCLUSION

The Bush administration leaves a commendable record of achievement
in Africa in both aid and trade. But the current worldwide economic
and financial crisis and competing views on priorities in a new Obama
administration call for careful steps to preserve this legacy and improve upon it in a way consistent with the new realities and the changing circumstances in Africa. The following recommendations recap
some of those discussed earlier in this chapter:

1. *Appoint an NSC coordinator for African development, not
separate ones for health, trade, or agriculture, and the like.* (For
other reasons, there could be a separate NSC coordinator for
global health but who would defer to the Africa coordinator
for implementing any such strategies in Africa). Charge this
individual with getting quick coordination and new program
initiatives among aid agencies for existing or largely agreed
new priorities, such as between PEPFAR and USAID to
improve health infrastructure, and other agencies working on
trade capacity, food security, and postconflict reconstruction.
A coordinator at the undersecretary level in State should be
appointed to chair a coordinating body of agencies to work on
developing the specific programs that flow from this process
and implementing them.

2. *Defer any major reorganization of the aid program until these new
coordination efforts are under way and tested and priorities are
better established.* Charge a high-level commission to undertake
with Congress an examination of all the issues related to any

reorganization and seek consensus that would ease implementation of any major changes.

3. *In its first assistance budget, the Obama administration should preserve the major achievements and the current, if not modestly enhanced, budget levels for the major ongoing programs and in the process preserve the bipartisan consensus around them, to include PEPFAR, AGOA, malaria and TB programs, food security, and improved governance.* The MCC should be maintained sufficiently to test the efficacy of its compacts as disbursements grow and not be dismantled or changed before then. Appropriation for new MCC compacts (not yet under negotiation) can be deferred for the first year or two.

4. *The NSC coordinator should charge an appropriate body to examine the long-range problems associated with climate change, the directions in world trade, and the current financial crisis to recommend major changes as needed in the approaches to development in Africa in the future.* This planning should be done in conjunction with the international financial institutions, the UN Economic Commission for Africa, the African Union, and OECD's Development Assistance Committee. The results would be a major input to the commission studying reorganization proposals and form the basis for the administration's FY 2011 assistance budget.

5. *The NSC coordinator should develop with relevant agencies a trade and development strategy for Africa that would be pursued in the renewed Doha negotiations, with the key African players in those negotiations and with relevant aid agencies.* A new program for building trade capacity, integral to that strategy and involving all the relevant agencies, should be presented to Congress for FY 2011.

6. *The administration should make a singular effort to inspire and assist a moral regeneration in Africa and its partners, taking advantage of President Obama's particular credibility.* This effort should be pursued through statements and speeches, high-level visits, support for the strengthening of democratic and governance institutions, conditioning some forms of assistance on such reforms, and a pledge to pursue and prosecute foreign

corporations or individuals who act to corrupt African governments or citizens. This approach could be the foundation of a distinctly Obama legacy that in eight years would profoundly improve Africa's hopes for development and peace. It could well be a more important legacy than doubling aid.

APPENDIX

STUDIES ON AID REFORM

Adams, Gordon. "The Politics of National Security Budgets." Policy Analysis Brief. Muscatine, Iowa: Stanley Foundation, February 2007.

Atwood, J. Brian, and Peter McPherson. "Foreign Assistance Reform: Rebuilding U.S. Civilian Development and Diplomatic Capacity in the 21st Century." Testimony before the House Committee on Foreign Affairs, 110th Cong., 2nd Session, June 25, 2008.

Atwood, J. Brian, Peter McPherson, and Andrew Natsios. "Arrested Development: Making Foreign Aid a More Effective Tool." *Foreign Affairs* 87, no. 6 (2008).

Birdsall, Nancy. "Building on International Debt Relief Initiatives." Testimony before the U.S. Senate Foreign Relations Committee, 110th Cong., 2nd Session, April 24, 2008.

Brainard, Lael, and Vinca LaFleur. *Making Poverty History? How Activists, Philanthropists, and the Public Are Changing Global Development.* Brookings Blum Roundtable 2007. Washington, D.C.: Brookings Institution, 2007.

Campbell, Kurt, Alexander T.J. Lennon, and Julianne Smith. *The Age of Consequences: The Foreign Policy and National Security Implications of Global Climate Change.* Washington, D.C.: Center for Strategic and International Studies and Center for a New American Security, November 2007.

DATA. *The DATA Report 2008: Keep the G8 Promise to Africa.* Washington, D.C.: ONE, 2008.

InterAction. "Proposed Major Components and Organization of a Cabinet-level Department for Global and Human Development." Policy paper, InterAction, Washington, D.C., June 2008.

Lancaster, Carol. *George Bush's Foreign Aid: Transformation or Chaos?* Washington, D.C.: Center for Global Development, May 2008.

Modernizing Foreign Assistance Network. *New Day, New Way: U.S. Foreign Assistance for the 21st Century*. Washington, D.C.: Center for Global Development, June 2008.

Morrison, J. Stephen, and Kathleen Hicks. *Integrating 21st Century Development and Security Assistance: Final Report of the Task Force on Nontraditional Security Assistance*. Washington, D.C.: Center for Strategic and International Studies, January 2008.

Morrison, J. Stephen, and Johanna Nesseth Tuttle. *A Call for a Strategic U.S. Approach to the Global Food Crisis*. Washington, D.C.: Center for Strategic and International Studies, July 2008.

Oxfam. *The World Is Still Waiting: Broken G8 Promises Are Costing Millions of Lives*. Oxfam Briefing Paper 103. Oxford: Oxfam International, May 2007.

Oxfam America. *Smart Development: Why U.S. Foreign Aid Demands Major Reform*. Boston: Oxfam America, February 2008.

Radelet, Steve. "Foreign Assistance Reform in the New Administration: Challenges and Solutions." Testimony before the U.S. House Foreign Affairs Committee, 110th Cong., 2nd Session, April 23, 2008.

———. "Modernizing Foreign Assistance for the 21st Century: An Agenda for the Next U.S. President." In *The White House and the World: A Global Development Agenda for the Next U.S. President*. Washington, D.C.: Center for Global Development, March 2008.

Radelet, Steve, and Sami Bazzi. "U.S. Assistance to Africa and the World: What Do the Numbers Say?" CGD Notes. Washington, D.C.: Center for Global Development, February 15, 2008.

Ramachandran, Vijay. "Power and Roads for Africa." In *The White House and the World: A Global Development Agenda for the Next U.S. President*. Washington, D.C.: Center for Global Development, March 2008.

U.S. Commission on Helping to Enhance the Livelihood of People around the Globe. *Beyond Assistance: The HELP Commission Report on Foreign Assistance Reform*. Washington, D.C.: HELP, December 2007.

STUDIES ON TRADE ISSUES

African Global Competitiveness Initiative. *2007 Compendium of Trade-Related Success Stories*. Washington, D.C.: USAID, July 2008.

Constantin, Anne Laure. *Turning High Prices into an Opportunity: What Is Needed?* Minneapolis: Institute for Agriculture and Trade Policy, April 2008.

Lande, Stephen, and Tony Carroll. "Proactive Approach for Incorporation of a Sub-Saharan African Dimension into U.S. Trade Policy." Unpublished paper, Manchester Trade, Washington, D.C., November 2008.

———. "Suggestions for U.S. Economic Policy towards Sub-Saharan Africa (SSA): Focus on Regional Integration." Unpublished paper, Manchester Trade, Washington, D.C., November 2008.

Lande, Stephen, and Sudha Meiyappan. "Strategy for Economic Partnership Agreements (EPAs)." Unpublished paper, Manchester Trade, Washington, D.C. November 2008.

Office of the U.S. Trade Representative. *2008 Comprehensive Report on U.S. Trade and Investment Policy toward Sub-Saharan Africa and Implementation of the African Growth and Opportunity Act*. Washington, D.C: Office of the U.S. Trade Representative, May 2008.

Oxfam America. "Presidential Transition Brief: Trade and Development." Oxfam America, Washington, D.C., November 2008.

Oxfam International. *Partnership or Power Play? How Europe Should Bring Development into its Trade Deals with African, Caribbean, and Pacific Countries*. Oxfam Briefing Paper 110. Oxford: Oxfam International, April 2008.

Smaller, Carin. *Can Aid Fix Trade? Assessing the WTO's Aid for Trade Agenda*. Minneapolis: Institute for Agriculture and Trade Policy, September 2006.

NOTES

The author is grateful to Katy Robinette, research associate for Europe and Africa, Council on Foreign Relations, for research assistance.

1. Steve Radelet and Sami Bazzi, "U.S. Development Assistance to Africa and the World: What Do the Numbers Say?" Center for Global Development Note, http://www.cgdev.org/content/general/detail/15423, 3–5.

2. Ibid, 5.

3. Oxfam America, *Smart Development: Why U.S. Foreign Aid Demands Major Reform* (Boston: Oxfam America, February 2008), 12, http://www.oxfamamerica.org/newsandpublications/publications/briefing_papers/smart-development/smart-development-may2008.pdf.

4. Chairman Howard Berman, "Opening Remarks," U.S. House Foreign Affairs Committee, *Foreign Assistance Reform in the New Administration: Challenges and Solutions*, 110th Cong., April 23, 2008, http://foreignaffairs. house.gov/press_display.asp?id=507.

5. A much more extensive approach is proposed in the HELP Commission Report, which recommends a totally new department of foreign affairs, patterned after the Pentagon with its secretaries of the Army, Navy and Air Force. This new department would be led by a secretary, but development, including related trade issues, would be under a secretary-level official, with other secretary-level officials over political affairs and public diplomacy. The U. S. Commission on Helping to Enhance the Livelihood of People around the Globe, *The HELP Commission Report on Foreign Assistance Reform: Beyond Assistance* (Washington, D.C.: HELP, December 2007).

6. Anne Laure Constantin, *Turning High Prices into an Opportunity: What Is Needed?* (Minneapolis: Institute for Agriculture and Trade Policy, April 2008), http://www.iatp.org/iatp/publications.cfm?accountID=451&refID=102867, 8.

7. Ibid., 18–19.

8. For details of these and other special allowances for AGOA-eligible countries, see the Office of the United States Trade Representative, *2008 Comprehensive Report on U.S. Trade and Investment Policy toward Sub-Saharan Africa and Implementation of the African Growth and Opportunity Act* (Washington, D.C.: USTR, May 2008), http://www.ustr.gov/assets/Trade_Development/ Preference_Programs/AGOA/asset_upload_file203_14905.pdf?ht=, 7–8 and 17–27.

9. For details of USAID trade and investment programs and specific achievements, see African Global Competitiveness Initiative, *2007 Compendium of Trade-Related Success Stories* (Washington, D.C.: U.S. Agency for International Development, July 2008), http://pdf.usaid.gov/pdf_docs/PNADM772.pdf.

10. For example, opening EU and U.S. markets to more agricultural imports would most likely have benefited large export-capable countries like Brazil, India, and South Africa but not the largely subsistence farming communities of Africa's poorer countries. See Constantin, *Turning High Prices,* 11. It is not entirely clear, moreover, that reducing subsidies would lower food prices in a way helpful to food importing countries, of which there are many in Africa. Moreover, some of the Doha provisions might inhibit African countries from protective measures for their agricultural sectors. See Jagdish Bhagwati and Arvind Panagriya, "How the Food Crisis Could Solve the Doha Round," op-ed, *Financial Times,* June 22, 2008. That does not take away from the benefits African cotton farmers would receive from an end to U.S. cotton subsidies, nor to the longer-term potential for African farmers that open markets might provide.

11. K.Y. Amoako, "Africa's Trade Priorities in Wake of Probable Doha Failure," Attachment B to the statement of Realizing Rights: The Ethical Globalization

Initiative and the Council on Foreign Relations, *Trade and Development in Africa: A Policy Approach in Light of the Suspension of the WTO Round Negotiations,* November 2006.
12. Stephen Lande and Sudha Meiyappan, "A Possible Strategic Approach toward EPAs" (Unpublished Paper, Manchester Trade, May 2008).

7

CHINA'S ENGAGEMENT IN AFRICA

DAVID H. SHINN

THE CHANGING AFRICAN CONTEXT AND
AMERICAN INTERESTS

The end of Cold War interests in Africa and more recently a predominant U.S. focus on counterterrorism and humanitarian assistance have led to a decline in U.S. influence on the continent. At the same time, the dramatic expansion of China's economy in recent decades has resulted in a huge increase of imported raw materials, especially oil, from Africa and a more vigorous and complex engagement between Beijing and various African capitals. China's policy has changed since the 1960s from ideological support for liberation groups and revolutionary governments to a pragmatic and comprehensive political and economic relationship with most states on the continent. While China is not the only emerging power expanding its ties with Africa, the speed and scale of China's expansion in the past decade warrant special attention from U.S. policymakers, both in seeking areas of potential collaboration and in mitigating potential tensions and differences.

China's growing role has provided African leaders with an alternative source of support and contributed to the decline of Western influence. Furthermore, China's interests and approach to Africa are strategic and long term. China needs long-term access to Africa's raw materials and the political support of as many as possible of its governments.

ECONOMIC AND HUMANITARIAN AID

The Bush administration has trebled the amount of resources going into Africa but, in contrast with China, has been selective in its political engagement, focusing mainly on crises in Sudan and more episodically in the Democratic Republic of the Congo (DRC), postelection Kenya, Somalia, and Zimbabwe. Increased U.S. resource flows to Africa have generated only modest political leverage because they consist heavily of emergency food aid and funding to combat HIV/AIDS. Both programs are well received by African leaders and individuals, but over the years they have tended "to expect" this kind of help from the United States. The Millennium Challenge Account (MCA) provides large grants to low-income countries after it has been determined that the aid will reinforce good governance, economic freedom, and investments in people. The MCA potentially offers greater political leverage. Its larger programs, however, are available to relatively few African countries deemed to be politically and economically well governed.

Total Chinese aid to Africa is much lower than that provided by the United States. In addition, the United States offers grant assistance, while China provides mostly concessionary loans. African countries perceive that Western aid comes with many strings attached and that Chinese aid does not. While there is considerable truth to this perception, China insists on acceptance of the "One China" policy and often ties its loans to projects built by Chinese companies with substantial Chinese equipment and labor. Like the United States, China has built a record of eventually canceling debt, which may continue with some of China's newer loans. It is important, however, to leave out of China's foreign aid figures the multibillion dollar loans to countries such as Angola, the DRC, and Niger that are tied to infrastructure projects built by Chinese companies with the loan repaid largely in oil or mineral exports to China. These are effectively commercial barter arrangements in which China benefits as much, if not more, than the recipient African country. Even though these loans do not qualify as foreign aid, they are highly desired by the African leaders who receive them because they are largely used to build infrastructure.

IMPORTS AND INVESTMENTS

In recent years, the average growth rate of gross domestic product across Africa has risen more than 5 percent annually. The impact, however, is mitigated considerably in many countries by a high population growth rate. Africa's mineral wealth, fisheries, timber, and even a few specialty crops have enjoyed high prices in recent years because of growing demand, especially in markets such as China and India. As a whole, the continent has about 10 percent of the world's known oil reserves. It remains the least-explored region in the world, opening the possibility of significant additional discoveries. In 2006, the United States obtained about 22 percent of its oil imports from Africa, including North Africa, while China received about 33 percent of its imports from Africa. In absolute terms, China's import percentage of total African oil production was only about 9 percent, while the United States accounted for about 32 percent. Both China and the United States are projected to obtain a growing percentage of their oil imports from Africa, although China is increasing its imports of African energy at a faster rate than the United States. Ultimately sustaining the import of oil from Africa will become an increasing security concern for both countries.

Africa's improving economic situation and China's rapid economic growth—at least until the onset of the global financial crisis—have had a telling impact on U.S. and Chinese trade with the continent. U.S. exports to Africa doubled between 2000 and the end of 2006, while imports (mostly oil) almost trebled. But during the same period, Chinese exports to Africa more than quintupled, while imports (mainly oil and minerals) nearly quintupled. Based on current projections, China will likely surpass the United States in 2010 as Africa's single most important trading partner. Chinese products are found throughout Africa, primarily because of their low prices and effective distribution systems that often rely on Chinese traders.

Current direct investment figures are elusive for both countries. The Office of the U.S. Trade Representative (USTR) estimated that by the end of 2005 U.S. direct investment in sub-Saharan Africa was about $15 billion. Chinese direct investment in sub-Saharan Africa almost certainly exceeds this amount and is growing more rapidly than U.S. investment. The effort by just one Chinese company makes this point. Huawei Technologies Company, a huge conglomerate, has more than 2,500 employees in 40 African countries and 300 Chinese staff in Lagos alone. No U.S. company has ever made that kind of staffing commitment to Africa. It is not surprising that Chinese companies like Huawei and ZTE are replacing U.S. and European manufacturers of telecommunications equipment across Africa. It appears China will increasingly penetrate the communications sector, among others, in the foreseeable future.

The impact on U.S. and Chinese companies of a slowing global economy is likely to reduce business activity for both countries and negatively affect Africa. But China is in a league of its own. It has a $2 trillion supply of foreign reserves, a current account surplus, minimal links to foreign banks, and a budget surplus that offers considerable room to boost spending. China's economy will probably slow to perhaps 8 percent annual GDP growth, but it will not collapse. This growth will help put a floor under commodity prices and assist economies in Africa. In the short term, the international financial crisis may weaken Africa's ties with the West and push African countries toward emerging markets, especially China.

China tends to view Africa's political and economic situation more positively than most Western companies. Large state-owned companies and smaller private companies from China (and a number of other emerging countries) are taking greater business risks than their Western counterparts, as manifested in relatively more rapid growth of trade and direct investment. Recent attacks on Chinese nationals in Ethiopia, Nigeria, and Sudan and concerns about corruption have caused some revaluation in Beijing, and China's sense of optimism about Africa may eventually be proved wrong. So far, however, it has paid off.

DIPLOMACY

The U.S. and Chinese diplomatic presence in Africa provides another example of moving in different directions. Beijing has more diplomatic offices in Africa than does the United States. The United States has diplomatic relations with all 53 countries in Africa, while China has relations with only 49 (Burkina Faso, Gambia, São Tomé and Principe, and Swaziland recognize Taiwan). The United States and China have the same number of embassies in Africa—48. With the exception of Somalia, where for security reasons neither the United States nor China has a presence, China has an embassy at the level of ambassador in every African country with which it has diplomatic relations. For cost-saving and security reasons, the United States closed its embassies in Comoros, Guinea-Bissau, and Seychelles, while China pointedly maintained its embassies in all three countries. The United States never opened one in São Tomé and Principe. The United States has six independent consulates and one branch office in Africa's 53 countries, while China has nine independent consulates in Africa.

China's implementing agent for carrying out its Africa strategy is the Forum on China-Africa Cooperation (FOCAC), which China and Africa established in 2000. China followed the forum with a comprehensive Africa policy statement in January 2006. At the third FOCAC summit in Beijing in November 2006, all 48 African states that recognized China at the time sent delegations, 43 of them led by the head of state—another indication of the progress China has made in strengthening its position in Africa. Preparations are well advanced for the next FOCAC summit in Cairo in 2009.

China has been a regional power for some time. It is now a global economic power well on its way to becoming a global political and military power. In its march toward global influence, it has made a special effort in Africa. As Michael Oksenberg and Elizabeth Economy wrote more than a decade ago: "China has rejoined the world. No aspect of world affairs is exempt from its influence."[1] They identified the following as China's global strategies: to play a balance-of-power role, to steer between the major powers, retain flexibility in the conduct of foreign policy and avoid entangling alignments, to demonstrate a credible resolve to employ military power and develop military capability as conditions permit, to use ethnic Chinese outside mainland China as sources of influence, and to seek influence without shouldering responsibility. These strategies apply in varying degrees to Africa and have evolved in some cases. China is, for example, shouldering more responsibility by participating in African peacekeeping operations and increasing foreign assistance.

Oksenberg and Economy concluded in 1998 that "no relationship will have greater impact for the United States in the decades ahead than that with China. The time to set relations on a firm path is now."[2] In the case of China-Africa relations, that statement is even more salient today.

AN ASSESSMENT OF THE BUSH ADMINISTRATION'S APPROACH TO CHINA IN AFRICA

The policy of the Bush administration on China's engagement in Africa has generally been consistent and appropriate. Nonetheless, the administration was late in recognizing the exceptional scope and impact of that engagement. It was then tardy in realizing that this engagement warranted a U.S. policy approach different from that toward other significant external actors in Africa.

CHINA AS A "GLOBAL PARTNER"

The 9/11 attacks led to a major shift in the Bush administration approach to China overall, with greater emphasis placed on seeking areas of collaboration. In his presidential campaign, candidate Bush gave the impression that the United States was prepared to confront China on issues where it disagreed with Beijing, and the relationship during President Bush's tenure did not begin auspiciously. Three months after the inauguration, an American EP-3 reconnaissance aircraft collided with a Chinese F-8 fighter plane in international airspace over the South China Sea. China captured the American crew and released them only after 11 days of hard negotiations. After 9/11, as Thomas Donnelly and Colin Monaghan pointed out, the administration's tone toward China changed, and the president no longer referred to China as a strategic competitor.[3] "China pledged to play a constructive role in international counterterrorism efforts," wrote Donnelly and Monaghan, "and the Bush administration pledged to pretend that the Chinese were doing so." The president's 2002 *National Security Strategy* welcomed "the emergence of a strong, peaceful, and prosperous China," adding that the United States will pursue "a constructive relationship with a changing China."[4]

Secretary of State Condoleezza Rice echoed this theme in March 2005, asserting that "America has reason to welcome the rise of a confident, peaceful, and prosperous China. We want China as a global partner, able and willing to match its growing capabilities to its international responsibilities."[5] Then Deputy Secretary of State Robert Zoellick began a strategic dialogue in Beijing in August 2005 and enunciated before the National Committee on U.S.–China Relations in September what became the framework for the Bush administration's policy toward China, calling on China "to become a responsible stakeholder" in the international system. He added that "China has a responsibility to strengthen the international system that has enabled its success."[6]

ENGAGING WITH CHINA ON AFRICA

Those responsible for African policy subsequently followed Zoellick's guideline as they mapped out a policy for engaging with China on Africa. Based on public statements, the Africa Bureau of the State Department first focused on China's increasing engagement in Africa in July 2005. Deputy Assistant Secretary of State for African Affairs, Michael Ranneberger, gave a comprehensive presentation on the subject before a hearing called by the House Subcommittee on Africa, Global Human Rights and International Operations. Ranneberger identified the following direct U.S. interests with respect to Africa and China's presence there:

- To ensure that our respective engagement on the continent promotes open, vibrant markets that operate in a constructive and transparent fashion.

- To ensure that our respective policies supporting political, economic, and commercial engagement promote economic prosperity, stability, good governance, democracy, and human rights.

- To ensure that the United States remains a close partner of African countries and institutions on key regional and international issues.

- To foster conflict resolution and to limit arms sales that could make that more difficult.

- To identify areas where interests converge, while remaining aware of potential differences. Peacekeeping is one area of converging interest.

According to Ranneberger, China's growing presence in Africa can increase the potential for collaboration between the United States and China "as part of a broader, constructive bilateral relationship."[7] He pointed out that China should have many of the same interests in Africa as the United States, based on a shared reliance on the global oil market, shared desire to diversify sources of imported oil away from the Middle East, and shared concern over volatile oil prices. Both countries should share interests in conflict resolution, promotion of national and regional stability, and economic frameworks that promote trade, markets, resource exploration, and production in a sustainable way. Ranneberger concluded: "The future of U.S.-China relations in Africa has yet to be charted, but a focused, direct dialogue is an essential starting point. The administration will continue to advance U.S. interests in Africa actively and to engage China directly, at all appropriate levels, to seek to develop new concepts of cooperation that can advance our common interests."

Assistant Secretary of State for African Affairs Jendayi Frazer followed up the Zoellick strategic dialogue with China in November 2005. She met with Chinese officials in Beijing specifically on Africa. She concluded after the meetings that she did not believe that "China's interest or engagement in Africa is in direct competition to the United States."[8] A Chinese foreign ministry spokesperson in December 2005, referring to the Frazer visit, noted simply that "China and the United States share common concerns on African affairs and will strengthen further cooperation in this regard." He added that "it is baseless to say that China poses a threat to the United States in Africa." His brief remarks were positive but terse.

China reciprocated the 2005 meeting in March 2007 when Chinese Assistant Minister Zhai Jun met with Frazer in Washington. This meeting dealt more specifically with debt sustainability, peacekeeping operations, and conflict resolution in the Horn of Africa and Great Lakes region, Chinese companies' reputational risks in Africa, and transparency in the extractive industries. It also covered the situation in Darfur, a subject of considerable Chinese-American dialogue with a variety of officials, including Deputy Secretary of State John Negroponte during the fourth round of the U.S.-China Senior Dialogue held in June 2007. Although China has never agreed to support U.S.-proposed sanctions against Sudan, most objective observers agree that the numerous Chinese-U.S. talks on Darfur have resulted in a more constructive and flexible Chinese approach to the problem.

The Chinese "reaction" to Frazer's second round of meetings on Africa was much more effusive. He Wenping, a senior researcher in the government's Institute of West Asian and African Studies at the Chinese Academy of Social Sciences, published a long article in *China Daily* in April 2007 entitled "Sino-US Cooperation Can Benefit Africa Even More." Although apparently written on the eve of the Frazer visit, the article set forth a comprehensive agenda for U.S.-China cooperation in Africa. He Wenping concluded: "All said, if China and the U.S. cooperate more closely and substantially on development projects in Africa, this will promote the healthy development of China-U.S. ties while increasing benefits for the African people."

The third round of U.S.-China talks on Africa took place in Beijing in October 2008. On that occasion, Frazer said that there may be opportunities for the United States and China to cooperate in building Africa's infrastructure and its agriculture and health sectors. She added that coordinating U.S. and Chinese aid would prevent overlapping projects and lead to more efficient use of resources. While expressing concern about Chinese lending practices and China's failure to endorse the Extractive Industries Transparency Initiative for Africa, she praised China's efforts in encouraging the government of Sudan to cooperate on peace talks on Darfur.

Throughout 2007 and 2008, a number of State Department officials, particularly Deputy Assistant Secretary of State for African Affairs James Swan, made numerous presentations on China-Africa relations. The themes have been consistent. Swan and Deputy Assistant Secretary for East Asian and Pacific Affairs Thomas Christensen testified on this topic in June 2008 before the Senate Subcommittee on African Affairs.[9] They commented that China's growing engagement on the continent is a "potentially positive" force for economic development there. They did not see evidence that China's commercial or diplomatic activities in Africa are aimed at diminishing U.S. influence. They described China's embrace of market-based economics and openness to most aspects of globalization as a positive example for African nations. After expressing some concerns about Chinese practices on good governance, human rights, and transparency in Africa, they identified several areas for cooperation. They cited UN peacekeeping operations, countering endemic diseases such as malaria, and joint development projects in the agricultural sector. They offered appreciation for China's help on Darfur but expressed concern about Chinese arms sales to countries such as Sudan and Zimbabwe.

A ZERO-SUM GAME?

While the State Department has tended to emphasize the positive aspects of China's engagement in Africa, the Treasury Department has focused on a negative issue. In 2006, Treasury released a paper that raised concerns about Chinese lending practices before Treasury Secretary Henry Paulson visited China. The paper questioned the advisability of a $500 million loan to Ghana and $2.3 billion for financing a dam in Mozambique. Paulson urged China to be a "responsible stakeholder" but obtained no commitment from Beijing to curb its questionable lending practices. The Treasury Department and China's Ministry of Finance have a continuing dialogue, including issues related to Africa.

During a stop in Ghana in February 2008, a reporter asked President Bush about China's growing involvement in Africa. Bush responded: "I don't view Africa as zero sum for China and the United States," adding that "I think we can pursue agendas without creating a great sense of competition." Although the "zero sum" terminology had been used previously by other U.S. officials in describing the situation, the president's reference got the attention of the Chinese. At a Howard University conference on China-Africa relations in March 2008, Chinese Ambassador Zhou Wenzhong called explicitly for China-U.S. cooperation in Africa. He added: "Our respective relations with Africa are not confrontational, or harmful rivalry, or a zero-sum game. President Bush stated this point in public during his recent visit to Africa. China appreciates this statement."

The Bush administration consistently pursued the most appropriate policy on China's engagement in Africa, taking into account U.S. interests in Africa and China-U.S. relations. The tone of the dialogue has been good, and increasingly the Chinese have reacted positively.

OPPORTUNITIES FOR COOPERATION WITH CHINA

Implementing a policy that envisages the United States and China working cooperatively in Africa was less successful. First, the administration was slow to recognize the enormous impact China was having in Africa, dating back to the early 2000s. Washington's first comprehensive public statement on the topic was Ranneberger's testimony in July 2005, and it took place only as a result of a request from a House subcommittee. The bureaucracy subsequently addressed the issue energetically.

Second, the administration was slow to move forward with tangible projects for cooperation with China. Cooperative activity on UN peacekeeping in Liberia and more recent collaboration between U.S. Peace Corps volunteers and Chinese volunteers in Ethiopia met with some success. Proposed cooperation on an agricultural project in Angola, however, did not materialize because of lack of Angolan interest. In the last round of U.S.-China talks on Africa, the two sides agreed to pursue security sector reform in the DRC and consider possibilities for cooperation on irrigation in Ethiopia.

At least until very recently, part of the problem stems from the perception in the State Department's Africa Bureau that China should be treated like any other country that has significant interests in Africa. Yet China's political and economic impact in Africa is significantly greater than that of any single country other than the United States, and in a number of African countries China has more influence. To treat China's presence and influence in Africa today as though they are similar to those of France, Germany, Russia or the UK misunderstands what China is doing in Africa. The United States should not, of course, allow China's engagement in Africa to drive its Africa policy, but it must be more realistic about the enormous change China has brought to Africa and will likely continue to bring in the foreseeable future.

RECOMMENDATIONS FOR THE
OBAMA ADMINISTRATION

The Obama administration will have important opportunities for engaging China more vigorously in Africa. Comments made by President-elect Obama and his campaign team on China and Africa before the inauguration seem to indicate a willingness to work cooperatively with China in Africa. The president-elect said his administration will not demonize China, will try to draw it further into the international system, and will work with China on shared political, economic, environmental, and security objectives. Obama has indicated that he favors expansion of military-to-military relations to improve transparency and U.S. understanding of China's military development goals. He has said he will seek cooperation with China to combat climate change and to develop more secure, affordable, and dependable energy supplies.

The president-elect pledged to help root out corruption, push for 100 percent debt cancellation for the world's heavily indebted poor countries, and promote research aimed at creating a green revolution in Africa. Obama commented to Fareed Zakaria in July 2008 that the United States needs to cooperate with China to solve significant global problems, especially economic issues. In countering terrorism, the Obama team has promised to focus on programs such as funding for training and border security and rely less often on military responses, making counterterrorism cooperation with China possible. On the other hand, Obama has said he will support democratic activists living under the most repressive regimes and press China to respect human rights. Such actions will produce some tension with Beijing.

Following a trip to Africa in 2006, Senator Obama told the Congressional Black Caucus that "one of the striking things about traveling through Africa is everybody says that the United States' absence is as noticeable and prominent as the Chinese's presence." He wrote in 2008 that China's growing influence in Africa is "among the most significant developments on the continent since the end of the Cold War." The Obama team has spoken extensively about the problem of Darfur in Sudan, an issue where it will bump up against a different approach by China. Obama noted that China is supporting one of the "most reprehensible regimes" in the world. He promised to use all available tools, including a no-fly zone, whose need is questionable and implementation problematic, to end the mayhem. He said he will demand that "China use its influence to prevent Sudan" from acting contrary to international law. Presidential candidate Obama had conversations on Darfur, among other subjects, with the Chinese ambassador to the United States and China's ambassador to the United Nations. Obama promised to impress upon China's leaders that their support for regimes in Sudan and Zimbabwe runs counter to the well-being of the people in those countries and to China's longer-term interests in becoming a global leader.

The Obama team clearly appreciates the need to come up with a strategy for dealing with China's engagement in Africa. Campaign documents noted that China's growing presence in Africa challenges the United States to improve its own policies and programs. This will, in turn, require strengthened U.S. support for democracy, good governance, and the rule of law in Africa. Obama added that the United States should seek to find common ground upon which both countries can better contribute to Africa's development. He concluded that it would be mutually beneficial if Africa and the United States developed strategies for cooperating with China in critical areas such as poverty alleviation, health care, and protection of the environment. From all indications, the incoming Obama team understands that the China-Africa relationship is just too important to leave near the bottom of the foreign policy priority list.

MANAGING INTERNAL U.S. POLITICS

Recommendations for the Obama administration must take into account U.S. interests in Africa, the China-U.S. relationship, and recent shocks to the global economy. They must also take account of widely diverse congressional views on China. Some in Congress champion a cooperative relationship with China in Africa. For example, Senator Russell Feingold (D-Wis.), chairman of the Senate Africa Subcommittee, commented at a hearing on China and Africa in June 2008 that "the appropriate response to China's rising role in Africa is more U.S. engagement with both Africans and Chinese to show that we acknowledge the growing strategic importance of this continent and are committed over the long term to its stability." Senator Richard Lugar

(R-Ind.) commented in 2006 when he was chairman of the Senate Foreign Relations Committee that it was crucial for Washington to broaden its energy cooperation with China.

But Congress could also potentially limit the ability of the new administration to engage in greater cooperation with China on Africa. In 2005, for example, Representative Chris Smith (R-N.J.), at the time chairman of the House Subcommittee on Africa, stated that "the Chinese intend to aid and abet African dictators, gain a stranglehold on precious African natural resources and undo much of the progress that has been made on democracy and governance in the last 15 years in African nations."[10] At the same hearing, Representative Donald Payne (D-N.J.), now chairman of the House Subcommittee on Africa, said that China's economic and political pursuits in Africa "appear to be undermining United States success in alleviating poverty and expanding U.S. influence." The new administration will need to make a strong case to China-Africa skeptics that building on areas of common interest and seeking ways to engage collaboratively with China in Africa will ultimately serve both U.S. and African interests.

The following recommendations are linked specifically to China's increasing engagement in Africa. They are designed to advance U.S. interests and benefit Africans while being acceptable to China and, in some cases, even advancing Chinese interests in Africa.

POLITICAL AND ECONOMIC ISSUES

- The United States should raise the level and increase the frequency of the U.S.-China dialogue on Africa. Discussions at the assistant secretary level should occur at least annually. To the extent possible, the assistant secretary of state for African affairs should be included as part of a more senior level U.S.-China dialogue followed immediately by a U.S.-China session specifically on African issues at the assistant secretary level.

- U.S. embassies in Africa and the embassy in Beijing should report more vigorously on China's activities in Africa and solicit the views of host governments, business communities, and civil society on ways that the United States can cooperate with China in Africa. They should also be urged to submit suggestions for developing a strategy that might ameliorate those issues on which the United States and China disagree.

- As part of a broader dialogue on global energy security, the United States should engage China on greater collaboration in Africa. Discussions could include developing oil derivatives and renewable energy, encouraging efficient energy consumption, developing energy technology, and increasing the safety, efficiency, and environmental protection of oil extraction in Africa.

- The new administration should support an expansion of the G-7 to include China and more systematically engage China in multilateral forums that focus on African development.

SECURITY ISSUES

- The U.S. Africa Command (AFRICOM) should engage its Chinese counterparts in dialogue and possibly establish joint projects such as UN peacekeeping operations and maritime security. AFRICOM Commander General William Ward has expressed willingness to work with the Chinese military in Africa.

- The United States should follow up on successful collaboration in Liberia's security sector and seek to identify other areas where the two countries can work together in Africa on peacekeeping operations or training for peacekeepers.

- Washington and Beijing should expand cooperation to African coastal states to help reduce smuggling, illegal fishing, piracy, drug shipments, and threats to offshore oil facilities. The U.S. Coast Guard has been particularly successful in cooperating with its Chinese counterpart organizations. China has provided patrol boats and training to both Sierra Leone and Nigeria and most recently has joined international efforts to curb piracy off the coast of Somalia.

- The United States should encourage China to add small arms and light weapons to the list of items it reports to the United Nations. An opportunity could develop in this area, since there are some indications that China is becoming increasingly concerned that small arms it supplies to African governments are appearing in conflict zones such as Darfur and the eastern Congo.

- The United States should encourage U.S.-China-Africa discussions on narcotics trafficking in Africa. The continent has become a location for money laundering and a transit route for illegal drugs, especially heroin that moves from South Asia across Africa to Europe and North America. A number of African drug smugglers and dealers have been arrested in China. An operation in September 2007, for example, led to the arrests in Beijing's diplomatic quarter of nearly two dozen Africans for drug trafficking.

ASSISTANCE ISSUES

- The United States should ensure that a foreign assistance dialogue with China and the U.S. Agency for International Development (USAID)—to which China has agreed in principle—takes place. China has established a positive aid relationship with the UK's Department for International Development (DFID), and DFID offices and Chinese embassies are beginning to build close relationships in several African capitals. These are encouraging signs, especially because Chinese foreign assistance lacks transparency. China has begun to provide more significant amounts of disaster aid in Africa, and disaster assistance is an obvious area for greater coordination.

- In conjunction with other donors, the United States should encourage China to join the Paris Club, an informal group of financial officials from 19 of the world's richest countries. Its primary focus is debt restructuring, debt relief, and debt cancellation. China has already established a record of canceling debt but is also offering many new concessionary loans.

- Together with other donors, the United States should encourage China to engage in a dialogue on coordinating development assistance to Africa to avoid duplication and ensure more effective distribution of limited resources. The best mechanism for such coordination is the Development Assistance Committee of the OECD. That 23-member group works to increase the efficiency of donor efforts to support sustainable development. China would need to join the committee, at least as an observer. In any event, China should be encouraged to accede voluntarily to the OECD Declaration on Financial Cooperation Programs.

- The United States and China should seek to establish joint assistance projects in public health. The United States supports building the capacity of health infrastructure and funding for HIV/AIDS, malaria, and TB, while China has since 1963 sent medical teams throughout Africa and is especially active in malaria-control programs. It is building 10 antimalaria centers in Africa and has a factory in Tanzania that produces the antimalaria drug artemisinin. China is one of the world's major producers of artemisinin, which medical experts in both the United States and China agree is a highly effective program for preventing malaria, when used in combination with other drugs and as part of a holistic program that includes insecticide-treated bed nets. The Clinton Foundation recently agreed to purchase artemisinin from two Chinese suppliers. Tanzanian President Jakaya Kikwete lavished praise on the multidonor antimalaria program in his country, adding he would welcome participation by China in that effort, an idea endorsed by then U.S. Ambassador to Tanzania Mark Green.[11]

- Neglected tropical diseases offer another public health issue for U.S.-China collaboration, particularly hookworm infection and schistosomiasis, which each afflict some 200 million Africans. USAID and the Gates Foundation are working to reduce both diseases in Africa, and China has experience in combating them. It is also among the largest producers of praziquantel, the principal drug for treating schistosomiasis. A multidonor program that includes China could achieve considerable progress in reducing those diseases.

- The United States should increase its already significant support for African civil society organizations and launch new programs for aiding African higher education. These are areas where the United States has a comparative advantage vis-à-vis China.

TRADE AND MISCELLANEOUS ISSUES

- The United States and China should work to build greater trade capacity in Africa, which Africans have identified as a priority. Both the United States and China are in a position to help African states boost their competitiveness in the global market, especially for products other than raw materials. The United States has its Africa Growth and Opportunity Act, while China has a more modest program that eliminates duty on about 600 items for those African countries that are on the UN list of less-developed countries. China has a loan fund that could be used to encourage Chinese businesses to establish manufacturing operations in Africa.

- The United States should engage China in a dialogue that encourages Beijing to be more supportive of African countries at the World Trade Organization. China supported India during the recent collapse of the last Doha round, which worked to the detriment of African agricultural exports. The Doha round offers the United States an opportunity for improving its ties with Africa, particularly if it is able to engage China in supporting African aspirations more fully.

- The United States should continue to encourage China to support the principles of the Extractive Industries Transparency Initiative (EITI), which aims to strengthen governance by improving transparency and accountability in the extractive sector. So far, China has been disinclined to engage with EITI, a coalition of governments, companies, civil society organizations, investors, and international organizations. Those African countries that are candidates for EITI compliance may be the most effective interlocutors in convincing China to consider participating in this effort.

- Both the United States and China have recently demonstrated concern over the negative impact of climate change and environmental degradation, and the new administration should engage both African states and China on environmental stewardship. At the same time that China appears increasingly receptive to taking steps to end environmentally damaging practices, growing recognition of the potential impact of climate change on Africa could open opportunities for constructive discussion and cooperation.

- Both China and the United States should identify funding on both sides of the Pacific that will enhance contact among Chinese and U.S. Africanists. This might include funding for university and think-tank representatives to attend conferences, host professor exchanges, and engage in joint research with African scholars. The Ford Foundation funded a program in the 1990s to bring Chinese scholars to the United States to study African affairs at the graduate level in U.S. universities. This program no longer exists, and today there is limited contact between U.S. and Chinese scholars on Africa.

WORKING THROUGH AREAS OF DISAGREEMENT

While several areas hold promise for potential U.S. cooperation with China in Africa, the United States and China disagree on important issues concerning China's engagement in Africa. In some cases, a number of African states also disagree with the U.S. position. It does not serve U.S. interests, however, to ignore these problems, and dialogue with China and African states, which has already begun on many of these concerns, should continue. Furthermore, the United States should encourage and empower African civil society organizations and regional bodies to engage more actively with the United States, China, and other external actors. Key areas for engagement should be:

- *Encouraging democracy and good governance in Africa.* Although China will continue to object to the Western concept of liberal democracy, it may well conclude that good African governance is in China's interest. If it does not encourage good governance, African civil society groups will have an increasingly strong negative reaction.

- *Improving the human rights situation in Africa.* This issue will remain difficult as certain African governments and China support each other in international forums.

- *Increasing Chinese transparency in Africa.* China has a long history of opaqueness, but there is reason to believe this could change, particularly if African governments, civil societies, and regional organizations demand it.

- *Taking tangible steps to reduce African corruption.* China has already shown some willingness to rein in corruption because of the negative effects it has had in China.

- *Adopting better environmental practices in connection with Chinese trade, investment, and assistance projects.* Awareness that it must pay more attention to the environment is growing in China.

- *Ending the purchase by China of illegally harvested African hardwoods, ivory, and endangered species.* Past embarrassments have underscored the need to improve the practices of Chinese companies.

- *Improving worker safety and fair labor practices on Chinese projects and by Chinese companies.* This is not a priority in China, which will make it hard to convince Beijing to enforce such practices in Africa.

- *Stopping harmful and counterfeit Chinese products such as medicine and consumer goods from entering Africa.* Embarrassing cases are forcing China to improve in this area.

- *Implementing business standards and translating the principles into practice.* China has given no sign that it is ready to accept these standards.

- *Urging China to be more selective in its choice of arms partners and establishing better control over arms sales to African countries.* China talks a good line on arms sales but then quietly continues harmful past practices.

NOTES

1. Michel Oksenberg and Elizabeth Economy, *Shaping U.S.-China Relations: A Long-term Strategy* (New York: Council on Foreign Relations, 1998), 6.

2. Ibid., 48.

3. Thomas Donnelly and Colin Monaghan, "The Bush Doctrine and the Rise of China," Legacy Agenda, Part III, *National Security Outlook*, American Enterprise Institute, April 2007, http://www.aei.org/publications/pubID.26066/pub_detail.asp.

4. The White House, *The National Security Strategy of the United States of America*, September 2002, 30, http://www.whitehouse.gov/nsc/nss/2002/nss.pdf.

5. Secretary of State Condoleezza Rice, remarks at Sophia University, Tokyo, March 19, 2005, http://www.state.gov/secretary/rm/2005/43655.htm.

6. Deputy Secretary of State Robert B. Zoellick, Remarks before the National Committee on U.S.-China Relations, September, 21, 2005, http://www.

america.gov/st/washfile-english/2005/September/20050922120813TJkcollu B0.9864008.html.

7. Deputy Assistant Secretary of State for African Affairs Michael Ranneberger, testimony before the, Subcommittee on Africa, Global Human Rights, and International Operations of the Committee On International Relations, House Of Representatives, July 28, 2005, "China's Influence in Africa," available at http://commdocs.house.gov/committees/intlrel/hfa22658.000/hfa22658_0.htm.

8. Assistant Secretary of State for African Affairs Jendayi Frazer, remarks at the Foreign Press Center, Beijing, China, December 5, 2005, available at http://fpc.state.gov/57627.htm.

9. Deputy Assistant Secretary for East Asian and Pacific Affairs Thomas Christensen, testimony before the Senate Foreign Relations Subcommittee on African Affairs, June 4, 2008, available at http://foreign.senate.gov/hearings/2008/hrg080604a.html.

10. Hearing, *China's Influence in Africa.*

11. Response to question by the author at a meeting with President Kikwete and Ambassador Green in Washington, D.C., August 2008.

8

CRISIS DIPLOMACY

TIMOTHY M. CARNEY

Violent conflicts in Africa undermine long-standing U.S. foreign policy goals. They destabilize nations and generate human suffering, crip-
ple economic development, and open space for terrorism. Continuing
civil wars in Africa, many of which spill over national boundaries, pose
special challenges that prevent the United States from achieving its objectives. Every conflict has its own complex set of causes. Predatory
governments, ethnic rivalries, religious divisions, competition over resources, and economic and political marginalization of one group by
another have destabilized large areas of the continent, displaced millions of people, and left hundreds of thousands dead since 2000.

The new administration of Barack Obama will face a series of conflicts—in the Horn of Africa, Sudan, and the Democratic Republic of
Congo (DRC)—that will demand immediate attention and pose tough
challenges in conflict resolution. Sustained diplomatic engagement
with national leaders and regional organizations, with allies and concerned nations in Europe and Asia, and with the United Nations (UN)
Security Council will be essential for forging a stronger multilateral
strategy to end or dampen these conflicts.

None of these conflicts lends itself to fast or easy solutions, and each
will require a long-term, patient, and sustained approach, backed by
adequate diplomatic, intelligence, and development capacities. If the
new administration chooses to rely heavily on special envoys as a lead
element of U.S. policy, these will need to be very carefully managed,
deployed, and resourced to be effective.

THE BUSH LEGACY

President Obama inherits from the Bush administration a mixed legacy of using diplomacy to end conflict. The record illustrates the contradictions inherent in U.S. approaches to Africa since the continent's independence period of the mid-1950s and the 1960s. These contradictions include U.S. policies driven more by domestic agendas than by the broader national interests of the United States; actions forced by the "CNN effect," rather than a cool assessment of prospects for effective U.S. action; and reliance on regional states that have neither the capability nor the intention to resolve conflict effectively. At the same time, policymakers sometimes use the CNN effect to crystallize action. A lagging diplomatic effort to enhance the capabilities of the UN mission in the DRC, for example, succeeded in late 2008 largely because the press turned its lenses on the disastrous humanitarian consequences of violent conflict in eastern Congo. Similarly, heightened media attention to piracy off the coast of Somalia in 2008 helped spur a much more vigorous U.S. and international maritime response.

On the positive side, the Bush legacy also includes success in using a combination of U.S. prestige and a detailed grasp of history and culture to engage regional and international allies and friends in conflict resolution; the administration also demonstrated a keen appreciation of the role of the United Nations and the international financial institutions as guarantors and monitors of peace accords and agreements.

THE BUSH ADMINISTRATION'S NATIONAL SECURITY STRATEGY AND AFRICA

In two National Security Strategies, 2002 and 2006, the Bush administration addressed conflict in Africa. The first specifically cited Africa and, more broadly, identified violence—internal and regional—as threats to human dignity and as impediments to combating terrorism. The 2002 strategy called for creating coalitions and cooperative security arrangements to confront civil wars and prevent them from spilling across borders and becoming regional battlegrounds. Under this strategy, U.S. diplomacy concentrated on developing "anchors for regional engagement," with Ethiopia, Kenya, Nigeria, and South Africa as the key African players. At the same time, official U.S. policy was to coordinate with European allies and international institutions for "constructive conflict mediation and successful peace operations."[1]

The 2006 National Security Strategy cited Sudan and Liberia as successful U.S.–led negotiations and abandoned the clearly failed reliance on specific regional anchors. In fact, Nigeria continued to have a strong role in seeking to resolve the Darfur crisis, and South Africa not only facilitated negotiations in Burundi but also was the principal (albeit unsuccessful) mediator in Zimbabwe. The 2006 security strategy recognized more broadly the need for capable partners to address regional conflicts and set forth three levels of engagement: conflict prevention and resolution, conflict intervention, and postconflict stabilization and reconstruction. Diplomacy, cited implicitly as "a timely offer by free nations of 'good offices' or outside assistance," was seen as a measure to prevent or help resolve conflict. Recognizing the lack of international capacity for peace operations, the 2006 strategy specifically cited the 2004 G-8 Summit decision to train peacekeepers for service in Africa under the Global Peace Operations Initiative discussed in more detail in chapter 2 in this volume.

THE CONFLICTS

The United States confronts two primary kinds of armed conflict in Africa: fighting between countries and civil war within states. Over the past decade, African states have made war on each other by direct attack or, more usually, by fomenting insurgencies or stoking civil wars. Internal insurgencies themselves, banditry, and government repression account for much of the worst violence in Africa. Weak state structures, poor leadership, and the lack of a strong sense of national—as opposed to ethnic—identity have made ending these internal conflicts difficult.

EXTERNAL AGGRESSION

The most recent wars between two countries have occurred in the volatile Horn of Africa. In May 1998, Eritrea attacked the Ethiopian town of Badme, one of three areas disputed between the two countries. Fighting resulted in an estimated 70,000 casualties on both sides and Ethiopian control over about one quarter of Eritrea. The conflict lasted until the two sides signed the Algiers Agreement of June 2000. Provisions of the agreement have not been fully honored, and, as a result, the UN secretary-general has ended the UN mission on the border between the two countries with some fear that prospects for resumed fighting are high.

In 2006, Ethiopia sent its troops into Somalia to quash the Islamic Courts Union (ICU), an Islamist movement, elements of which received assistance from Eritrea and had ties to al Qaeda. Ethiopian troops and Ethiopian-backed forces of the Somali Transitional Federal Government (TFG) drove the ICU from Mogadishu in late 2006 and the key port of Kismayo three days later. A small U.S. military team was with Ethiopian forces, and a handful of U.S. missile strikes in January 2007 targeted senior al Qaeda figures in Somalia.

In the aftermath of the invasion, the United States focused its diplomatic efforts on the establishment of an authorized 8,000-strong African Union mission in Somalia (AMISOM). Less priority was given to pressuring the Somali TFG to expand its governing coalition or establish a modicum of legitimacy on the ground. The AMISOM mission, comprising 3,500 Ugandan and Burundian troops at its peak, had little impact on the ground, and the TFG failed to move beyond internal fissures and disputes or to offer any real vision of national reconciliation. With the imminent withdrawal of Ethiopian forces in late 2008, the Bush administration made a last-ditch effort at the UN Security Council to convert AMISOM to a UN peacekeeping force, but, with no peace to keep and no viable process in place, the effort failed to rally support among potential contributors. At the beginning of 2009, as Ethiopian forces withdraw, the situation in Somalia remains extremely fluid, with emboldened and radicalized Islamist militias expanding their control in Mogadishu and southern Somalia, as well as to areas previously under TFG control.

The broadest African warfare has been fought in the DRC. Uganda and Rwanda successfully backed insurgencies there from 1996 to 1998. Other regional states—Angola, Namibia, Zimbabwe, and, briefly, Chad—sent troops in support of DRC authorities from 1998 to 2003, opposing resumed Ugandan and Rwandan intervention. In 1999, a UN mission (MONUC) began with a relatively limited mandate to monitor an international cease-fire.

Following the 2001 assassination of former DRC leader Laurent Kabila and the inauguration of his son, Joseph, as president, the country has slowly moved toward resolution of conflict with regional and international mediation. MONUC, a major peacekeeping mission with a Chapter 7 mandate authorizing the use of force, had nearly 17,000 troops and 1,000 civilian police at the end of 2008.[2] The MONUC mandate was initially intended to effect peace between the DRC and the forces of both its invading and its protecting neighbors. It was later broadened to include deterring any use of force that would threaten the political process in the DRC, a provision aimed at the eastern Congo warlord, Laurent Nkunda, now in Rwandan hands.

More commonly, nations have waged wars indirectly by arming and supporting insurgencies, as Chad and Sudan have been doing recently and reciprocally along their Darfur border. This is nothing new. In 1978 Tanzania invaded Uganda in support of a rebellion that overthrew the dictator Idi Amin. In the 1970s and 1980s, South Africa and Angola waged proxy wars against each other. Angolans, backed by a Cuban military presence, supported a rebel movement in South African–occupied Namibia. South Africa, in turn, assisted an Angolan insurgency.

Some of these conflicts should force an examination of what constitutes a just war. When should a neighboring country exercise the more modern concept of the Responsibility to Protect?[3] What, if any, ongoing conflicts warrant such intervention? In this context, Sudan constitutes a particularly thorny problem. The Darfur insurgency of 2003 owed its funding and armament to Chad and other third-party countries, but its inception lay in the domestic grievances in Darfur against the central government of Sudan.

INTERNAL INSURGENCIES, BANDITRY, IDEOLOGY,
AND REPRESSION

During the past decade Africans have experienced terrible violence within their countries, from bandits, to warlords, to ideologically based insurgents. In some cases, government-sponsored terror and repression are responsible for much of the killing and hardship. African politicians, as their counterparts in other parts of the world, have also exploited ethnic differences to maintain power.

Warlords hold territory and have wielded ruthless authority in many parts of Africa. In West Africa, for example, the governments of Sierra Leone and Liberia have wrested power from them, but in the DRC, Somalia, Sudan, and Uganda, warlords control large swathes of land and operate outside any government control.

The Bush administration's strategy for resolving these internal conflicts varied depending on the nature of the fighting, on the actual or potential level of violence, and on the existence of interested, engaged, and credible third countries or other international players. The United

States used diplomacy to engage its allies in the European Union (EU) or interested countries in Asia, notably China, as well as regional and international bodies such as the African Union, the Economic Community of West African States (ECOWAS), and the UN in negotiations to end conflicts. The administration approved all proposed UN peacekeeping operations in Africa with robust (Chapter VII) mandates.

During the past eight years, U.S. diplomacy has helped resolve conflicts in Burundi, Liberia, and Sierra Leone. A concerted diplomatic push ended the civil war between northern and southern Sudan. This achievement in Sudan, however, has been overshadowed by the continuing conflict in Darfur that also threatens to undermine the north-south agreement. A look at how the Bush administration has dealt with conflict suggests diplomatic approaches that the next administration might take to end conflicts.

Sierra Leone

In West Africa, the Bush administration gave diplomatic support, notably at the UN, to British efforts in Sierra Leone, where the nine-year-old civil war had spilled into neighboring Guinea and Liberia. An initial effort by forces of the Monitoring Group of ECOWAS proved inadequate, and in 1999 the UN Security Council authorized a mission in Sierra Leone (UNAMSIL) with 6,000 troops. Resumed fighting overwhelmed the UN effort. British troops entered Sierra Leone in May 2000, enforced a cease-fire, and stabilized the country, paving the way for the second Abuja Agreement of May 2001, which became the foundation for a disarmament, demobilization, and reintegration program. U.S. diplomatic engagement with Pakistan, which in 2001 had a 4,000-strong brigade as part of the UN mission, helped accelerate the UN military campaign. By the end of October 2001, the Pakistani contingent of UNAMSIL had gained control over the diamond-bearing areas of eastern Sierra Leone that had funded rebel forces.[4] In 2002, the small British force withdrew and UNAMSIL itself slowly began to withdraw, finally completing its mission on January 1, 2006.

Côte d'Ivoire

In Côte d'Ivoire, once considered one of Africa's most stable countries, the death of long-time ruler Félix Houphouët-Boigny in 1993 triggered a crisis over issues of national identity, eligibility for citizenship, and land tenure. From a bloodless military coup in 1999, the country had descended into a vicious civil war by 2002. The United States backed French efforts to end the fighting, which included supporting a series of UN Security Council Resolutions that gave French troops an important role in peacekeeping. The UN Security Council also encouraged key African states to help resolve the conflict. The UN and France focused heavily on programs to disarm, demobilize, and reintegrate combatants into civilian life as well as prepare for the presidential and parliamentary elections, currently slated for 2009.

Liberia

Liberia proved to be a greater challenge, although ultimately senior-level U.S. attention and diplomatic pressure helped end the conflict there. Civil war, sparked by the 1989 coup and the brutality of its leader Sergeant Samuel Doe, devastated the country. Charles Taylor, supported by neighboring countries, rose to become first a warlord and, in 1997, president of Liberia. His rule spurred greater conflict both in Liberia and in the broader region, and in August 2003 ECOWAS sent in a military force to protect the capital city Monrovia from advancing rebel groups. A U.S. naval task force, stationed offshore, dispatched a small group of marines to liaise with the ECOWAS troops. The marines secured the airfield, permitting the ECOWAS soldiers to focus on securing the peace. As a result of U.S. pressure and negotiations with Nigerian President Olusegun Obasanjo, Taylor left Liberia for asylum in Nigeria in August. A UN Mission in Liberia (UNMIL) was created in September. Taylor's exile paved the way for the creation of a transitional government at the end of 2003, followed by successful presidential elections in October 2005. UNMIL maintained the peace and order during the elections, which Harvard-trained economist Ellen Johnson-Sirleaf won.

The United States has maintained a robust engagement with Liberia in support of the country's reconstruction. President Bush expressed his admiration for Liberia's recovery from war when he visited Monrovia in early 2008 as part of his second Africa tour. He noted that U.S. funds had trained the Liberian troops that he and the Liberian president reviewed but emphasized the importance of education, health, and other U.S. programs.

Burundi

In Central and East Africa, the Bush administration relied heavily on regional states, in this case leaning on South Africa, identified in the

2002 National Security Strategy as a regional anchor. South Africa proved especially helpful in Burundi, where two ethnic groups—the Tutsi and the Hutu—have been at odds since the country's independence in 1962. The international community was particularly worried about the volatile political situation in Burundi following the disastrous example of Rwanda and the 1994 genocide. Following a period marked by political assassinations and sporadic violence, South Africa became a mediator to the conflict in 2001 and helped the Hutu and Tutsi reach a power-sharing agreement. South Africa then provided troops, airlifted to Burundi by the United States, for what began in 2004 as a Chapter VII UN Peacekeeping operation, the UN operation in Burundi. The UN Security Council mandated the operation to help Burundi reform its security forces and judicial system, as well as to reform its institutions and to advise and assist the country in organizing elections. The UN supervised free and fair elections in 2005. The following year, South Africa helped negotiate a comprehensive cease-fire between the Burundi authorities and the remaining large rebel group. The UN mission formally ended on December 31, 2006, its presence evolving into a UN Integrated Office that monitors the cease-fire and helps establish the rule of law and good governance. After the September 2006 cease-fire agreement, the African Union created a special task force to guarantee the integration of Burundi's rebel forces, with 1,100 troops contributed by South Africa.

Kenya
In Kenya, timely senior-level U.S. intervention, in concert with international and regional partners, forestalled a worsening postelection crisis in early 2008. Decades of misrule and flagrant official corruption caused the country to unravel in late 2007, following national elections distinguished by gross irregularities, if not outright fraud. Fighting among ethnic groups broke out, and hundreds of thousands were displaced by the end of January 2008. The United States, the European Union, and the UN engaged to resolve the conflict. U.S. Secretary of State Condoleezza Rice worked closely with Kofi Annan, former UN secretary-general, who mediated the current fragile agreement between President Mwai Kibaki and opposition figure Raila Odinga, who became prime minister. Assistant Secretary for Africa Jendayi Frazer visited Kenya early in the conflict to press both sides to accept a mediator.

Sudan

In examining the legacy of conflict diplomacy that the Obama administration inherits from its predecessor, the situation of Sudan stands out. The Bush administration maintained an important and sustained effort at a high level, with a range of diplomatic resources, strategies, and partners engaged. Sudan provides an illustration of the U.S. process of assessing interests and then moving to realize the interests through a comprehensive, logical, and focused process.

The conflict that existed when the administration entered office in 2001 was the long-running insurgency of the south against the established government of Sudan in Khartoum. This civil war was by no means the only event in Sudan that had impact on U.S. interests. U.S. interests started with the obvious security issues related to terrorism. Since 1969 Sudan had become the haven for a large number of Middle East terrorist groups. Following the 1989 Islamist coup against the elected government of Prime Minister Sadiq al Mahdi, the country increasingly supported activities of terrorist entities, notably against Eritrea and Ethiopia. In June 1995, was complicit before and after the fact in the attempted assassination of the Egyptian President Hosni Mubarak as he arrived for the Organization of African Unity Summit in Addis Ababa. Sudan, under its then intellectual leader, Hassan Turabi, also sought to play a more important role among Islamist movements, clearly believing that political Islam was on a worldwide roll. Aside from menacing regional neighbors by support of violent Islamist groups, the Sudanese also backed the bizarre Lord's Resistance Army, in its guerrilla operations against the Ugandan government.[5]

Beyond the security rubric, the United States also has an important interest in stability in Sudan. The country is the largest in Africa and has important riches that include arable land and the water to irrigate it, as well as minerals, notably gold and chrome. Since 1998 Sudan has pumped large quantities of crude oil, reaching 500,000 barrels per day. With nine neighbors and such riches, Sudan is thus a potential engine of subregional prosperity, but not if the country is given to civil war and massive insurgency and remains subject to external stirring of its internal conflicts. While regional prosperity is a valid future goal, the immediate need for security and stability is more urgent.

Finally, powerful and vocal constituencies within the United States—most notably conservative Christian evangelicals and members of the Congressional Black Caucus, focused respectively on allegations of

Christian persecution and slavery in Sudan—galvanized President Bush to invest significant capital in taking on the theretofore intractable Sudanese conflict.

After an unsuccessful effort to isolate Sudan, the Clinton administration had accepted a long-standing Sudanese invitation and sent a counterterrorism team to Khartoum in early 2000. Those talks bequeathed to the Bush administration a productive dialogue. President Bush himself took a direct interest in Sudan, naming the USAID administrator as special humanitarian coordinator for the Sudan in May, and otherwise signaling very early in 2001, together with Secretary of State Colin Powell, that Sudan would be a priority. This interest resulted in a fruitful collaboration among his special envoy, the Episcopal priest and former senator John Danforth, the Department of State, and the governments of the UK, Norway, and, eventually, Italy. Appointed six days before 9/11, Senator Danforth argued for a primary role for the regional East Africa membership organization, the Intergovernmental Authority on Development, with Kenya in the lead, as mediator between Khartoum authorities and the armed, rebel Sudan Peoples Liberation Movement/Army (SPLM/A).[6]

Both the Kenyan mediator and the international community, notably the United States, accepted the vital decision to restrict the negotiations to the two principal parties, the Khartoum authorities and the SPLM/A. This controversial decision cut out the opposition political parties in Khartoum, including former Prime Minister Sadiq el Mahdi's Umma Party. It left the SPLM/A to represent the interests of the National Democratic Alliance of opposition northern elements and sidelined the Sudan Alliance Forces, a northern-based group that had taken up arms against Khartoum. Nor were southern elements, some of which argued that the SPLM/A was entirely too much under the control of the Dinka ethnic group, invited to be part of the talks. While Sudanese civil society groups regularly presented their views to the negotiators, the political and armed opposition did not. Critics argued that any agreement ultimately reached would not be durable without the missing elements.

The negotiations that began in 2002 ended in the signature of the Comprehensive Peace Accord (CPA) on January 9, 2005. The success for U.S. diplomacy resulted from a number of calculations related to external and internal elements that will continue to bear on the new administration's efforts in Sudan. Sudan remains an urgent issue because the peace agreement ends in 2011 when the south of Sudan can opt for independence through a referendum, a key provision in the agreement.

U.S. domestic concerns underlay the choice of an Episcopal priest to elicit a considered, rather than an automatically negative, response from evangelical Christians, many of whom mistakenly believe that the south of Sudan has a majority, or even a very large, Christian population. (In fact, Christian populations make up, at most, 10 percent of the southern Sudanese, with the vast majority following traditional religions.) The Department of State team working on Sudan from 2001 ensured creation of a troika of international countries, later expanded to four, so that international pressure and focus on the Kenyan mediator and the Sudanese parties could continue if the U.S. government effort were halted or limited. The fear was that U.S. domestic opposition could result in legislative branch–imposed sanctions or even further limitations on U.S. diplomacy beyond the continuing—to this day—congressional opposition to naming a U.S. ambassador to Sudan.

The U.S. strategy to reach peace through negotiation demanded an intensive effort, with the United States closely following the talks and staying in constant touch with international and regional partners. In the spring of 2002, the Department of State established a separate office to follow Sudan, the Sudan Programs Group.[7] The U.S. embassy in Nairobi sent a political officer to Naivasha when the talks moved there, and visitors from the Sudan Programs Group and more senior Washington officials regularly visited. U.S. officials made suggestions for compromises and, in March 2004, insisted on a formula, accepted by the two sides as the Abyei Protocol, to resolve the disagreement over whether the disputed area of Abyei lay in the north or the south. The United States also positioned itself as a resource for the negotiators, with an especially effective effort from the Center for Strategic and International Studies that centered on educating both the south and the north on wealth sharing, notably the facts about oil exploration, exploitation, and marketing.

The senior leadership of the Department of Defense, however, had little time for Sudan. DOD nonetheless played an important role during the period of talks from 2002, largely because the embassy in Khartoum had, in essence, a stealth defense attaché—not formally named, but who provided an important and knowledgeable liaison among the various military bodies formed to implement the early monitoring agreements in the Nuba Mountains and to protect the population. The Nuba Mountains agreement was a joint Swiss-U.S. mediated effort that showed the way forward to a structured cease-fire and tapped into a broad Sudanese desire for peace.

The negotiations were occasionally marked by false starts and bad tactics. At one point, Kenya's mediator tried to force acceptance of a comprehensive agreement that both sides rejected. An infelicitous U.S. tactic was to seek to push the negotiations to conclusion by holding out an invitation to the sides for a seat at President Bush's January State of the Union address. This effort created resentment, as Sudanese from both Khartoum and the SPLM/A wondered why they should fall in line on Washington's timetable. A year later, by the January 2005 signature, the crisis in Darfur had become such an issue that the U.S. administration did not contemplate an invitation to the president's speech.

Working with the international community—including international agencies, international financial institutions, and the UN itself—demanded careful timing and focused agendas. Khartoum authorities had long been chary of a role for the UN Security Council, in part because U.S. and European opponents of Khartoum during the civil war seemed to dominate the council. As the twenty-first century moved on, Khartoum authorities, especially the military, raised concerns—well taken as events related to Darfur have demonstrated—that human rights issues might figure in indictments before international legal bodies. The UN played little role during the beginning and middle period of negotiations. In 2004, Senator Danforth moved from special envoy of the president to become U.S. permanent representative to the United Nations. He used the UN body to close the agreement: during the period when the United States held the Security Council presidency, Danforth convened a UN Security Council session in Nairobi at which both Sudanese sides committed to making an agreement by the end of the year.

Other international entities have tried to guarantee the Comprehensive Peace Accord. The CPA Assessment and Evaluation Commission, a key body for ensuring the implementation of the agreement, was chaired first by the Norwegians, now by the British. The World Bank did the necessary study to determine aid levels to the national government and to both regional areas after signature of the CPA. A pledging session gave the international community the occasion to put up the needed development money.

In summary, Bush administration policy toward Sudan's north-south conflict had an effective combination of serious policy and sensible strategy, both the domestic and the international will to realize it, high-level (including presidential) attention as needed, and, finally, a continuing bureaucratic focus. Much of that changed as Darfur overwhelmed the Sudanese themselves and, with domestic criticism, tied the hands of the U.S. administration. Since the departure of Senator John Danforth, a succession of U.S. special envoys has come and gone, unable to reenergize the U.S. effort, largely because U.S. domestic pressure has constrained the possibilities for diplomatic action.

Events in Sudan since 2003 have evolved to include an important and violent international element related to the insurgency in Darfur. Nor is this new. The north-south war had included arms supplies and, in 1997, a major military incursion by Uganda, with Eritrean and Ethiopian elements in support of the SPLA. In the Darfur conflict, Khartoum and Ndjamena used proxies to push fighting briefly into each others' capitals in 2007 and 2008, with the government of Chad surviving in considerable part due to a French troop presence there.

The Democratic Republic of the Congo
Violent conflict in the DRC had an important international dimension in the 1990s as discussed above. Warlordism is now the major threat to peace in the DRC. Recently arrested rebel leader and former Congo military figure Laurent Nkunda was active in the area north of Lake Kivu. Nkunda claimed to be protecting Tutsi in the eastern Congo from Hutu militias (FDLR) responsible for the 1994 genocide in Rwanda, whom the DRC government has failed to disarm or eliminate as a threat to civilian populations in the region. The United States played a significant role in pushing for a January 2008 peace agreement with the national authorities, but the agreement collapsed in late August when Nkunda renewed fighting with the ineffective and undisciplined DRC army. A UN monitoring panel report in December 2008 accused the Rwandan government of supporting Nkunda's forces and the DRC government of collaborating extensively (not neutralizing) the FDLR. The UN reports that renewed fighting has displaced an additional 100,000 people, contributing to what is perhaps the world's worst humanitarian emergency. Human rights groups accuse Nkunda's forces, the DRC army, and the FDLR of murder, rape, and use of child soldiers.

As this volume goes to press, General Nkunda has reportedly been captured by his former Rwandan backers. If so, new diplomatic opportunities may now open up for pressing the DRC government to professionalize its forces and, with UN support, disarm the FDLR and for ensuring that the Rwandan government continues to play a constructive role. A practical issue, however, is the likelihood of a freer hand for the Rwandan military to fight in the eastern Congo.

Zimbabwe

Zimbabwe's extended period of crisis began in 1999 when President Robert Mugabe launched a chaotic and largely self-serving land reform program, with the principal aim to consolidate his authoritarian rule. Since then, Mugabe has ruthlessly suppressed all opposition, driving the country and its citizens into economic and financial ruin. Zimbabwe police and soldiers have killed and tortured thousands of fellow citizens and driven hundreds of thousands more from their homes. The United States, which has little direct leverage, has played a small role, essentially reduced to statements of condemnation backed by very limited sanctions, such as imposing travel restrictions and foreign asset controls on selected Zimbabweans. The international community has largely left resolution of the internal conflict in Zimbabwe up to the Southern African Development Community, which selected the former South Africa President Thabo Mbeki to lead mediation efforts. During a visit to South Africa in July 2003, President Bush, against the advice of Secretary Powell and Assistant Secretary for African Affairs Walter Kansteiner, endorsed Mbeki as mediator and chose a deliberately nonconfrontational approach. Mbeki proved unable or unwilling to play the role of balanced broker between the ruling ZANU-PF and the opposition Movement for Democratic Change, and the decision by President Bush ultimately led to a lowering of the U.S. profile and interest in Zimbabwe within the interagency process.

Mbeki did little until the disastrous 2008 elections, which the government, despite terrorizing the opposition, clearly lost. Under pressure from the international community as well as other southern African leaders, Mbeki embarked on negotiations to reach a power-sharing arrangement between Mugabe's government and opposition leader, Morgan Tsvangirai. But neither Mbeki nor the Southern Africa Development Committee has proved willing to isolate Mugabe or impose diplomatic or economic pressures that would force a more equitable sharing of power or induce Mugabe to leave the political scene.

As this publication goes to press in late January 2009, Morgan Tsvangirai and the Movement for Democratic Change have tentatively agreed to join a government of national unity, monitored jointly with ZANU-PF, to oversee power sharing. Allocation of key ministries and enforcement mechanisms remain unclear, and the United States should view the agreement with a great deal of caution and skepticism. The humanitarian situation in Zimbabwe continues to deteriorate, but the donor community must ensure that its responses overall do not empower or embolden Mugabe and that both parties adhere to the terms of the agreement. In addition, the administration should be prepared for alternative scenarios, including continued stalling over the division of ministries or a break within the ruling ZANU-PF that may lead to a violent and chaotic succession struggle.

PROSPECTS

The new U.S. administration will have to quickly develop policies to deal with violence and humanitarian crises in the DRC, Somalia, Sudan, and Zimbabwe. It will also have to develop policies to prevent potential conflict in several regions over natural resources, such as oil and, increasingly, water. The United States will have to manage evolving relationships with key countries like South Africa and Nigeria, where bilateral ties have foundered, internal competition for political power has intensified, and widespread corruption in Nigeria could degenerate into violence.

In looking at the most urgent contingencies, Sudan stands out. Should the 2009 national elections go badly, the prospects for a 2011 referendum on southern autonomy will be bleak. Recent suggestions that the government of South Sudan is buying T-72 tanks from Ukraine and speculation that some oil money are going into a government war chest raise possibilities of a return to conflict there. The heavy Khartoum attention to Darfur has meant short shrift for realizing the some 1,100 specifics listed to implement the 2005 CPA. A resumption of conflict between the north and the south would surely spill over into Sudan's neighbors, actively involving Kenya, Uganda, and Horn of Africa states in expanded violence. Elements in Chad would engage more deeply with insurgent ethnic groups in Darfur. Egypt, which has a good understanding of matters Sudanese, would be in a policy dilemma, not wanting to see yet another state added to the headwaters of the Nile.

The new administration will be under terrific domestic pressure to engage against Khartoum, with strident calls for regime change and few spare foreign assistance resources in either the current or the likely future economic environment to augment the already major U.S. humanitarian commitments to Sudan. This situation argues all the more strongly for heightened international focus on Sudan with the goal of realizing the CPA. A major effort to engage the international community, notably including China, which has become more responsible and constructive on the Darfur question, is the beginning of such diplomacy.

Although of somewhat less cosmic regional proportions, the situation in the DRC looks increasingly precarious. Congolese President Joseph Kabila and Rwandan President Paul Kagame must be pressed to fulfill their sovereign responsibilities, and the United States cannot blink, even for a period of transition to the new administration, lest it miss opportunities that Nkunda's departure generates to curb one of the world's most horrific humanitarian situations.

In Somalia, the situation may be on the verge of spinning out of control. Islamist groups could very well seize parts of Mogadishu, leading to new battle lines and intensified fighting among a multiplicity of groups. U.S. interests are at risk in such a scenario. Even a bolstered African Union peacekeeping force is unlikely to prove effective in stemming violence, and the UN Security Council has little stomach for a peacekeeping effort. Given the fluidity of the situation, a U.S. approach will need to be nimble, well-informed, and long term in vision and undertaken with strong multilateral cooperation.

Eritrea and Ethiopia, too, demand a strong U.S. focus, but others need to join in as actors. As Isaias Afewerki becomes increasingly erratic, room for solution under U.S. auspices narrows. Ethiopia chose a hard-line solution to Somalia, and pressures in Ethiopia exist to do the same with Eritrea. This situation requires a major effort of the African Union and the UN, perhaps sparked by the Intergovernmental Authority on Development and strongly backed by the West and the rest of the international community.

Two matters at issue in southern Africa include the situation of Zimbabwe, where negotiations to share power appear to require much more international muscle to be brought to conclusion. In this context,

South Africa could be an important player but so far has been unwilling to play a credible, balanced role in the mediation process. Internal events in South Africa have put the country's future role in conflict resolution it question, both in Zimbabwe and in other African conflicts. The political downfall of Thabo Mbeki, the rise of Jacob Zuma (who is supported by the left wing of the ruling African National Congress that seeks a continuing National Democratic Revolution), and the formation of the Congress of the People party (a breakaway faction of ANC) may undercut the country's appetite and capacity for external engagements. The new U.S. administration should embark on a far more serious, mature U.S. relationship with South Africa, one shaped less by euphoria about the end of apartheid and more by a focus on the needs of twenty-first century Africa. Fostering civil society in South Africa should be of the highest priority.

Besides Zimbabwe, a number of conflict areas, including Nigeria and Burundi, might benefit from a review to examine whether an increased U.S. role can catalyze resolution or can usefully shore up agreement reached to resolve earlier conflicts. This would require far more U.S. diplomatic muscle.

As it manages the multiple crises enumerated above, the new administration must take steps to bolster the long-term capacity for U.S. conflict diplomacy.

1. *The new administration should acknowledge and reaffirm the centrality of sustained diplomatic effort in responding to conflicts in Africa.* African Union or UN peacekeeping operations cannot sustainably be the default option for conflict mitigation. Peacekeepers deployed into situations in which there is no peace to keep or where the prospect of a negotiation process will be vulnerable and ultimately ineffective, and such deployments will undermine the legitimacy of their respective institutions. Far greater emphasis should be given to mobilize political and domestic will to invest in substantial and sustained diplomatic deployments.

2. *The new administration must make a strong case to Congress to add resources and professional incentives to the State Department's Africa Bureau and to U.S. embassies in Africa.* Additional resources may be difficult to come by in these tough budgetary times, although in real terms even doubling the budget of the Africa Bureau would not be exorbitant.

3. *The new administration must channel more resources into gathering facts on the ground, understanding the motivations of the various actors, and developing affordable policies based on an analysis of this information.*

4. *The new administration should work toward a more robust and creative new multilateralism.* It should work in greater concert with regional leaders as well as with European and Asian nations to pool resources to achieve mutual objectives.

5. *The new administration will need to make available to negotiators adequate and flexible funding that can be quickly mobilized either to consolidate gains or to seize on quickly emerging opportunities.* Further, given the fragility of many of Africa's peace agreements, the administration must plan for sustained robust engagement after the deals are signed, particularly where the costs of backsliding, as with Sudan's CPA, are intolerably high.

6. *Should the new administration choose to rely on special envoys in resolving African conflicts, it must ensure that they are competent, skilled, and well resourced and serve to support, not undermine, the efforts of the U.S. embassy.* To be effective, such envoys need to be adequately empowered and resourced and focused on concrete actions.

At bottom, given the overextension of the U.S. armed forces and the global economic crisis, diplomacy must trump military engagement in Africa to manage crisis and conflict. This situation calls for a very careful approach to using the newly created U.S. Africa Command, a promising evolution of the classic U.S. geographic combatant command structure aiming to better coordinate military and civilian agency engagement (discussed in chapter 2 in this volume).

NOTES

1. U.S. State Department, "An Overview of President Bush's African Policy," July 11, 2003, that quotes from the September 2002 U.S. National Security Strategy.

2. Chapter 7 of the UN Charter permits the UN Security Council to authorize the use of force to carry out its mandate.

3. The Responsibility to Protect doctrine resulted from the former UN secretary-general's response to failure to forestall the Rwanda genocide. It shifts linguistically from humanitarian intervention to protection and consists of an elaborated doctrine of prevention, reaction, including military intervention, and rebuilding.

4. Personal communication from the former assistant secretary of state for African affairs, Jendayi Frazer.

5. More detail on Sudan's role in support of terrorist groups is in my chapter, "The Sudan: Political Islam and Terror," in *Battling Terrorism in the Horn of Africa,* ed. Robert Rotberg (Washington, D.C.: Brookings Institution Press, 2005).

6. A large body of literature on the Sudan negotiations exists. Much is online at the United States Institute of Peace, including my own USIP Special Report, "Some Assembly Required: Sudan's Comprehensive Peace Agreement," November 2007. The advocacy body, International Crisis Group, also has extensive commentary. Apart from treatment of Darfur, recent books on north-south relations or larger Sudan issues are scarce, although the paperback edition of the late Robert O. Collins, *A History of Modern Sudan* (New York: Cambridge University Press, 2008), has a chapter on war and peace in the south.

7. See the "Chronology of U.S. Engagement in the Sudan Peace Process," U.S. Embassy Nairobi, January 8, 2005, available at http://www.state.gov/r/pa/prs/ps/2005/40459.htm.

9

AFRICA'S LOOMING MEGA-CHALLENGES

MICHELLE D. GAVIN

Successive administrations have been hard pressed to tackle long-term, sweeping challenges in Africa, with breaking developments and crises on the continent too often threatening to consume more resources and attention than are typically available. Yet "mega-trends" like demographic patterns, climate change, and increasing food insecurity will affect the region's stability and development and put at risk gains made through other targeted U.S.-backed initiatives. The magnitude, time horizon, and diffuse consequences of these dynamics, and the limited capacity of the United States to influence them, tend to relegate these considerations to the background in the policymaking process.

The Bush administration took tentative steps to address these issues and took strong emergency action when it became apparent in late 2007 that a global food crisis was under way, but overall, efforts to address these profoundly influential trends were modest. To bolster stability, prevent crises, and protect gains made to date, the new administration should be far more ambitious, addressing these issues in a focused rather than an ad hoc way.

This chapter is concerned with three interconnected trends likely to play a significant role in shaping Africa's future: steady growth in youth populations and urban centers, climate change, and increasing food insecurity.

YOUTHFUL, INCREASINGLY URBANIZED POPULATIONS

Most of sub-Saharan Africa will be gripped by a population "youth bulge" for the foreseeable future, meaning that young adults (aged 15 to 29) will account for a disproportionately large share—in many cases more than half—of the total adult population. Because fertility rates remain high throughout most of the continent and life expectancy continues to be relatively low, African population structures thus tend to have vast numbers of children and increasingly large numbers of young adults. More than 70 percent of all Ethiopians, Kenyans, Liberians, Nigerians, Ugandans, and Zimbabweans are under the age of 30, and the youthful nature of these populations is not projected to change in the near future. In fact, sub-Saharan Africa is the one youth-heavy region of the world in which the youth bulge is not expected to decline significantly over the next 15 years.

As a result, the region will have to provide for vast numbers of young children and create jobs for the fastest-growing labor force in the world.[1] Over a dozen sub-Saharan countries are expected to experience a 100 to 157 percent growth in their labor force between 2005 and 2030.[2] Large populations of young people can act as engines for economic growth but only in contexts in which they have access to education and labor markets are able to absorb them. In most of Africa today, education levels continue to lag, and even those who are highly educated often find themselves unemployed or underemployed after graduation.

At the same time, African societies are urbanizing rapidly, and the region's urban population is expected to increase from 294 million to 742 million between 2000 and 2030.[3] By 2025, more than half of Africa's population will live in urban areas.[4] Currently, 72 percent of Africa's urban populations live in slums. The concentration of young people coping with poverty, unemployment and underemployment, and few avenues of social mobility and economic opportunity can lead to a volatile mix of alienation and frustration, especially as media images from the industrialized world continue to penetrate deeply into the region, magnifying the sense of relative deprivation. Young people can be agents of change that transform societies for the better, but they can play this role only when there is space for them to act constructively.

A significant body of research has found a strong correlation between the likelihood of civil conflict and the existence of an urbanized youth bulge. Population Action International, for example, found that countries with more than 67 percent of the population under the age of 30 have been four times as likely as countries with an older age structure to experience civil conflict.[5] Large youth populations can also contribute to increased migratory pressure, as young people unable to realize their aspirations within their own societies seek to exit them entirely in the hopes of finding opportunity elsewhere. This migration, too, can have destabilizing, dislocating effects, within the continent and farther afield.

These dynamics have serious implications for U.S. interests in the region. Strong partnerships are hard to build with politically volatile states, and development goals are rarely achieved in contexts of conflict. Demographic trends may not cause conflict and instability, but in Africa they can create a context in which insecurity thrives.

VULNERABILITY TO CLIMATE CHANGE AND ENVIRONMENTAL DEGRADATION

Global climate change is particularly bad news for sub-Saharan Africa. Africa currently accounts for just 5 percent of greenhouse gas emissions[6] but is particularly vulnerable to global climate change. African ecosystems are already changing at a faster rate than anticipated.[7] Because the region has so little control over the causes of climate change, adaptation is the most important element of a response in Africa.

The effects of climate change will vary across the continent, but in total, the region confronts a likely loss of arable land largely due to desertification,[8] an increased frequency of natural disasters (both flood and drought), public health risks due to shortages of clean water and changes in the patterns of infectious disease vectors like mosquitoes, decreased biodiversity, and the prospect of inundated coastal communities. The Intergovernmental Panel on Climate Change has expressed high confidence in the assertion that food security in Africa will be "severely compromised" by climate change and variability, with crop yield reductions as high as 50 percent in some countries by 2020. The organization predicts that 75 to 250 million more Africans will be put under water stress because of climate change by 2025.

In addition to the economic, development, and humanitarian costs, all of these factors promise to contribute to destabilizing displacement and rising competition for resources, both potential drivers of conflict.[9] Africa could be caught in a vicious circle, as weak governing institutions and poverty make it difficult to adapt to climate change, leading to consequences that only exacerbate state failure and insecurity.

Climate change is not the only environmental challenge confronting the region. Africa's environmental treasures—forests, wildlife, and fisheries—are in peril. Carbon sinks like the Congo Basin forests have global significance, as does the region's rich biodiversity. But unsustainable logging and mining practices, the thriving bushmeat trade, and human migratory patterns cause deforestation and biodiversity loss and threaten to further impoverish rural communities and indigenous people who depend upon forest and freshwater resources for their livelihood. Meanwhile, the pressures of demographic growth and climate change promise to increase the challenge of conserving natural resources.

FOOD INSECURITY

The global food crisis became a front-page topic in 2008, but in sub-Saharan Africa, food security trends have been moving in the wrong direction for several years. While some countries have made progress in combating hunger, the aggregate picture is grim. Africa has lagged behind the rest of the world in agricultural productivity: by 2006, sub-Saharan Africa's grain yield was only about 40 percent of what the developing world was achieving. Currently, the region has the highest undernourishment rates in the world.

The causes of chronic food insecurity in the region are complex. Underdeveloped infrastructure and limited access to appropriate seeds, fertilizers, and technologies play an important role. In May 2008, the U.S. Government Accountability Office (GAO) found that in addition to low productivity, "limited rural development, government policy disincentives, and the impact of poor health on the agricultural workforce" all contributed to the problem.

International investment in agricultural development has been declining since the 1980s, and the United States has been no exception to this trend.[10] U.S. assistance for agricultural development declined from $2.3 billion in 1980 to $624 million in 2006.[11] Research has suffered as well, with U.S. support for the Consultative Group on International Agricultural Research declining from $46 million in 1986 to $25 million in 2006, with further cuts on the way.[12]

The global trading system tends to disadvantage farmers in the poorest countries, and even the U.S. flagship African trade initiative, the African Growth and Opportunity Act, does little to improve market access for most African agricultural products. The apparent collapse of the Doha round of trading talks further darkens the outlook for addressing this element of the problem.

Global dynamics beyond African control deepened the problem by the end of the Bush administration's tenure. Weather-related disruptions curtailed supply, and the surge in demand for biofuels in turn generated a sharp increase in demand for key crops. High oil prices added to production costs, driving food prices even higher. The World Bank estimates that ranks of the chronically food insecure have recently grown by over 100 million, with most of the hardest hit countries in Africa.[13] The current decline in commodity prices mitigates some of these factors but does nothing to address the extreme vulnerability of millions of Africans to price fluctuations in the future.

Add increasing population growth and the impact of global climate change, and it is clear that Africa's food security challenge is not likely to diminish in the near future. The International Food Policy Research Institute has found that if all the effects of climate change are considered, it is possible that the number of undernourished Africans may triple from 1990 to 2080.[14]

Food insecurity is more than a humanitarian problem and more than an obstacle to economic development. Food insecurity can tip fragile states into instability. The recent spike in global food prices led to riots several African countries during the past year, including Burkina Faso, Cameroon, Côte d'Ivoire, Ethiopia, Madagascar, Senegal, and Somalia. The 2008 coup in Mauritania has been blamed in part on the democratically elected government's inability to satisfy consumers frustrated with rising food costs.

THE BUSH ADMINISTRATION'S RECORD

The Bush administration's record of engagement and accomplishment on these issues ranges from minimal to modest, with some of the most important efforts on climate change and food security taking place too late in the administration's tenure to bear much fruit. Emergency food aid was a notable exception: the administration ramped up food assistance dramatically to respond to crises on the continent. Faced with multiple competing priorities, the necessity of responding to urgent crises, finite resources, and the challenges of coming to agreement with Congress, any administration will find it difficult to devote significant effort and resources to long-term trends through investments and programs that do not lend themselves to immediate, measurable results.

DEMOGRAPHICS

The Bush administration engaged only peripherally with the changing nature of Africa's demographic landscape. Political sensitivities contributed to a lack of enthusiasm and support for reproductive health and family-planning services abroad—programs that can assist ongoing demographic transition by ensuring that women can bring fertility rates down if they so desire. Since 1995 U.S. funding for international family-planning programs has declined by 40 percent (adjusted for inflation), while the number of women of reproductive age in the developing world has increased by nearly 300 million. Some studies have found that over 60 percent of the 201 million women around the world with an unmet need for family-planning services are in Africa.[15]

Skepticism about the UN Population Fund (UNFPA) led the administration to withhold funds from the organization, making bilateral programs that much more important to the overall U.S. contribution. But the Bush administration's overall budget requests for U.S. Agency for International Development (USAID) family-planning and reproductive health programs have been consistently low. In both FY 2008 and FY 2009, the administration proposed cuts in excess of 25 percent to these programs. The administration directed larger portions of available resources to some African countries, resulting in meaningful increases from funding levels of the mid-1990s for programs in countries like Ethiopia, Ghana, and Mozambique, but others including Kenya, Mali, and Uganda have experienced significant declines in U.S. bilateral support for family-planning and reproductive health over the same timeframe.

Bolstering girls' access to education can also help facilitate demographic transition, and the Bush administration has provided some 85,000 scholarships for girls under the auspices of its Africa Education Initiative, launched in 2002. In addition, the administration's robust efforts to combat malaria were an important contribution, since reducing infant and child mortality can ultimately lead to long-term declines in desired family size.

But the broader issue of engaging with Africa's demographic reality and finding new ways to promote civic participation and economic opportunity specifically for young Africans was not a focus of the Bush administration energies. Youth are targeted for awareness-raising interventions in the context of the President's Emergency Plan for AIDS Relief, but these educational efforts are narrowly focused on promoting abstinence and preventing HIV/AIDS transmission. Relatively small projects in a handful of countries seek to improve young people's employment prospects through job skills training, and similar types of training are regularly provided to young ex-combatants in postconflict situations. The latter efforts often fail to recognize that these young people do not wish to "reintegrate" into old roles and communities, and this disconnect is symptomatic of a failure to recognize the transformational nature of this demographic group and the tremendous gap between youth aspirations and current realities.[16]

CLIMATE AND THE ENVIRONMENT

The Bush administration's initial reluctance to acknowledge the phenomenon of global climate change and its persistent discomfort with many proposed policy responses and multilateral strategies for addressing it constrained, but did not entirely preclude, action to address this issue in Africa.[17]

Various elements of the U.S. government are involved in climate change–related work that affects Africa. The National Oceanic and Atmospheric Administration's Climate Program Office does important global research. The U.S. Forest Service engages in sustainable forest management projects throughout Africa. The National Air and Space Agency (NASA) and USAID, in partnership with other international organizations and nongovernmental organizations, have been involved the Regional Visualization and Monitoring System (SERVIR) that has helped increase access to important climate-related data throughout Latin America. In 2008, NASA, CATHALAC (the Water Center for the Humid Tropics of Latin America and the Caribbean), and the Regional Center for Mapping of Resources for Development established SERVIR Africa in Nairobi to monitor and forecast ecological changes and respond to natural disasters.

USAID's Global Climate Change Program has supported natural resource management, clean energy, and climate change adaptation projects in Guinea, Madagascar, Malawi, Mali, Senegal, South Africa, and Uganda, as well as regional programs in Central and West Africa. The scale of these efforts has been relatively modest, accounting for about $27.4 million in 2007. The agency has also provided some funding for collaborative climate change research. (Another effort to promote research and training in Africa and elsewhere, the Center for Capacity Building at the National Center for Atmospheric Research, closed because of budgetary constraints in 2008, four years after its launch.)[18] Perhaps the most important climate change–related effort undertaken by USAID has been the production in mid-2007 of a guidance manual for development, "Adapting to Climate Variability and Change," pointing the way toward the integration of climate considerations in mainstream development work.

The Bush administration contributed to the World Bank's Global Environmental Facility (GEF), which works with governments, international organizations, and nongovernmental organizations (NGOs) to address a wide variety of environmental issues. The climate change–related portion of the U.S. GEF contribution totaled about $26 million in 2007, and an estimated $36 million of its total $106.8 million GEF budget request for 2008 will go toward climate-related activities.[19] But to date, two funds within the GEF that are especially relevant to Africa's climate change adaptation challenges, the Least Developed Countries (LDC) Fund and the Special Climate Change Fund, receive no support from the United States, as the Bush administration has argued that these are Kyoto related. Congress is pushing back on this decision; the Senate Appropriations Committee's version of the FY09 Foreign Operations Appropriations bill calls for providing $20 million to the LDC Fund if certain conditions are met.

In contrast to the administration's ambivalence about climate change, conservation efforts enjoyed significant support during the Bush years. The most important initiative, affecting the Congo Basin forests, has clear climate implications, since Central Africa's forests are second only to the Amazon in serving as vitally important carbon sinks. The administration launched the Congo Basin Forest Partnership in 2002 and through the Central African Regional Program for the Environment funded this effort with roughly $15 million annually ($17.5 million for FY08). The UK and Norway have launched a more expansive Congo Basin Forest Fund, which they are financing with $150 million over four years. The Bush administration took action to protect African forests when it supported multilateral sanctions on Liberia's timber exports while former President Charles Taylor still held office, taking an important stand linking unsustainable logging to the destabilizing, criminal nature of the Taylor regime.

Toward the end of President Bush's second term in office, the administration took new steps to acknowledge the importance of climate change, laying the groundwork for more energized engagement by the next president. In December 2007 the administration signed onto the Bali road map, which establishes an adaptation negotiating track to develop a more effective framework for helping vulnerable regions adapt to climate change in the future. In his 2008 State of the Union address, President Bush called for the creation of a multilateral Clean Technology Fund (CTF) that would, among other goals, help leverage private sector engagement by making clean energy projects in the developing world more appealing, a concept supported by the G-8. The CTF is less important for Africa than a serious commitment to support adaptation, but these steps help to clear away some of the antagonism that had developed between the United States and much of the world on this issue and contribute to heightened expectations about what a new administration might do to address climate change.

FOOD SECURITY

Despite early indications that the Bush administration might reenergize U.S. engagement on agricultural development, emergency food aid has received far greater emphasis than development work aimed at building sustainable agricultural capacity (see figure 9.1). This mirrors international donor trends, which have, since the late 1980s, seen a decrease in assistance to agriculture and steep increases in emergency assistance (see figure 9.2).

Pressed to respond to numerous food crises, the United States has contributed about 44 percent of the World Food Program's total budget (largely in the form of commodities, not cash) since 2000 and has repeatedly requested and received significant emergency supplemental appropriations for food aid. However, numerous analyses point out that the primary method by which the United States provides food assistance is tremendously inefficient because it requires that most aid be purchased in the United States and then shipped on U.S. carriers to crisis zones, resulting in slower, more costly, and often market-distorting assistance. While the administration has repeatedly requested that Congress relax these problematic food aid requirements, it has met with only limited, late success.[20]

Meanwhile, despite the impassioned case for restoring USAID's focus on agricultural development made by Andrew Natsios at his 2001 Senate confirmation hearing to be the agency's director, the Bush administration never coalesced around a strategic decision to prioritize agricultural development (see figure 9.3). The Partnership to Cut

Figure 9.1. Comparison of USAID Funding for Emergencies and Food Aid Funding for Development Activities in Sub-Saharan Africa under Title II of Public Law 480, Fiscal Years 1992–2007

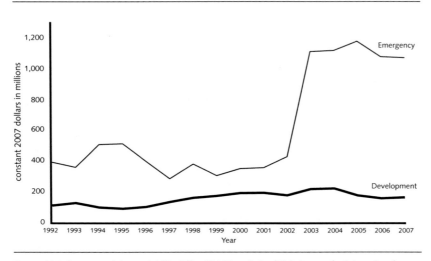

Source: U.S. Government Accountability Office (GAO) analysis of U.S. Agency for International Development data.

Figure 9.2. Worldwide ODA to Africa for Emergencies Compared with ODA to Africa for Agriculture, 1974–2006.

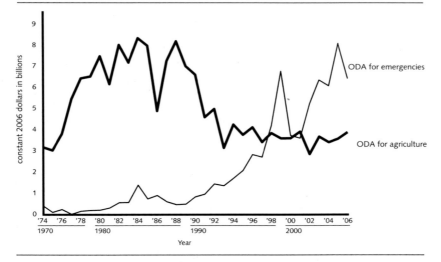

Source: GAO analysis of Organization for Economic Cooperation and Development (Development Assistance Committee) data.

Figure 9.3. Trends in U.S. Official Development Assistance to Agriculture for Africa, 1974–2006

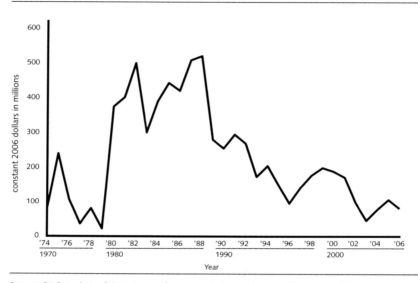

Source: GAO analysis of Organization for Economic Cooperation and Development (Development Assistance Committee) data.

Hunger and Poverty in Africa found that U.S. support for agricultural development declined by 3 percent in real terms over the course of the administration's first term in office, and the GAO has indicated that the situation did not improve over the course of the second term. The President's Initiative to End Hunger in Africa, launched in 2002, proved to be little more than a new name for ongoing, modest efforts. Rather than forging an interagency strategy, it involves only USAID, operates in only eight countries (in addition to regional programs), and did not receive new funding. The initiative became merely an organizing scheme for existing efforts involving about $200 million a year.

A more significant administration initiative, the Millennium Challenge Account, did provide new funding for agricultural development. Agriculture is one of six focus areas of the Millennium Challenge Corporation (the closely related issues of infrastructure and transportation are two of the others), and the GAO found that as of mid-2007, 39 percent of the $605 million pledged in signed compacts thus far was for agriculture-related projects.

Despite these positive steps, for the most part, the Bush administration dealt primarily with the symptoms, not the causes, of food crises in Africa. It has not been alone; the World Bank and other bilateral donors have followed the same trend for years. The soaring food prices of 2007 and 2008 provided a wake-up call for the donor community. World Bank President Robert Zoellick has pledged to double the bank's lending for agricultural development by 2010 as part of his call for a "New Deal for Global Food Policy."

Providing less specificity but still signaling renewed commitment to the issue, leaders of the G-8 Summit in July 2008 pledged to increase funding for agricultural development. While the administration's primary reaction to the global crisis was to release $200 million in emergency food reserves and to appeal Congress to for $770 million in additional emergency aid, senior officials have described a three-pronged approach that also includes increasing agricultural productivity and stimulating agricultural trade and investment.[21] James Kunder, acting deputy administrator of USAID, laid out an ambitious new agenda for promoting food security in the developing world in testimony before the House Agriculture Committee in July 2008, but it was too late in the administration's tenure for effective action.

RECOMMENDATIONS FOR A NEW ADMINISTRATION

Because of the transformational nature of the mega-trends and their implications for African stability, the new administration should go beyond an ad hoc, episodic approach to addressing these interrelated dynamics. Mainstreaming youth, climate, and food security–related concerns into ongoing policies and development projects makes sense, but without a strategic plan and clear lines of responsibility for addressing these issues, responding to and influencing these trends will consistently take a backseat to mitigating the crisis of the day. Someone must be accountable for U.S. policy in these critical issue areas, rather than allowing multiple officials to be relevant to—but in no way responsible for—sound U.S. policy.

In addition to ensuring that the appropriate institutional capacities are in place, the new administration should engage key congressional and nongovernmental actors early on to develop consensus around the merit of targeted new initiatives. Because most efforts to engage youth, build capacity for adapting to climate change, and increase food security are unlikely to yield quick, easily measured results, clarifying U.S. goals and identifying metrics for evaluating interventions will be essential to maintaining lasting support.

Of course, the new administration inherits a difficult economic climate, making it all the more important to leverage each foreign assistance dollar for maximum efficacy. Where possible, existing programs should be reformed to incorporate more focus on youth, to be mindful of climate change adaptation, or to contribute toward a new agricultural economy in the region. It is critical that the United States work multilaterally, engaging energetically in international negotiations on climate change, seizing on European sensitivities to migration to develop new opportunities for African youth, and working with existing efforts to strengthen African agriculture.[22]

ADJUSTING ENGAGEMENT TO REFLECT DEMOGRAPHIC REALITIES

As African societies become more youthful and more urban, the United States should make a concerted effort to ensure that engagement strategies do not leave the United States disconnected from the most demographically powerful groups on the continent.

ENGAGING YOUTH MORE PURPOSEFULLY

The new administration should aim to organize its diplomatic presence to reflect more closely the demographic realities in Africa, expanding U.S. presence and engagement in Africa's growing cities. U.S. embassies should be given the explicit task of engaging next-generation leaders, be they young legislators, civil society activists, student leaders, or community activists in nonelite settings. Opening lines of communication, fostering ongoing dialogue between young Africans and the U.S. government, and making a concerted effort to stay abreast of youth concerns can help the United States build relationships that will pay dividends in the future and anticipate changing trends on the continent. In a similar vein, the new administration should work with NGOs and educational institutions within the United States to scale up exchange opportunities that involve young people.

The new administration could launch an initiative to strengthen civic participation among young African adults as a part of its democracy and governance programming. Rule-governed systems can be sustained only if Africa's tremendous youth cohort has a stake in them, and efforts to improve youth voter participation, provide young people with the tools to engage in peaceful civic activism, and encourage young Africans to use information provided by transparency and accountability initiatives to demand better governance can all help build stronger societies and partners on the continent.

STRENGTHENING LINKS BETWEEN EDUCATION AND EMPLOYMENT

Efforts to improve access to education deserve ongoing support, but in this context far more attention must be paid to the issue of what happens after graduation. By engaging the private sector and U.S. universities well versed in creating mechanisms that link students and graduates with apprenticeships, mentors, entrepreneurial infrastructure, and employment opportunities, the administration can make educational interventions far more meaningful and at the same time broaden U.S. engagement with African youth. For the vast numbers of young Africans whose experience with formal education ends with secondary school or even before, initiatives designed to improve access to credit and to create space for small-scale entrepreneurs will be particularly important. Programs directed at young ex-combatants should be more directly linked with actual job opportunities. The United States should work with other donors and organizations to share best practices in addressing the needs of marginalized and at-risk youth.

EMPOWERING YOUNG WOMEN: FAMILY PLANNING, EDUCATION, EMPLOYMENT

Finally, as a part of efforts to improve overall primary health care infrastructure, the next administration should support efforts to expand access to family-planning and reproductive health services to address unmet needs in Africa. It should continue support for girls' education, including new efforts to improve girls' security at schools. And the new administration should ensure that young women are not marginalized in professional mentoring, job training, or job creation initiatives.

PRIORITIZING ADAPTATION TO CLIMATE CHANGE AND ENVIRONMENTAL PROTECTION

Given the magnitude of the U.S. contribution to global emissions, the new administration has a responsibility to devote far more effort to this issue, investing in concrete, on-the-ground programs, particularly those that improve water management, storage, and distribution.[23]

STRENGTHENING INSTITUTIONAL AND COMMUNITY CAPACITIES

The new administration should develop a specific adaptation agenda that strengthens the capacity of institutions and local communities to respond to climate changes. Adaptation efforts should involve senior government officials and governing institutions capable of creating incentives for new agricultural and resource management practices. But top-down efforts alone will not work; the new administration must recognize that natural resource management is primarily a local responsibility, and empowering citizens at the community level with awareness-raising efforts and support for appropriate adaptation efforts will be critical to the success of such an effort.

As the new U.S. Africa Command refines its mission on the continent, disaster preparedness training and assistance could become a major priority. The command is well positioned to help African states develop their capacity to plan for and respond to coastal flooding and other climate-related crises.

- *Work with International Partners.* The African Union (AU) is expected to adopt a common African position on climate change at its summit in the summer of 2009. The new administration should be prepared to offer a constructive response to the agenda set by the AU, laying the groundwork for effective partnership.

  The new administration should seize the opportunity presented by the Bali road map to improve existing multilateral mechanisms for funding adaptation efforts, which are often confusing and slow. Influencing the development of a better approach will require a meaningful U.S. commitment to participate, and the upcoming UN Climate Change Conference in Copenhagen in December 2009 provides a focal point and structure for this effort. The new administration is likely to work with Congress to enact cap-and-trade legislation, and revenues generated from auctions of emissions should be seriously considered as a source of funds for adaptation contributions.

  Investments in urban infrastructure will be critical to Africa's successful adaptation to climate change. The new administration should make a special effort to reach out to China in this regard, which is deeply involved in infrastructure projects on the continent. Such an effort could help defuse some of the unnecessary tension that has developed around China's engagement in

Africa and could set the stage for working cooperatively with the Chinese on a code-of-conduct effort for major external actors that would set new norms for incorporating climate and conservation priorities and sensitivities in development projects.[24]
Finally, the new administration should leverage the interest, expertise, and ongoing effort of nongovernmental actors, including research institutions, universities, environmental protection organizations, philanthropic foundations, and private sector actors already engaged in climate change adaptation and resilience work, focusing on how U.S. policy can strengthen their hands.

- *Promote Clean Energy and Protect Carbon Sinks.* While adaptation should be the primary focus of efforts to address climate change in Africa, the new administration should seek opportunities to promote clean energy technologies in Africa. As growing economies and urban areas experience surging energy demands, opportunities to promote clean energy strategies should be aggressively embraced. The African Development Bank is putting together its own Clean Energy and Development Investment Framework, which may be worthy of the new administration's attention. The World Bank has also noted that many African countries have a comparative advantage in biofuel production—another potentially job-creating opportunity that could be worthy of U.S. government and private sector support.[25]

  Addressing climate change globally requires protecting carbon sinks like the Congo Basin forests, and the new administration should increase U.S. investment in the Congo Basin Forest Partnership and work multilaterally and with NGOs to increase the costs for actors involved in unsustainable and illegal logging.

- *Invest in African Agriculture.* The 2008 global food crisis focused international attention on the need for a new approach to African agriculture and helped mobilize political will within the United States that could make bold new action possible.[26]

  International organizations, several African governments, and NGOs are in the process of reinvigorating their own efforts, making this a valuable opportunity to establish a new, collaborative dynamic between the United States and other international actors.

- *Use Presidential Leadership to Launch Ambitious Food Security Initiative.* There are strong indications that bipartisan support for a bold new approach could be mustered in Congress. Most notably, the Global Food Security Act of 2008, introduced by Senators Richard Lugar and Robert Casey, offers an ambitious approach to reforming and strengthening U.S. policy. This kind of initiative could gain traction in the new Congress, but given domestic economic constraints and diminishing media attention to the issue, presidential leadership will be required to sustain momentum.

- *Revisit How the U.S. Provides Emergency Food Aid.* The new administration should work to reduce the portion of assistance that must be purchased in the United States and then shipped abroad and increase the portion that can be used for local and regional purchase. While the current system promotes strong support for food aid among a powerful coalition of American constituencies, this approach leads to inefficient use of taxpayer dollars and limits the ability to provide the most timely and constructive help to communities in humanitarian crisis. With the right strategy, change is politically possible. Other politically sensitive issues also need to be addressed, including U.S. subsidy policies (especially for biofuels) and trade barriers.

- *Put a Focus on Agricultural Development.* In addition to pushing a new political discourse on food security, the new administration should refocus energy on agricultural development in Africa. USAID should recruit new agricultural expertise to the agency and should make sustainable agricultural growth in Africa one of the agency's top priorities. This should be part of a stronger interagency mechanism aimed at driving a cohesive, goal-oriented agenda on agricultural development. A high-level interagency working group should be established for this purpose, and senior officials from participating agencies should be held responsible for achieving specific benchmarks relative to research capacities, agricultural yields, and other indicators within specific timeframes by Congress and the president.

    There is broad agreement on how to effectively promote the growth of sustainable agriculture in Africa. Farmers need increased access to better seed varieties, fertilizer, extension services, credit, crop insurance, market information, and markets themselves. More intensive research on Africa's crops is needed, with a particular sensitivity to climate change and a focus on alternative crops and new drought-resistant crop varieties. Other priorities should include bolstering technical capacity, modernizing rusty facilities, and promoting partnerships with agricultural centers of excellence. Ministries of agriculture should be strengthened and encouraged to attract capable scientists and managers, and central governments may need to undertake land tenure reform efforts to clear barriers to agricultural investment. Appropriate water conservation infrastructure is urgently needed, and transportation infrastructure requires continued investment, through the Millennium Challenge Corporation or possibly through collaborative work with China.

Given the scope and scale of needs, meaningfully improving agricultural sustainability must be a multilateral endeavor—but U.S. leadership will be vitally important. The United States should develop its efforts to be explicitly complementary to the Comprehensive Africa Agriculture Development Program (CAADP) of the New Partnership for Africa's Development, while urging African governments to meet their own CAADP commitments to devote significant resources to agriculture. A collaborative approach that engages African civil society could also help move the debate surrounding genetically modified organisms beyond the mutually accusatory stalemate that persists today. The United States should work with other UN member states to reform the Food and Agriculture Organization, which is currently too slow and bureaucratic to meet the urgent needs of Africa's agricultural sector.

In addition to partnering with other governments and international organizations, the new administration should draw on the private sector, where actors from around the world can help to point the way toward needed reforms to increase private capital flows quickly. Similarly, academic and research communities and philanthropic efforts like the Alliance for a Green Revolution in Africa (an initiative of the Bill and Melinda Gates and Rockefeller Foundations), may generate promising new approaches appropriate for rapid scaling up.

- *Link to Demographic and Climate Change.* Africa's mega-trends are interlinked. The new administration should avoid the temptation to address agricultural development needs with a purely rural strategy. As Africa becomes increasingly urbanized, urban and peri-urban agriculture will demand increased attention, and links between urban markets and rural farms will be even more important. U.S. policy should encourage ministries of public works and municipal authorities to collaborate with ministries of agriculture to provide supportive regulatory frameworks to peri-urban agriculture. Job opportunities should be developed in urban areas where value can be added to raw agricultural goods. Urban youth are unlikely to be coaxed back to rural communities to take up farming, but some can become a part of a sophisticated new agricultural economy. Job creation in programs that aim to improve resilience to climate change and strengthen food security should receive priority.

CONCLUSION

Demographic, environmental, and food security mega-trends intertwine in complex ways, making them easy to set aside as amorphous, overwhelming phenomena threatening to consume massive resources without tangible results. When so many other urgent issues compete for policymakers' attention, these issues rarely take priority. Indeed, confronted with numerous crises on the continent, committed to a historic effort to combat HIV/AIDS, guided by a skeptical view of climate change, and constrained by domestic political imperatives, the Bush administration often had little to offer in the way of energy and resources to address the mega-trends reshaping the African landscape. The new president and his team can find opportunity in these challenges. Policy interventions to respond to and influence the mega-trends will promote new multilateral, public-private, and civic partnerships that can make U.S. policy stronger. Better yet, successful policy responses can do more than stave off disaster; they can promote meaningful economic growth and even positive political change.

NOTES

1. UN Department of Economic and Social Affairs, *2007 World Youth Report*, 96–97.
2. Adele Hayutin, "How Population Aging Differs across Countries: A Briefing on Global Demographics," Stanford Center on Longevity, March 2007.
3. UN Population Fund, *State of World Population 2007: Unleashing the Potential of Urban Growth*, 2007, http://www.unfpa.org/swp/2007/english/introduction.html.

4. UN Human Settlements Program (UNHABITAT), Global Urban Observatory and Statistics Unit, Africa Trends, http://ww2.unhabitat.org/habrdd/africa.html.

5. Richard Cincotta et al., *The Security Demographic—Population and Civil Conflict after the Cold War* (Washington, D.C.: Population Action International, 2003); and Elizabeth Leahy et al., *The Shape of Things to Come: Why Age Structure Matters to a Safer, More Equitable World* (Washington, D.C.: Population Action International, 2007).

6. World Economic Forum, *Africa at Risk Report*, 2008, http://www.weforum.org/pdf/Africa2008/Africa_RiskReport_08.pdf. The Intergovernmental Panel on Climate Change estimates Africa's emissions at 3.8 percent of the global total, an even lower estimate than the 5 percent cited.

7. Michel Boko et al., "Africa," in *Climate Change 2007: Impacts, Adaptation and Vulnerability,* Intergovernmental Panel on Climate Change Fourth Assessment Report, 2007, http://www.ipcc.ch/pdf/assessment-report/ar4/wg2/ar4-wg2-chapter9.pdf.

8. Ibid. As many as 232,000 square miles of arable land may become untenable for agriculture because of to climate change.

9. Estimations of the negative economic impact on Africa as a result of climate change fluctuate. The *Stern Review on the Economics of Climate Change* estimated that the income effects of climate change are 1.9–2.7 percent of GDP in Africa. See http://www.hm-treasury.gov.uk/sternreview_index.htm.

10. The GAO found that the share of official development assistance from both multilateral and bilateral donors to agriculture for Africa has significantly declined, from about 15 percent in the 1980s to about 4 percent in 2006. See GAO, *International Food Insecurity: Insufficient Efforts by Host Governments and Donors Threaten Efforts to Halve Hunger in Sub-Saharan Africa by 2015* (Washington, D.C.: GAO, May 2008), 5.

11. Keith Bradsher and Andrew Martin, "World's Poor Pay Price as Crop Research Is Cut," *New York Times*, May 18, 2008.

12. Statement of Peter McPherson, president of the National Association of State Universities and Land-Grant Colleges, "Food Security in Africa," before the House of Representatives Committee on Foreign Affairs Subcommittee on Africa and Global Health, July 18, 2007.

13. Statement of James R. Kunder, acting deputy administrator, U.S. Agency for International Development, "U.S. Response to the Global Food Crisis: Humanitarian Assistance and Development Investments," before the U.S. House of Representatives Committee on Agriculture, July 16, 2008.

14. Joachim von Braun, *The World Food Situation: New Driving Forces and Required Actions* (Washington, D.C.: IFPRI, 2008), p. 20.

15. Shusheela Singh et al., *Adding It Up: The Benefits of Investing in Sexual and Reproductive Health Care* (New York: Guttmacher Institute, 2003), http://www.unfpa.org/upload/lib_pub_file/240_filename_addingitup.pdf.

16. For an excellent discussion of these issues, see Marc Sommers, "Embracing the Margins: Working with Youth amid War and Insecurity," in *Too Poor for*

Peace? Poverty, Conflict, and Security in the 21st Century, ed. Lael Brainard and Derek Chollet (Washington, D.C.: Brookings Institution Press, 2007), 101–18.

17. The Bush administration's record regarding policies aimed at reducing U.S. emissions that contribute to global warming is obviously relevant in a broad sense but is not the focus of this chapter.

18. Andrew Revkin, "Climate-Change Program to Aid Poor Nations Is Shut," *New York Times*, August 7, 2008.

19. FY 2008 Federal Climate Change Expenditures Report to Congress (May 2007), available at http://www.whitehouse.gov/omb/legislative/index.html.

20. The last and most serious skirmish on this front involved the 2007 Farm Bill, which became law in 2008. The Bush administration had requested authority to use up to 25 percent of available funds for PL 480 Title II food aid to purchase food in theater. Congress responded by authorizing only a $60 million, four-year pilot program.

21. Statement of Henrietta Fore, administrator and director of foreign assistance, USAID, "Responding to the Global Good Crisis" before the Senate Foreign Relations Committee, May 14,2008; and remarks of Ed Schafer, secretary of agriculture, at the UN Food and Agriculture Organization Conference, June 5, 2008, available at http://www.usda.gov/wps/portal/usdahome?conten tidonly=true&contentid=2008/06/0150.xml.

22. For a discussion of the need to improve evaluation measures on youth employment initiatives, see World Bank, "A Review of Interventions to Support Young Workers: Findings of the Youth Employment Inventory" (World Bank Social Protection Discussion Paper 0715, October 2007).

23. For a helpful discussion of the issues at stake in planning for more robust international support for adaptation in the developing world, see Heather McGray, Anne Hammill, and Rob Bradley, *Weathering the Storm: Options for Framing Adaptation and Development* (Washington, D.C.: World Resources Institute, 2007).

24. This could be particularly important given China's reported plans to build new roads in the Congo Basin.

25. "Suggested Action Items on Food Prices for Consideration by the G-8," The World Bank. July 2008, available at http://wwww.reliefweb.int/rw/rwb. nsf/db900sid/ONIN-7G6MEA?OpenDocument.

26. For a more detailed discussion of appropriate U.S. policy responses to the global food crisis, see *A Call for a Strategic U.S. Approach to the Global Food Crisis* (Washington, D.C.: CSIS, July 2008), http://www.csis.org/media/ pubs/080728 food security.pdf. See also *World Development Report 2008: Agriculture for Development* (Washington, D.C.: World Bank, 2007) for a detailed discussion of lessons learned from past, unsuccessful agricultural development interventions, available at http://econ.worldbank.org/WBSITE/EXTERNAL/ EXTDEC/EXTRESEARCH/EXTWDRS/EXTWDR2008/0,,menuPK:2795178 ~pagePK:64167702~piPK:64167676~theSitePK:2795143,00.html.

10

CONCLUSION

CHESTER A. CROCKER

The chapters of this volume represent a comprehensive and balanced effort to capture key aspects of the Africa policy legacy of the 2001–2008 years. The purpose of these concluding pages is not to summarize the preceding material, which contains a wide range of analyses and recommendations for future policy. Rather, the aim is to capture from the perspective of a former Africa policymaker some possible guideposts for the Obama administration's policy team—both those charged with full-time responsibilities for Africa and those charged with a broader focus.

THE DOMESTIC DIMENSION OF A SMART AFRICA POLICY

Several issues on the domestic front should be considered. Policymakers will face the usual temptations to change things for the sake of doing so and being seen to do so. In practice, it is better to start by building rather than by dismantling and reorganizing all the bureaucratic, interagency, and personnel elements of policy. Starting with clearly established reporting relationships between the Africa Bureau and the State Department's senior leadership, while also setting in place regular procedures for interagency coordination on a standing basis. Those involved in Africa policy require reliable and credible "air cover" from the deputy secretaries and principals to overcome the reality of the region's severe fragmentation and its large concentration of relatively weak states, many of them landlocked entities with very small economies. Africa has never been a top priority in U.S. foreign policy, a situation unlikely to change anytime soon. But that is not the point. U.S. policy toward the region cannot develop traction unless it has the explicit backing of the White House and the president's lieutenants at the State Department and the Department of Defense (DOD).

Perhaps the most important mandate the secretary of state should give to the senior Africa policy people is to take seriously their responsibility to make the bureau a center of personnel excellence. Recruitment and retention of top-quality people and the maintenance of bureau (and field) morale and connectedness are essential. The bureau has a lot of opportunity to offer career people, who will be the primary instrument for developing and implementing day-to-day policy. If the incentives are right, top-quality people will want to work in Africa and in the Africa Bureau.

Reorganization and possible upgrading to cabinet rank of the U.S. assistance bureaucracy should not be an early priority. But a fresh review of assistance priorities within the U.S. International Affairs Budget (known as the "150 account") and authorities to transfer funding between the Department of Defense and State should be undertaken. It will be particularly important early on to sort out the bureaucratic relationships governing assistance provided under sections 1206 and 1207 (now 1210) of the National Defense Authorization Act.[1] A range of goals is supported by various U.S. assistance resources. Overall weightings and priorities need a fresh look to make sure that these resources are rigorously integrated and geared toward support of overall U.S. goals and requirements in Africa—energy security, conflict management and peacemaking, health (prevention, infrastructure, treatment), rule of law and governance support, regional integration, agriculture and food security, population and women's health, and so forth. The reality, however, is that these programmatic thrusts will be implemented in the context of specific countries and regions and that connections should make strategic and diplomatic sense.

FRIENDS, DEMOCRATS, AND AUTOCRATS

It is commonly, and often credibly, argued, first, that democratization has stagnated in Africa during the past eight years and, second, that U.S. efforts to promote democracy have taken a back seat to other priorities, especially to counterterrorism. Whether there is a direct relationship between these two trends is not really the point. The challenge is to define an approach to democracy and governance based on African political realities as well as U.S. interests (including our values agenda and our view that democracies make better, more successful partners). Looking back, the balance sheet is mixed. The United States, in the end, did play a positive role (working with African partners) in shepherding the departure of Charles Taylor from Liberia and fostering a supportive environment for the transition to Ellen Johnson-Sirleaf (and supporting her once in office). Bringing an end (at least for now) to the Kenyan political crisis of 2008 was the work of many actors, principally African but also Western, and the United States made a significant contribution to sobering up the leadership of Kenyan President Mwai Kibaki. The tools for supporting democratic rule have also been strengthened substantially with the advent of the Millennium Challenge Corporation.

Having said that, Africa remains a zone in which personalized rule and dominant incumbent power structures are the norm and genuine democratic alternations of power as in Ghana in early 2009 are the exception. And it remains the case that many African states are institutionally weak and vulnerable to clientelism, ethnic factionalism, and potential decline under the impact of economic, demographic, health, and climate stresses. In this context, U.S. policymakers may want to consider some basic rules of thumb.

One of these is to avoid destabilizing friends who may have a marginal performance on governance issues: Africa does not need more arcs of instability. But that does not mean averting our eyes and writing blank checks. It should mean that we speak candidly when African states engage in behavior that could endanger themselves and that we should underscore the upside of governance improvements through the use of our multilateral diplomatic and assistance tools. As the United States charts its course and pursues its priority programs with African partners, it requires heightened awareness of the potential traps. When we announce that we are in the market for counterterrorist allies, we will find them aplenty. Some could produce problems of "blowback," in which the unintended consequences of U.S. support lead us to ignore the bad agendas with which we become identified or the dubious actors who purport to speak for us.

The question of so-called anchor states or key partners is also important. The problem here is that sometimes the anchors drag or become problem relationships. High-profile articulation by U.S. officials that a given state has achieved the status of "anchordom" may not be the best way to retain one's freedom of action and may persuade African audiences that we have simply decided to embrace a given leader. The problem of anointing the leaders of other countries, whether in Russia or in Africa, has bedeviled the diplomacy of both the Clinton and the George W. Bush administrations: it is better not to talk so much about it. In the case of Nigeria, anchordom may have been warranted in regional conflict-management terms but at the cost of not addressing some of the most pressing domestic challenges of governance and stability. In the case of South Africa, anchordom may explain the development over the past dozen years or so of an immature relationship characterized more by pander than by candor. Ethiopia may at various points have appeared as a haven of hope in a sea of disorderly and failing governance, but it is only a matter of degree.

Another rule of thumb concerns the importance of sustaining and vigorously protecting existing democracies. That is why the Kenya case was so important—for Africa, for Africans, and for us—and why the Zimbabwe case is such an exemplary illustration of Africa's failure to set and sustain its own normative order. The United States and other Western countries made a variety of efforts—a few of them sincere—to draw lines over Zimbabwe. Initiatives to enable the survival of democratic voices and to thwart the predatory appetites of regime members at the margins have been useful. A new administration has a golden opportunity to speak with unprecedented moral authority to the leaders of southern Africa on this crisis and to convey that Americans care about the success of the subregion but can do little to bolster its prospects as long as the cancer of thuggery continues unabated in Harare.

SECURITY AND CONFLICT ISSUES

A word of context is needed to grasp the trend lines of African conflict. Africa experienced a steady rise of conflict during the decolonization and Cold War years. In the early post–Cold War period, African conflicts surged toward the peak years of 1993–94 when some 40 percent of African states were caught up in one form or another of serious conflict events. The 1990s, in fact, were the bloodiest decade Africans have experienced in modern times. Since the 1993–94 peak, the number of ongoing significant conflicts has declined steadily, especially those involving government armed forces as distinguished from conflicts between nongovernment factions and militias. According to data generated by the leading conflict research centers, one can say this: (1) the number of significant African conflicts has fallen from a range of 15–18 in the early 1990s to 5–8 today, depending on criteria and coding methods used; (2) the region continues to account for some 75–80 percent of all UN peacekeeping operations (deployed troops), and its conflicts continue to occupy over 50 percent of the UN Security Council conflict agenda; and (3) while the number of major African conflicts is down, the region accounts for some two-thirds of the so-called nonstate conflicts (those without direct involvement of government forces) occurring in such places as Chad, the Democratic Republic of Congo (DRC), Ethiopia, Nigeria, Somalia, and Sudan.

The number of African countries affected by violent conflict today is somewhat lower than during the final phase of the Cold War, but violence continues to plague some of Africa's largest and most important states. Experts debate the factors that have helped to reduce African wars and encourage negotiated settlements. Clearly, major diplomatic and political energy has been invested in peacemaking and peacekeeping, by the UN system, by African regional and subregional organizations, by individual powerful states such as the United States, and by nongovernmental organizations that play a gradually increasing role in conflict management. A positive doctrinal shift is occurring in favor of negotiated solutions, the Responsibility to Protect[2] (however imperfectly applied), and notions of expanding good governance. A third factor has been a continental learning process as Africans observe the ingredients of success (and failure) in other societies struggling to make their way in a globalized international environment.

Even while we celebrate the end of wars in Angola, Burundi, Côte d'Ivoire, much of the DRC, Liberia, Mozambique, Namibia, Sierra Leone, Sudan (north-south), and Uganda (we hope), it is important to recognize (1) that the human and economic toll of African conflicts since the end of the Cold War has been massive; (2) that the ongoing burden of the remaining conflicts is substantial and their impact is increasingly transborder in scope; and (3) that some troubled postconflict countries are far from out of the woods. Security in a number of postconflict countries remains fragile. Negotiated settlements can and often do break down under the burden of their own complexity and the sad tendency of peacemakers to disengage at precisely the moment when they are most sorely needed as implementers and peace builders.

Decisionmaking on conflict and postconflict challenges is increasingly fragmented—internationally and within conflict-torn societies—a tendency that threatens vitally needed coherence and coordination among the key actors. And the case of Zimbabwe reminds us of the risks that repressive dictatorships pose to regional stability.

The Obama administration will have to decide its priorities in the face of this legacy. Questions abound: Where should the United States engage? Where and when should the United States push others to the fore? In which situations is regional African leadership up to the challenges of conflict management (and where is it not), and which conflict and security issues are best managed by the UN or an ad hoc multinational grouping? U.S. leadership on conflict issues has been quite narrowly focused on Sudan (and to a much lesser extent Liberia and the DRC) in the past eight years. In the Africa of today, Washington cannot afford to be so timid about engaging or to treat conflicts in the DRC and Nigeria as second- or third-order priorities.

While unprecedented attention has been given to developing security relations with African states, the political messaging associated with these efforts—the Africa Contingency Operation Training and Assistance Program and the associated Global Peace Operations Initiative, the U.S. Africa Command (AFRICOM), the Africa Partnership Station, the Trans-Sahara Counter-Terrorism Partnership, the Combined Joint Task Force–Horn of Africa—has been confused and lacking a coherent link to conflict management. The messaging mechanisms should be fixed promptly, and the doctrinal and policy links between programs sorted out. The creation of AFRICOM itself was eminently sensible and, in fact, long overdue as a mechanism for coordinating a wide range of U.S. defense and security-related activities on the continent. AFRICOM has the potential to focus more defense resources on Africa in support of core policy goals. U.S. officials should be unapologetic about using these activities, first, to empower our partners to acquire greater capacity for conflict management and peacekeeping operations at the regional level and, second, to enhance the capacity of African states to control national territory and maritime zones better so they do not become a safe haven for terrorist groups or a transit and operational area for criminal mafias and pirates. Countering the buildup of hideouts and staging areas for international and regional terrorists and criminals is an important priority for the United States and its African partners.

Moreover, to be effective in African conflict arenas, U.S. policy needs a proper, balanced appreciation of the wide range of destructive and conflict-related activities that can thrive in ungoverned or undergoverned spaces beyond the current control of fragile states. The United States has strong common interests in partnering with African states to bring these destructive activities under control: arms, narcotics, and human trafficking; environmental and fisheries violations; piracy; natural resource predation; and related criminal enterprises. From an African perspective, terrorism is one of many security challenges, and not necessarily the most salient one.

The policymaker's attention naturally gravitates first to questions involving the use of force for peace and stability operations and for humanitarian intervention. Inexorably, however, the focus is turning toward regional and subregional institutions as they increasingly take a leading role either by themselves or as part of hybrid (e.g., African Union/UN) operations. As the incoming Obama team sorts through these challenges and choices, it could organize its responses in such areas as:

- *Conflict prevention*: How to organize the resources of the State Department and the process of interagency coordination to get a jump on conflict-inducing political and security dynamics; how to link up operationally with parallel efforts in allied capitals and the UN to create the germ of a standing mechanism for coordination when the need arises.

- *Negotiation and mediation capacity:* How to ramp up the capacity of the UN's Department of Political Affairs, the African Union Commission, and the Department of State itself to launch and sustain high-quality, appropriately staffed mediation missions.

- *The "postsettlement" end-of-the-conflict life cycle:* How to ensure that Africa gets the bureaucratic and budget support to receive vital diplomatic and development tools for such things as training, capacity building, security sector reform, mediation and negotiation, cease-fire monitoring, and peace-building support.

THE SOURCES OF U.S. INFLUENCE

It has become a commonplace to note that Washington seems to have lost a step in its African reach and clout. The point has merit. Never before have U.S. policymakers and diplomats enjoyed the current (fiscal year 2009) level of official resources dedicated to programs and projects in Africa. Yet it appears that U.S. views are often ignored and U.S. goals diverted or caught up in a web of complex detours. U.S. civilian capacity appears to lack heft, even as attention has shifted to the launch of AFRICOM.

To remedy these problems, the starting place is to grasp the context and reasons for declining U.S. mastery of the African policy playing field. First, the *relative* influence of the United States has been on the decline almost everywhere; one could have parallel conversations about the U.S. position in Latin America and Southeast Asia, for example. Africa is not unusual in the sense of standing out from other places where the United States is doing a lot better. Nor is the United States regarded negatively in African public opinion; on the contrary, Africans rank first in the world in their favorable views of the United States.

The problems are elsewhere. The African playing field has changed. There are more major players engaged in Africa—diplomatically, commercially, and militarily and in terms of official development assistance—than at any time in the postcolonial era. Much attention is given to China's arrival as a major actor in Africa, and rightly so. But this should not obscure the strong, continuing roles of our European and Japanese allies, of other major Asian nations such as India and South Korea, or of Brazil and Russia. Moreover, Africans themselves are shaping the playing field and charting their own course more decisively than before, a process that is both natural and in most respects positive, even if it means a relative decline in our own influence. Another factor is the overwhelming U.S. preoccupation in recent years with the challenges of the Middle East and the demands of a counterterrorism-oriented global policy. The United States has had little political capital and policy energy left over for fresh initiatives and the exercise of diplomatic leadership on the major African crises and challenges.

To develop greater policy reach and influence again, Washington will want to do four things more effectively in the coming years:

- *Build Africa as a major factor into our broader bilateral and multilateral policies so that our primary global partners get the message that Africa matters to us.* It is past time for Africa to be mainstreamed and not viewed as a policy ghetto within our own bureaucracy and in our diplomacy with major non-African states.

- *Leverage our expanded policy resources to support our primary political-strategic and development goals more directly.* Part of the reason why there is a sense of not getting the policy bang for the resource buck is the heavy concentration of those resources in generic programs and regionwide initiatives that fail to translate into direct bilateral or subregional influence.

- *Make better use of multilateral burden-sharing opportunities.* The example of UN peacekeeping is an obvious but overworked case in point. Much the same could be said for modest efforts to upgrade the capacity of the UN's Department of Political Affairs for undertaking facilitation and mediation roles.

- *Expand the application in Africa of the cutting-edge policy tools developed in the counterterrorism field and battle against money laundering and the narcotics trade.* Properly used, many of the instruments and tools used by the intergovernmental Financial Action Task Force could serve the needs of combating illicit trafficking, gun-running, corruption, and cross-border criminality that threaten Africa's fragile state structures.

NOTES

1. Section 1206 of the 2006 National Defense Authorization Act provides DOD with authority to train and equip foreign military forces, with the "concurrence" of the secretary of state. Section 1207 authorized the secretary of defense to transfer up to $100 million per year for two years to the Department of State for programs that support security, reconstruction, or stabilization. Congress extended this authority in Section 1210 of the 2008 Defense Authorization Act.

2. This concept holds that if sovereign governments fail to protect their own people from genocide, ethnic cleansing, or other major crimes against humanity, then the wider international community must take whatever action is appropriate to do so.

ABOUT THE CONTRIBUTORS

Joel D. Barkan is professor emeritus of political science at the University of Iowa and a senior associate at Center for Strategic and International Studies. A specialist on issues of democratization and governance across Anglophone Africa, he served as the first regional democracy and governance adviser for eastern and southern Africa at the U.S. Agency for International Development from 1992 to 1994. Since 2000, he has served periodically as senior consultant on governance in the Africa region at the World Bank. He has written extensively on democratization and governance. He received an A.B. from Cornell University and a Ph.D. in political science and African studies from the University of California at Los Angeles.

William Mark Bellamy is director of the Africa Center for Strategic Studies at the National Defense University and a senior fellow in the CSIS Africa and International Security Programs. A career diplomat, he has served as U.S. ambassador to Kenya, principal deputy assistant secretary of state for African affairs, and deputy assistant secretary for African affairs. He has had earlier diplomatic postings in Australia, France, South Africa, and Zimbabwe. Ambassador Bellamy holds a B.A. in history from Occidental College in Los Angeles and an M.A. in international relations from the Fletcher School of Law and Diplomacy at Tufts University.

Timothy M. Carney, a retired career Foreign Service officer, was the last accredited U.S. ambassador to Sudan. His 32-year career included service in areas of conflict from Indochina to South Africa and Haiti, as well as work in UN peacekeeping missions in Cambodia, Somalia, and South Africa. At the request of the Department of Defense, he joined Lt. Gen. (Ret.) Jay Garner's staff in Iraq in March 2003 as the senior authority in the Ministry of Industry and Minerals, serving three months then and four months in 2007 as coordinator for economic transition at the State Department's request. He regularly lectures on aspects of Iraq as part of a team preparing U.S. Army and National Guard units assigned to Iraq. Ambassador Carney graduated from MIT in 1966. He speaks Cambodian, Thai, and French.

Jennifer G. Cooke is director of the CSIS Africa Program, which she joined in 2000, and works on a range of U.S.-Africa policy issues, including HIV/AIDS, security, conflict, and democratization. With J. Stephen Morrison, she edited *Africa Policy in the Clinton Years: Critical Choices for the Bush Administration* (CSIS, 2001) and has written a variety of reports, articles, and commentary on U.S.-Africa relations. Previously, she worked for the House Foreign Affairs Subcommittee on Africa, as well as for the National Academy of Sciences. She earned a B.A. in government from Harvard University and an M.A. in African studies and international economics from the Johns Hopkins University School of Advanced International Studies.

Chester A. Crocker is the James R. Schlesinger Professor of Strategic Studies at Georgetown University, where his teaching and research focus on conflict management and regional security issues. He served as chairman of the board of the U.S. Institute of Peace from 1992 to 2004 and continues as a member of its board. From 1981 to 1989, he was U.S. assistant secretary of state for African affairs. As such, he was the principal mediator in the negotiations among Angola, Cuba, and South Africa that led to Namibia's transition to independence and the withdrawal of Cuban forces from Angola. He was also the architect of the U.S. policy of "constructive engagement" toward apartheid South Africa. Dr. Crocker received a B.A. with distinction from Ohio State University and an M.A. and Ph.D. from the Johns Hopkins University School of Advanced International Studies.

Michelle D. Gavin is senior director for Africa at the National Security Council. At the time of writing, Ms. Gavin was an international affairs fellow in residence at the Council on Foreign Relations, where she examined the implications of youth bulge in the developing world for U.S. foreign policy. Before joining the Council, Ms. Gavin served as legislative director to U.S. Senator Ken Salazar (D-Colo.), as well as the primary foreign policy adviser to Senator Russ Feingold (D-Wis.). She has also served as the staff director of the Senate Foreign Relations Committee's subcommittee on African affairs. Ms. Gavin earned an undergraduate degree from Georgetown University's School of Foreign Service and an M.Phil. in international relations from Oxford University, where she was a Rhodes Scholar.

David L. Goldwyn is president of Goldwyn International Strategies LLC, an international energy consulting firm. He is also a senior fellow in the CSIS Energy and Africa Programs and chairman of the Global Energy and Environment Initiative at Johns Hopkins University School of Advanced International Studies. Goldwyn has served as assistant secretary of energy for international affairs, counselor to the secretary of energy, national security deputy to the U.S. ambassador to the United Nations, chief of staff to the undersecretary of state for political affairs, and attorney-adviser in the Office of the Legal Adviser at the State Department. He has taught at Columbia and Georgetown Universities, has been a frequent commentator in the media, and is the author of numerous publications on transparency in the oil sector. He received a B.A. from Georgetown University, an M.A. from the Woodrow Wilson School of Public and International Affairs at Princeton University, and a J.D. from New York University.

Princeton N. Lyman is adjunct senior fellow for Africa policy studies at the Council on Foreign Relations and an adjunct professor at Georgetown University. Ambassador Lyman's career in government has included assignments as director of the U.S. Agency for International Development in Addis Ababa, deputy assistant secretary of state for Africa, U.S. ambassador to Nigeria, director of refugee programs, U.S. ambassador to South Africa, and assistant secretary of state for international organization affairs. Ambassador Lyman is a board member of several philanthropic and civic organizations and author of numerous articles on foreign policy, African affairs, economic development, HIV/AIDS, UN reform, and peacekeeping. He received a B.A. from the University of California at Berkeley and a Ph.D. in political science from Harvard University.

J. Stephen Morrison is director of the newly created CSIS Global Health Policy Center and senior vice president of CSIS. He has directed the CSIS Africa Program and the CSIS Task Force on HIV/AIDS and codirected the CSIS Task Force on Nontraditional Security Assistance and the CSIS Task Force on the Global Food Crisis. Dr. Morrison served on the secretary of state's policy planning staff during the Clinton administration, where he was responsible for African affairs and global foreign assistance issues and launched the Office of Transition Initiatives. He received a B.A. from Yale College and a Ph.D. in political science from the University of Wisconsin.

Phillip Nieburg is a senior associate with the CSIS Global Health Policy Center and a visiting scholar at Northwestern University. He is a pediatrician, also trained in infectious diseases, who became interested in public health while serving as a military physician in the early 1970s. Dr. Nieburg became a U.S. public health service officer at the Centers for Disease Control and Prevention (CDC) in 1977 and remained at CDC until 2003, eventually serving in senior positions in its Global AIDS Program and its National Center for HIV, STD, and TB Prevention. At CDC, he was extensively involved with famine and refugee relief operations, working with various U.S. government and international agencies. Dr. Nieburg received B.A. and M.D. degrees from Case Western Reserve University and an M.P.H. from Johns Hopkins University.

David H. Shinn is adjunct professor of international affairs at the Elliott School of International Affairs at the George Washington University. He served for 37 years in the U.S. Foreign Service with assignments at embassies in Cameroon, Kenya, Lebanon, Mauritania, Sudan, and Tanzania and as ambassador to Burkina Faso and Ethiopia. He serves on a number of boards of nongovernmental organizations and has authored numerous articles and book chapters on U.S. Africa policy. He is an expert on the Horn of Africa and China's rising engagement on the African continent and is currently working on a book concerning China-Africa relations. Ambassador Shinn holds a B.A., M.A., and Ph.D. from the George Washington University. He has a certificate in African studies from Northwestern University.